Introduction to Jazz History

Introduction to Jazz History

4TH EDITION

DONALD D. MEGILL
RICHARD S. DEMORY

MiraCosta College

PRENTICE HALL, Upper Saddle River, New Jersey 07458

Library of Congress Cataloging-in-Publication Data

MEGILL, DONALD D.
  Introduction to jazz history / Donald D. Megill, Richard S.
Demory
    p. cm.
  Includes bibliographical references, discography, and index.
  ISBN 0-13-210790-2
  1. Jazz—History and criticism. I. Demory, Richard S.
II. Title.
ML3506.M43 1996
781.65'90—dc20   95-19967
                                              CIP
                                              MN

Acquisitions editor: Norwell F. Therien
Production supervisor: Carole R. Crouse
Buyer: Bob Anderson
Interior design: Carole R. Crouse
Photographs: Courtesy of Frank Driggs Collection. © Copyright. All rights reserved.
Pen and ink drawings: David Musser

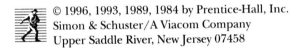 © 1996, 1993, 1989, 1984 by Prentice-Hall, Inc.
Simon & Schuster/A Viacom Company
Upper Saddle River, New Jersey 07458

Printed in the United States of America

10 9 8 7 6 5 4

ISBN 0-13-210790-2

PRENTICE-HALL INTERNATIONAL (UK) LIMITED, *London*
PRENTICE-HALL OF AUSTRALIA PTY. LIMITED, *Sydney*
PRENTICE-HALL CANADA INC., *Toronto*
PRENTICE-HALL HISPANOAMERICANA, S.A., *Mexico*
PRENTICE-HALL OF INDIA PRIVATE LIMITED, *New Delhi*
PRENTICE-HALL OF JAPAN, INC., *Tokyo*
SIMON & SCHUSTER ASIA PTE. LTD., *Singapore*
EDITORA PRENTICE-HALL DO BRASIL, LTDA., *Rio de Janeiro*

Contents

Preface

The people who play jazz create the complexities and individual nuances that make a history of jazz so difficult to formulate. No clear-cut category can encompass all jazz. Each performer's idiom is a style unto itself; if it were not so, the music would hardly be jazz.

Jazz, like almost all music, comprises three artistic activities: creating, performing, and listening. In traditional Western European music, these three activities are not always performed by the same individual, although they quite often are. In jazz, however, it is necessary for the performer to combine all three at the same time. Musical creation is an active part of any jazz performance and depends on the performers' understanding of the developing creation, an understanding gained only by their ability to listen well. They must react instantaneously to what they hear from their fellow performers, and their own contribution must be consistent with the unfolding themes and moods. Every act of musical creation in jazz is, therefore, as individual as the performer creating it.

Jazz occupies a unique place in American cultural history. Although it has been influenced by the music of many countries, it remains a purely American phenomenon. And because the creators of jazz, the performers, have been influenced by social and historical forces peculiar to America, an understanding of their life experiences and life styles is often essential.

It is almost impossible to present a history of jazz without looking closely at its great performers. Although we are concerned mainly with the music itself, the various styles can often be seen to have grown directly out of the substance of the performers' lives, and we have therefore given whatever biographical information is necessary to understand a musician's development.

Looking over the historical span of jazz, we cannot say one performer is more important than another, and we have had a difficult time choosing which performers to discuss. We have selected certain individuals for special biographical treatment because they stand out as leaders in the development of a particular jazz style. We have necessarily had to exclude a number of significant artists. Furthermore, we have gone into detail in the biographies of some musicians, not because they are more important than others, but because their lives have been bound up with the lives of so many other musicians. Such an approach allows us to examine many interesting interactions between musicians who have determined the direction of jazz over the years. Nevertheless, the subject of this book is jazz, not life histories, and we include biographical detail only to the extent that it illuminates the music.

This edition updates several of the ongoing stylistic trends in jazz today, including the modern big bands, piano styles, bebop, and crossover. New biographical sketches for recent and historical musicians have been added for balance and to provide background for the discussions of style. The overview appendix on rock has been expanded for a better understanding of its influence on contemporary jazz styles.

SPECIAL FEATURES

The book's format is best suited to students and professors concerned with the chronology of jazz styles and how they have influenced one another. The chapters are organized so that professors may include additional biographies and recordings. It is also possible to schedule short-term classes by using only the first chapters of each part for class discussion.

Listening Guides and recordings. Discussions of each stylistic period appear at the beginning of each chapter, and most of them are accompanied by a Listening Guide of a specific performance. For the sake of convenience, most of the recordings come from the *Smithsonian Collection of Classic Jazz* (SCCJ). This excellent collection is readily available to students. Furthermore, it contains extensive explanatory notes by historian Martin Williams that add much to its effectiveness. Every recording featured in a Listening Guide is labeled so that it can be located in the collection. For this edition, several Listening Guides for selections from SCCJ have been added, where appropriate, at the end of each part of the text. The Listening Guides are intentionally kept brief and point out musical landmarks. They have proven successful in the classroom because they leave professors free to help students draw their own aesthetic conclusions from the music. The guides have been designed primarily to help students at any level discipline their listening. A suggested discography appears at the end of each chapter to further augment the students' listening experience. A more comprehensive discography appears at the end of the book.

This edition again stresses the importance of listening by adding several new Listening Guides. There is a total of seventy Listening Guides. By using the *Smithsonian Collection of Classic Jazz* (five CDs) and the supplementary two tapes or CDs that accompany this text, there will be very little need to secure albums to facilitate examples for the Listening Guides.

Box biographies. Within the flow of the discussion, short biographical boxes appear that relate to the topic but not directly to the specific subject. In this way, background information can be presented without interruption.

Student study aids. Several other study aids are included to help prepare the student for the course: "The Elements of Music for the Nonmusician" and "The Elements of Jazz." The first is intended to supply the necessary rudiments of music to students who have little or no music background. The second presents specific musical elements in jazz and illustrates them with several examples; it also defines many of the jazz terms used throughout the book.

Student tapes. The tapes that accompany the text serve two purposes. First, the instructor can make listening assignments knowing that the recorded examples are immediately accessible—that is, in the Smithsonian collection and the student tapes. The second purpose is to supply more contemporary examples for the students to have after the course is finished.

Glossary. Glossary terms are printed in bold type at least once in the text for easy identification, and are readily found again in the extensive glossary at the back of the book.

Teacher's manual. Brief summaries of each chapter, topics for classroom discussion, and a bank of questions from which to construct exams are provided in a teacher's manual and will help the professor better use the material in the text. For this edition, additional listening guides are available in the teacher's manual.

Interactive listening software is now available to access the Listening Guides on the two-CD series that accompanies the text. This software allows the student to move anywhere in the listening example with just a mouse click on the description. There is additional background material on both the performer and the music and an interactive glossary.

TO THE STUDENT

As a student of jazz styles, you must keep one activity foremost in your studies: You must actively listen to the examples and observe the differences that identify each style. Reading and discussion alone will not convey the essence of the various styles. Only listening does, and listening requires total attention; approach jazz as you would any other serious musical art. Your appreciation of jazz and understanding of its history will be greatly enhanced by continued listening and reading about how jazz styles were born, grew, and changed.

ACKNOWLEDGMENTS

The drawings throughout the book are the work of California artist David Musser, who himself is a musician. Most of the photographs are by courtesy of Frank Driggs and Carl Baugher. We are also indebted to jazz authority Pete Welding of Capitol Records and writers Mack McCormick, Stanley Dance, and Frank Alkire, who generously shared their time and expertise. We are particularly grateful to James Cimarusti for his painstaking and thorough discographic research. Without it, our task would have been greatly prolonged.

Donald D. Megill
Richard S. Demory

Introduction
to Jazz History

The Roots of Jazz

Although jazz emerged as a recognizable form around the turn of the twentieth century in the southern United States, its roots extend backward over several centuries. It represents a synthesis of many cultural influences—both musical and nonmusical, religious and secular, African and European—that was achieved through the institution of slavery. This synthesis began over five hundred years ago, when the first black slaves were brought to Europe from West Africa by Portuguese explorers. The synthesis continued as Spanish, French, Dutch, and British merchants entered the slave trade over the next two hundred years, selling to plantation and mine owners in the West Indies. Slavery spread to North America in 1619, when the British imported the first blacks to their colonies in Virginia.

A slave-trade distribution pattern based on the nationalities of sellers and buyers soon developed. The pattern was even more clearly defined by the fact that each trading nation procured slaves from specific "factory" areas in West Africa. The Portuguese purchased slaves from black rulers in Senegal and sold them in Brazil. The English plundered the Ashantis of the Gold Coast and sold them in North America. The French bought slaves in Dahomey and sold them in Haiti and the Louisiana Territory. Each of these African tribes was a separate cultural entity, with its own social customs and religion, and its own music, songs, and instruments.

Two factors—one technical and the other sociological—distinguished African from European music. The technical factor was that African **rhythms** were complex. Several drummers usually performed at the same time, weaving a pattern of contrasting beats and accents. Such complex rhythms, called **polyrhythms,** had become well established in daily life. The second factor concerns the sociological aspects of African music making: Although most African societies allowed certain gifted individuals to assume a principal role in musical performances, they emphasized mass participation to a far greater degree than did European societies. Everyone within earshot was expected to participate. There were few passive observers. A typical performance would have a leader, accompanied by drummers and possibly other instrumentalists, who called out rhythmic words or phrases. The participating "audience," clapping in time and moving in unison, would shout a response. As the hypnotic beat quickened and became more insistent and persuasive, participants might become "possessed," tremble violently, and fall down. African music making thus was a collective experience in which everyone had the opportunity for self-transcendence through music. Although similar give-and-take situations existed in some European religions, where the pastor would quote a passage and the congregation would answer, African societies had brought the art to a higher state. Slaves in the New World colonies adapted these response-cries to their work routines and social and religious gatherings. White Americans called them **field hollers** and shouts, or when performed in a moving circle, ring shouts. Jazz musicians applied the term **call-response** to these plantation songs and later to the blues.

The collision of African and European societies in the New World produced distinctive cultural practices that are evident to this day. Foremost was the conflict between language and religion. French, Spanish, and Portuguese Catholic slaveowners were more tolerant of native African religious practices than were the puritanical English Protestants. Whereas North American slaveowners forebade their slaves to construct or play drums, or engage in tribal chants and dances, slaveowners in Haiti, Cuba, and Brazil, while urging their slaves to convert to Catholicism, left them relatively free to continue their African rituals and musical practices.

Because of the difference in restrictions, slave music evolved in different ways from region to region. Slaves in North America found the simple rhythms and isolated **melodies** of English ballads and dance tunes strange, but had to adopt them if they were to have any music at all. The slaves in Latin America found Spanish and Portuguese music less alien. The Moorish conquest of the Iberian Peninsula in the 700s, lasting as it did for the next seven hundred years, had already infused Spanish and Portuguese music with African inflections. The North African Moors themselves had previously assimilated sub-Saharan music through exposure to black Africans brought north in the intracontinental slave trade. Thus, more African sounds survive in Latin American than in North American black music.

Western European music also heavily influenced the development of jazz. These early influences came from four areas: church hymns, folk songs and dances, military marches and airs, and classical compositions. Not all forms were present in the Americas when the first slaves were brought over, but each eventually had an effect. The effect differed, however, depending on the African-European cultural mix. In Protestant North America, efforts to impose Christianity and suppress tribal worship led to the emergence of hymn and spiritual singing and the simplification of rhythms. In Latin America and Catholic North America, European music had the most influence on **harmony.** It might be said that of the three major elements of music, Africa's principal contribution was rhythm, Europe's was harmony, and both furnished melody; however, it was the Afro-Americans who combined all three elements into a whole.

INSTRUMENTS

The amalgamation of styles was not a simple task, considering that the black slave culture had very few instruments at its disposal. With the exception of the banjo, jazz is normally played on instruments of European design. Although African music seems to be dominated by drums and other percussion instruments, it did not lack melody or the instruments for producing it. Different tribes played various kinds of horns, trumpets, and stringed instruments such as the 10-to-14-string guitarlike *bandora;* the 3-string *koonting;* the harplike 18-string *korro* and 7-string *simbing;* the *sansa,* a thumb piano; and the marimbalike *balafou.* Another plucked instrument was the *banya,* which, when reconstructed in

America and anglicized, became the banjo. Why, then, were European instruments used exclusively in jazz? First of all, slaves captured in Africa brought no property. Once ashore, they had little opportunity to make instruments; as was mentioned, they were prohibited from doing so in most cases. Second, African musical **scales** varied from region to region, and slave musicians tuned their instruments in ways very different from those of Europeans. Therefore, the few Afro-Americans who did get the opportunity to play instruments in military bands or for the entertainment of their masters played European-style music on European instruments. These early marching bands became part of the black social organizations that flourished in the post–Civil War South. The bands, in measured step, would accompany funeral corteges to gravesites and then, on the return march, would strike up lively tunes to lift the spirits of the bereaved and joyfully usher the soul of the departed to the gates of heaven.

MUSICAL FORMS—THE SPIRITUAL

Slaveowners discouraged or prohibited African religious songs and dances but encouraged the singing of Christian hymns. Hymns therefore underwent a transformation at the hands of Afro-Americans. The *spiritual*, a religious folk song, became an expression of hope for release from oppression and sorrow, if not in this life, at least in the next. Protestant Christianity was introduced into slave life by means of individual and family conversions in the 1600s and early 1700s; black Protestant congregations began to form around 1780, a date that coincides with the beginning of the Great Awakening, an important religious movement that affected the colonial and frontier states for the next fifty years. Great Awakening activities included "camp meetings," which took place in temporary tent communities. They lasted as long as a week at a time and featured traveling preachers, some of whom became quite famous. Both blacks and whites attended, and the Afro-Americans injected their rhythmic style into the frequent mass hymn singing. The songs were primarily folk hymns that were *lined out*—that is, the preacher would call out a line of the **stanza** and the congregation would repeat it in song. This procedure was familiar to most blacks. Soon they were composing their own songs of worship. They employed symbolism specific to the black situation while using more free-swinging, **syncopated** melodies full of **blue,** or bent, **notes** (see Chapter 3). Over the next century, the singing of spirituals spread widely over the southern United States. In 1871 the Jubilee Singers of Fisk College, a black school in Nashville, toured the United States and Europe. Their programs, which included many spirituals, were received enthusiastically and helped establish the spiritual as a valid art form.

BEFORE THE BLUES

In addition to spirituals, secular songs dealing with loneliness, infidelity, rootlessness, or repression began to appear. Since most were composed and played by unschooled musicians, they were not written down but passed on orally, as is the case with most folklore. These songs were the forerunners of the common 12-measure blues discussed in Part 1 (see also Appendix B). The blues has been fundamental to the development of jazz; without it, jazz, if it should exist at all, would be vastly different.

MINSTREL SHOW MUSIC

The interchange of cultural elements between whites and blacks took several curious turns. In the 1840s white stage companies began presenting minstrel shows. These featured entertainers in blackface performing song, dance, and comedy acts that portrayed blacks as amusing, if not ridiculous, personalities. After the Civil War, Afro-Americans, seeing the popularity of minstrel shows, organized several such companies themselves. To be accepted in Southern cities, black showmen, and a few women, had to make up in blackface, too. Thus, a double deception emerged in which blacks imitated whites who imitated blacks. Prominent among the varied minstrel acts was the lighthearted but usually somewhat disparaging "coon song." It was sung by the lead vocalist in dialect and took a humorous, if patronizing, view of the blacks' condition.

THE CAKEWALK AND RAGTIME

Because Protestant strictures forbade working on Sunday, black slaves were allowed one day of rest. A favorite Sunday amusement among slaves was parodying European dances that they had seen the white gentry performing at balls and socials. These parody-dances were accompanied by syncopated tunes played on fiddles and banjos; they usually included a "walkaround," in which couples would parade around a square and improvise high-stepping, vigorous movements as they turned each corner. These entertainments were often performed before whites and were incorporated later in minstrel shows. Couples who were judged to be the most inventive would receive a prize, often a cake. Thus, the strutting, high-kicking dance to syncopated music became known as the *cakewalk*. In the 1890s the cakewalk craze swept the country; whites from coast to coast cakewalked. And so another double deception occurred, only in this case whites imitated blacks who were mimicking whites. The cakewalk craze may have spurred the composition of piano music with similar rhythms called *ragtime*. On the other hand, ragtime (discussed in Chapter 6) may have stimulated the cakewalk fad; whichever form provided the impetus, jazz was not far away.

    As will be seen in the following chapters, jazz originated from a mixture of African and European music and grew into the sophisticated form it is today. It is uniquely American music, and although it is composed of musical elements drawn from other cultures, it probably could not have developed anywhere but in the United States.

SUGGESTED LISTENING

New World Records

#205, *White Spirituals from the Sacred Harp*
#224, *Brighten the Corner Where You Are: Black and White Urban Hymnody*
#294, *The Gospelship: Baptist Hymns and White Spirituals from the Southern Mountains*

Work Songs:
Huddie Ledbetter—"Leadbelly"

2

Huddie Ledbetter—
"Leadbelly"

In most preliterate cultures, *work songs* have served as a means of coordinating large tasks that require many workers. History does not record exactly when the custom began, but it is likely that in the United States, the slaves themselves devised it in the 1600s. When plantation bosses and prison guards saw how effective work songs were, they encouraged their use. On prison work farms and on large plantations where tasks such as pulling up tree stumps, chopping cotton, or hauling heavy loads were common, a lead singer would set the pace by using the rhythm of a song. Most work songs told a simple story, one with which the workers were familiar. The singer would use heavy rhythmic **accents,** and the workers would join in with shouts (**call-response**) at regular intervals throughout the song. The shouts or grunts signaled the moment of coordinated effort.

The work songs were kept simple to allow the laborers to concentrate on the work. They were made even more effective by their hypnotic rhythms. When there was no need to coordinate single thrusts or pulls, work songs could take on more balladlike qualities. Even the slower songs, however, induced the workers to move in smooth-flowing motions that paralleled the song's rhythm. The **tempo,** or rate of speed, of each work song was adjusted to match the speed required for the task.

Effective work-song leaders were in demand, not only because they promoted efficiency, but also because they alleviated worker discontent. There were undoubtedly many locally famous lead singers, but it was not until the advent of the phonograph that one was brought into national, and even international, prominence. He was discovered in prison by two record talent scouts. His name was Huddie Ledbetter.

Ledbetter's rhythmic sense, combined with his strong, emotional voice, made him a valuable asset to any work team. As leader he received preferential treatment and avoided much heavy prison work; he sang and played while the others sweated.

LISTENING GUIDE

"Juliana Johnson"—ca. 1941 (Intro. to Jazz Disc 1, Cut 1)

Huddie Ledbetter—vocal, guitar

.00   Beginning: No introduction; clear, full voice; strong, even chords on the guitar; two chords per **beat.**
.13   New text ("gonna leave ya").
.24   New text, identical music ("done got married").
.34   New text ("I married Marty:"); these short musical phrases all end with the grunt where the workers would pull together; tempo begins to increase; spoken **fill.**

.43   Next phrase ("Marty promised").
.52   New phrase ("Goodbye Juli").
1.02   "Gonna leave ya."
1.17   Fade-out, end.

"Juliana Johnson" is an example of Ledbetter's talents. Although there are no workers' responses, one can easily imagine where they would occur.

Each verse is divided into two identical parts, and there are only two harmonies for each verse. This is a simpler structure than the standard 12-**measure** blues **progression** (see Appendix B). The guitar accompaniment is deceptively complex, however. Each strum of the guitar seems to contain only one beat, but Ledbetter actually strums twice. Thus, each measure contains eight strums (the first complete measure starts on the word "John-son"). Notice that the guitar accompaniment contains lead and rhythm elements, as well as an underlying bass line. Ledbetter recorded this song several times, and the text changed each time.

HUDDIE LEDBETTER—"LEADBELLY" (1885?–1949)

At an age when today's suburban youngsters are preparing for junior-high proms, Huddie Ledbetter was ranging around the Caddo Lake area of Louisiana, attending the numerous "sukey jumps" and "breakdowns" that made up nightlife on Saturdays in the rural South. Huddie found these late-night activities exciting and the music fascinating. Not content to be a mere observer, Ledbetter began teaching himself on the only available instrument, the accordion, and soon became, in his estimation, "as good as they had" on the "windjammer."[1]

Born in Mooringsport, Louisiana, in 1885 (according to the best estimates), Ledbetter went to work on his father's cotton farm at an early age. He was bigger and stronger than other boys his age, which probably contributed to his self-confident, aggressive nature. By age fifteen he was working away from home as a field hand, and his undisciplined nature soon led to problems. His habitual pursuit of women brought on a number of confrontations with husbands, parents, and jealous boyfriends. It is said he acquired his nickname "Leadbelly" after a fight in which it was alleged he had been shot.

Leadbelly's life involved a long series of scrapes with the law. The combination of whiskey, an explosive temper, and boundless physical energy was often too much for him to handle. In his youth he was in and out of prison half a dozen times; sentenced to chain gangs, he escaped only to get into trouble

[1]Excerpted from Frederic Ramsey, Jr., "Leadbelly's Last Sessions," *High Fidelity*, November–December 1953. All rights reserved.

again. In 1918, while in Texas serving a thirty-five-year sentence for murder in Sugar Land Penitentiary, he struck up a friendship with the warden, who introduced him to the governor. The governor was so impressed by a song beseeching his leniency that he pardoned Huddie in 1925. Seven years later, when he was serving a six-to-ten-year sentence for attempted homicide in Louisiana's Angola State Penitentiary, he got another break. Folklorists John and Alan Lomax, then touring prisons in the hope of discovering unpublished songs, heard Ledbetter and interceded on his behalf with the governor of Louisiana. In 1934 the governor commuted Huddie's sentence.

Leadbelly went to New York in 1935 and worked as a chauffeur for the Lomaxes. They sponsored stage and nightclub appearances for Huddie, whose authenticity won him almost instant acclaim. Popularity and financial security could not keep him out of trouble, however. Between 1937 and 1940 he went to jail two more times; but after his release in 1940, he managed to avoid any further arrests. His confinements were only inconvenient interruptions in his career. He continued to be a popular entertainer, touring off and on with such well-known performers as Josh White, Big Bill Broonzy, and Woody Guthrie.

He collected and remembered a very large number of songs in the years he spent rambling around the South. Historian Frederic Ramsey believes that the blues troubadour Blind Lemon Jefferson, who was twelve years younger than Ledbetter, exerted a significant influence on his musical style.[2]

Leadbelly made many recordings, including some touching performances before children, who seemed to see a tenderness in him that his prison record would belie. But he had trouble working in studio situations. More than once, recording companies refused to continue working with him because of the excessively long time it took to make an acceptable cut.

Huddie's appeal began to fade during World War II, and in the ensuing years he found few audiences for his music. In Paris, in 1949, a degenerative disease of the nervous system (amyotrophic lateral sclerosis), which had been gradually overtaking him, finally caught up. He was brought back to the United States virtually paralyzed. Leadbelly died in New York on December 6, 1949.

SUGGESTED LISTENING

The Library of Congress Recordings. Elektra EKL301.3. 3-LP set. Out of print.
Roots of the Blues. New World Records, 252.

[2]Ibid.

Stylistic Time Line

	1890	1900	1910	1920	1930	1940	1950	1960	1970	1980	1990

Blues
- Country Blues
- City Blues
- Rhythm and Blues
- Rock and Roll

Instrumental and Vocal Styles
- New Orleans Dixieland
- Chicago Dixieland
- Swing
- Modern Big Band
- Bebop
- Cool/West Coast
- Hard Bop (Funky)
- Third Stream
- Free Jazz
- Jazz/Rock, Fusion

Piano
- Ragtime
- Stride
- Boogie-Woogie

Legend: Solid black line = most active period.

Country Blues: Robert Johnson

3

The blues is the root from which and the foundation upon which all jazz has developed. Indeed, without the blues there would be no jazz as we know it today.[1] Every style of jazz, even the avant-garde, has been found to have a heritage in the blues.[2]

As we saw in the last chapter, work songs were structurally simple two-harmony songs that were sung by a leader and responded to by other workers. Another kind of song, the *country blues,* was developing at the same time, however. The first blues songs were sung by itinerant male singers in the South and the Southwest who went to bars and social gatherings singing songs full of earthy lyrics in exchange for liquor. Early blues singers drank, danced, and mingled freely with the patrons and guests, and their music was informal, unrestrained, and often *improvised* (composed on the spot). The themes of these songs were the basic human problems of sex and love, poverty and death. Such themes seemed to demand a slightly more elaborate form than did those of the work songs. Instead of a simple statement and answer, the early blues songs developed a 12-measure format containing three equal **phrases** (see Appendix B). The unsophisticated lyrics and uncomplicated **chords** flowed with a comfortable regularity that separated them from the city blues style that was to come later. The basic format, however, was widely adopted and remains virtually unchanged today.

Country blues has four other major characteristics: (1) It uses *blue notes* and personal inflection in the vocal line; (2) it is free from any traditional rhythmic restrictions; (3) it relies on only a few harmonies per verse; and (4) it conveys a feeling of simplicity and personal identity. All these qualities can be found in Robert Johnson's "Hellhound on My Trail."

Use of blue notes and personal inflections. Johnson's ability to decorate simple melodies with vocal inflections is legendary. He intensified words by "bending" notes away from their original **pitch,** thereby creating blue notes. This practice undoubtedly was based on African tonal scales. As the following example shows, the fundamental blues scale contains only seven notes:

Blues musicians using this scale traditionally lowered (blued) the two notes shown in the example. These notes are **flatted** approximately halfway between the major and the minor scale **tones** (see Appendix A). Sliding them away

---

[1]Some of the material in this chapter and the chapter on Scott Joplin appears through the generosity of biographer Mack McCormick. We have also benefited from access to an unpublished article written by Pete Welding of Capitol Records, whose research has included lengthy interviews with Johnny Shines, Henry Townsend, Son House, Honeyboy Edwards, and other friends of Johnson's.

[2]See Joachim Berendt, *The Story of Jazz* (London: Barrie & Jenkins, now a part of the Hutchinson Publishing Group, Ltd., 1978).

from the traditional pitch emphasizes specific words and gives listeners the impression that the song is being composed on the spot. Blues singers employ many other personalized inflections in addition to blue notes. They may growl or slide from note to note or swallow the sound. All these devices serve to highlight words and heighten emotion.

Freedom from traditional rhythmic restrictions. Robert Johnson took many liberties with the rhythm. At times, he would add a beat to a measure or drop one for expressive effect. He felt free to sing as the lyrics moved him, and his use of rhythm varied from performance to performance. Such fluctuations in rhythm intensify the mood being created.

Pronounced harmonic and textual repetition. The repetitive harmonic progression of the blues gives it a solid structure. The ordering of the three chords creates three equal phrases. The first phrase introduces a statement or a question, the second phrase repeats that statement, and the last phrase completes (or answers) the first two phrases. The three phrases combine to make one verse. The verses to "Hellhound on My Trail" illustrate the basic structure of a blues song. (These verses have been condensed from Johnson's actual performance to show the underlying structure. The recording, with all its repetitions and changes, should be compared with this skeleton.) The verses are numbered, and each one contains the same chord progression. Each line of text is a musical phrase, which is immediately followed by a vocal or an instrumental fill.

"Hellhound on My Trail"

1. I got to keep movin'. Blues fallin' down like hail.
   I got to keep movin'. Blues fallin' down like hail.
   I can't keep no money with a hellhound on my trail.
2. If today was Christmas eve, and tomorrow Christmas day,
   If today was Christmas eve, and tomorrow Christmas day,
   I would need my little sweet rider just to pass the time away.
3. You sprinkled hot-foot powder* all around my door.
   You sprinkled hot-foot powder all around my door.
   It keeps me with a ramblin' mind, rider, every old place I go.
4. I can tell the wind is risin', the leaves tremblin' on the tree.
   I can tell the wind is risin', the leaves tremblin' on the tree.
   All I need is my little sweet woman to keep my company.

The words are often difficult to understand because of vocal inflections and imprecise pronunciation. Notice the **fills** between the phrases. Johnson either talked or talk-sang these short, improvised interjections, which help personalize the story. This technique is still widely used today by blues singers like Ray Charles and B. B. King.

A feeling of simplicity and personal identity. By means of vocal inflections, which are extensions of their personalities, great blues singers are able to draw

---

*("Hot-foot powder" probably alludes to a magic, voodoo spell. "Rider" means lover.)

the listener into the story and the mood of the song. Country or rural blues has been called "primitive" or "undeveloped." While the blues sound may be natural and simple, it is never cold or stagnant. In "Hellhound on My Trail," notice the interplay between the melody, the fills, and the guitar. The feeling of improvisation is evident from the first chord.

LISTENING GUIDE

"Hellhound on My Trail"—1937 (Intro. to Jazz Disc 1, Cut 2)

.00	Introduction (4 measures): Strong, rhythmic strumming on the guitar.
.10	1st verse, 1st phrase: The guitar plays the melody as accompaniment.
.18	Fill between phrases: Chords are strummed on guitar with vocal echoes.
.25	2nd phrase: Begins with humming; the words are said quickly to catch up with the accompaniment.
.37	3rd phrase: The end of the phrase has a vocal echo of the text.
.50	2nd verse, 1st phrase: The guitar player is having technical problems (because of wrong notes?) and almost stops.
1.03	2nd phrase: The fill at the end of this phrase is spoken.
1.14	3rd phrase: The fill at the end is a talk-sing.
1.25	3rd verse, 1st phrase: The guitar plays a clear **chromatic scale.**
1.35	2nd phrase: Notice the bass line on the guitar.
1.44	3rd phrase.
1.58	4th verse, 1st phrase: The guitar almost stops completely; instead of chords, it plays one note at a time.
2.11	2nd phrase: Ends with humming (fill).
2.21	3rd phrase: Heavy bass notes are played on the guitar.
2.26	Abrupt ending.

Notice the fluctuations in rhythm; at times, the rhythm almost stops. No matter what problems may occur in the performance, there is always some activity to carry the music forward. Johnson reduces the activity on the guitar to a few sparse notes while singing the first part of each phrase. At the end of each phrase, the guitar becomes more rhythmic while he improvises melody and words to fill the gap between phrases. The musical fills are free and often show some of his best technique.

Notice the slowly changing chords. The three simple blues chords are relatively easy to play on the guitar and can be strummed or broken into single notes to create activity below the melody.

ROBERT JOHNSON (1912?–1938)

A complete biography of Robert Johnson has yet to appear. A number of accounts are in circulation, but they are contradictory in so many details that the truth is difficult to determine. As nearly as can be ascertained, Johnson was born about 1912 in Copiah County, Mississippi (just south of Jackson, Tennessee). His mother, Julia Majors, had already borne nine children by her husband, Charlie Dodds. Robert's father's name was Noah Johnson. (Robert's life has been difficult to trace, since he was known in his youth as Johnson, Dodds, or sometimes Spencer.) Robert grew up in the poverty of a plantation laborers' community near Robinsonville, Mississippi, remaining at home until 1930.

He was attracted musically to local and traveling blues musicians. Son House, an early established blues musician, remembers that Robert used to sneak away from his stepfather's house on the Polk plantation to come and listen to blues men play guitar and sing at Saturday-night parties and dances. Robert played blues harp (harmonica) but was more interested in learning guitar. He would pester the older musicians and try to play their instruments when they were taking breaks. House says he could only make noise. But, following a mysterious six-month disappearance, when House saw him at a dance in Banks, Mississippi, Robert reappeared with his own guitar and a fully developed playing style. the older blues man was astonished. He seriously believed Johnson must have struck a bargain with the devil to have made such miraculous progress.

The year was probably about 1933. Johnson had five years to live, and he spent them on the move. Henry Townsend, another blues musician, recalls his six-month association with Johnson in St. Louis in the early to mid-1930s:

> He was a slender-built fellow—brown skin. . . . He conducted himself very quietly at all times. . . . I was excited because, to me, he was a rare type of executor of music. . . . Played slide a lot. . . . Oh, the people was wild about it![3]

Guitarists play *slide* by inserting the little finger of the left hand into a broken-off "bottleneck," or short length of tubing or bone, and sliding this device up and down the fingerboard of the guitar while playing.

Even though it was the depths of the Great Depression, the two men worked quite steadily. They were making five or six dollars a night, which was better than bare subsistence in those days. Townsend was impressed by Johnson's lyrics but most of all by his musicianship.

> Each time, whatever he played was uniform. . . . His (harmonic) changes were actually correct all the time. Everything was timed out perfect, and he kept the words pretty well balanced.[4]

[3]Pete Welding, "Robert Johnson" (unpublished article, Capitol Records, n.d.), pp. 15–16.
[4]Ibid., p. 20.

In 1936 a salesman for the American Record Company, Ernie Oertle, discovered Johnson somewhere in Mississippi. There followed five recording sessions, which produced the twenty-nine blues masterpieces that preserve Johnson's artistry. Sixteen songs were recorded during the first three sessions, which took place on November 23, 26, and 27, 1936, in the Gunter Hotel in San Antonio, Texas. It was here that the most famous Johnson escapade occurred. One night before the sessions began, he was jailed for a minor offense. Record producer Don Law extricated him and returned him to his boarding house, giving him forty-five cents for breakfast and telling him to stay put. Law went back to an interrupted engagement but was shortly called to the phone. It was Johnson: "I'm lonesome and there's a lady here. She wants fifty cents and I lacks a nickel."

Johnson recorded the remaining thirteen songs in two sessions in Dallas on June 19 and 20, 1937. Recording conditions were excellent for the time. The engineer and the equipment had been sent from New York, and a studio was built in the corner of a warehouse. The microphone was placed in one room and the other equipment in an adjoining room. Despite their lack of technical polish, the songs came through with remarkable emotional intensity. Johnson's high, nasal voice was made for the blues, and he drew remarkable qualities from his guitar. Through poetic lyrics, he was able to speak of his buried longings, wanderlust, and torments. Through language unique to the blues, Johnson brought the imagery of the most basic human drives and fears to a height rarely achieved.

Johnson received several hundred dollars for these recordings. He was rich for that time and place, but only temporarily. Singer-guitarist David "Honeyboy" Edwards recalls meeting Johnson shortly thereafter on the streets of Itta Bena, Mississippi, playing for nickels and dimes. Edwards remembers Johnson during his last year:

> . . . Tall, brown skin, skinny, had one bad eye. . . . At the time he was with his people in Robinsonville. The biggest he'd do, he'd play on a Friday and Saturday night for dances. He'd stay home on through the week, work on the farm. And sometimes he'd get on out, get on the road somewhere. . . . His people wouldn't see him for a month or so.[5]

In the summer of 1938, Edwards recalls:

> Next time I met him was in Greenwood [Miss.]. A fellow give a dance, he lived in the country. . . . We went out there a couple of times and this fellow said Robert was messing around with his wife. . . . So he give some of his friends some whiskey to give Robert to drink. . . . I don't know was it poisoned or not, but that's the way I got it. I know he got poisoned out there. . . . About one o'clock Robert taken sick when he was playing. . . . He came back to town and he dies in Greenwood.[6]

[5]Ibid., p. 37.
[6]Ibid., pp. 40–42.

Robert Johnson died in 1938 at the age of twenty-six. The last eight years of his life had been extraordinarily creative. He had transformed the blues into an art form still capable of touching the deepest feelings of his listeners.

SUGGESTED LISTENING

Great Blues Singers. Riverside Records, 121. Out of print.
Robert Johnson: The Complete Recordings. Columbia C2K-46222.

City Blues: Bessie Smith

4

Bessie Smith

Although city blues shares the same 12-bar format with country blues, it differs from country blues in many subtle but unmistakable ways. It had its beginnings in minstrel and vaudeville shows, not in social gatherings or honky-tonks. It was sung from a stage, with the audience clearly separated from the performer, not in the midst of a crowd of people who mingled with the performers. City blues singers were usually accompanied by other performers, usually a pianist or a small ensemble, whereas country blues singers usually accompanied themselves on the guitar. As we have seen, the mood of country blues was informal and unrestrained, and the music tended to be relatively unstructured and included a good deal of improvisation. Moreover, it was usually sung by men; city blues was sung mostly by women. City blues replaced the intimacy of country blues with a refinement and sophistication that held audiences and played on their feelings. Bessie Smith was particularly talented in this regard. Later performers such as Ella Fitzgerald and Sarah Vaughan drew from Bessie's legacy.

The following table outlines some of the differences between country and city blues.

Country vs. City Blues

	Country Blues	*City Blues*
Accompaniment	Sparse, usually a single guitar	Several instruments and/or a piano
Rhythm	Quite free	Rigidly controlled by 12-**bar** structure
Lyrics	Earthy, dwelling on hardships of the downtrodden	Sophisticated, mature observations on love; verses carefully constructed to fit rhythm and meter
Vocalism	Undeveloped, but highly expressive	Refined, carefully considered

LISTENING GUIDE

For an excellent example of the formality of city blues, listen to "St. Louis Blues" in the *Smithsonian Collection of Classic Jazz*. Bessie Smith and Louis Armstrong join talents in an exciting demonstration of a blues dialogue. This technique is a distant relative of the call-response technique of field hollers and other plantation songs. You will remember that the call is a musical phrase sung by the lead vocalist, and the response is an exclamatory or answering fill sung or played by another soloist or group. In this example, the-call is much longer than the response, which may consist of only two or three notes. Bessie Smith sings the text while Armstrong plays softly in the background. The cornet fills the pause after each phrase with a little melody, which is always louder than the background it plays to the vocal part. These fills are entirely improvised, whereas the vocal part is written out.

This particular blues composition deviates from the traditional 12-measure structure. Two sections of 12 measures each use the same melody, a middle section of 16 measures introduces a new melody, and a final section of 12 measures uses yet a third melody.

Notice the relaxed dialogue between the two soloists. The blues feeling is carried by the three performers without the aid of rhythm instruments. There is neither a drummer nor a bass player. Furthermore, unlike the piano, the reed organ is not percussive; it can only supply long chords to underpin the melody. Nevertheless, the musicians provide their own compelling pulse.

"St. Louis Blues"—1925 (SCCJ Disc 1, Cut 3)

Vocal—Bessie Smith
Cornet—Louis Armstrong
Reed organ—Fred Longshaw

.00	Introduction of one chord.
.04	1st section, 1st phrase: Vocal.
.13	Cornet answers and continues as accompaniment, filling after each phrase.
.19	2nd phrase: Relaxed **lay-back** style.
.33	3rd phrase: Completes 12 measures; the fill is built on an expanding interval.
.48	2nd section, 1st phrase: Same melody, dialogue continues; the cornet helps define the harmony and supplies rhythm between the vocal phrases.
1.31	3rd section, 1st phrase: New chord progression.
1.45	2nd phrase.
2.00	3rd phrase.
2.13	4th phrase: Completes 16 measures.
2.26	4th section, 1st phrase: Cornet harmonizes with the vocal part, voice becomes more aggressive, using a slight throat-growl effect.
3.05	End.

BESSIE SMITH (1894?–1937)

A great deal has been written about Bessie Smith's life; and, because of the controversy over how she died, almost as much has been written about her death. Writers disagree about a number of facts. Was she born in Chattanooga, Tennessee, on April 15, 1894, or 1898? Was she discovered by Lonnie and Cora Fisher or by Ma Rainey? Was her death, following an auto crash, the result of a white-managed hospital's refusing to admit her? Or was she properly attended to and would have died of her injuries in any case?

The truth of these matters is not verifiable because few, if any, written records were kept in those days. But the details are of secondary importance. One can experience the essence of Bessie Smith by listening to her. The 160 phonograph records she made between 1923 and 1933 have been reproduced on long-play albums with the clicks, hisses, and distortions of the original 78-rpm records removed. The richness and the power of Bessie's voice remain undistorted. Jazz impresario John Hammond has said that Bessie was the greatest artist American jazz ever produced.

The Early Years

Bessie's father, William, a part-time preacher, died when she was very young. Her mother, Laura, died when Besse was nine, by which time two brothers had also died. The five remaining children were brought up by Viola, the oldest sister.

Before her mother's death, Bessie was singing on street corners to the accompaniment of her brother Andrew's guitar. What little she made went to support the family. Her character, which in later years was to be described as aggressive, self-centered, and overbearing, was nurtured in an atmosphere that could not have permitted much else.

When she was eighteen, Bessie began performing professionally, primarily as a dancer. She traveled with a show that toured the South and the Midwest, playing before black audiences. It was here that she met and was influenced by Ma Rainey, often called the "Mother of the Blues." Bessie gradually emerged from the chorus to become a featured singer. She joined and left several vaudeville and minstrel troups during the next eleven years. She received her bookings from the most influential agency handling black artists, the Theater Owners' Booking Association (TOBA). Because of the low pay, black performers said the initials stood for "tough on black artists," but the association soon recognized Bessie's value and paid her well for her work. Very little has been written about this period, but it is known that Bessie gradually built a devoted following.

Ma Rainey (Gertrude Malissa Nix Pridgett) (1886–1939)

Ma Rainey, born in Columbus, Georgia, was a popular cabaret singer in the first decade of the 1900s. Her husband, Pa Rainey, was a member of the Rabbit Foot Minstrels. Ma traveled for several years on the Negro vaudeville circuits until she began recording for Paramount in 1923. The recordings became very successful. They also displayed the talents of trumpeters Tommy Ladnier and Joe Smith, Lovie Austin's Serenaders, and Louis Armstrong.

Ma Rainey could project her voice over large ensembles. She had a strong, intuitive musical sense that became a model for aspiring singers such as Bessie Smith. Her skills were refined by her extensive club and vaudeville background. Because of her early recordings, she was one of the most popular of the new city blues vocal stylists. Her peak years lasted until 1929. She no longer recorded after 1930, and her fame diminished quickly. She retired three years later in Rome, Georgia, where she remained until her death in 1939.

The Years of Fame

Bessie would probably have been content to continue singing in theaters and clubs for TOBA if it had not been for the rapid increase in popularity of the phonograph in the early 1920s. Frank Walker promoted Bessie's first records. He headed the Columbia Company's "race" department, which marketed "race-records"—that is, recordings of black artists intended primarily for black buyers. In February 1923, Bessie recorded "Down-hearted Blues" and "Gulf

Ma Rainey's Georgia Jazz Band, 1925. *Left to right: Gabriel Washington, drums; Al Wynn, trombone; Dave Nelson, trumpet; Ma Rainey; Eddie Pollack, alto sax; Thomas A. "Georgia Tom" Dorsey, piano.*

Coast Blues" for Columbia. The two numbers, on opposite sides, sold 780,000 copies in less than six months, making Bessie a celebrity of national importance.

She began making records regularly for Columbia on a contract that yielded $20,000 a year. As her records sold in large numbers, her value to theater and club owners increased. Within three years she was receiving as much as $2,500 a week for personal appearances.

Her professional life became hectic and exhausting, and her personal life began to suffer. She was unable to manage large sums of money and squandered much of her income in pursuit of the glamor associated with success. Public exposure of her private life also aggravated many of her problems. Fortunately, her singing remained unaffected.

By 1928 Bessie's popularity had leveled off, although on a high plateau; and by 1930 her career began to wane as a result of the generally poor economic climate, vaudeville's replacement by the talking movies, and the relative decline in the popularity of the blues. To make things worse, TOBA, which had always booked Bessie's shows, folded in the summer of 1930. Bessie's hard-driving, high-flying life style had taken a toll also. Her voice had deepened and roughened—although as a singer of pure city blues she was still without equal.

The Last Seven Years

In 1930 Columbia renegotiated her annual contract with the guaranteed fee per side cut nearly in half; in 1931, Columbia dropped Bessie altogether. The next three and a half years were lean ones for Bessie, although not as lean as some biographers believe. Bessie left her first husband and moved in with a wealthy ex-bootlegger, who provided for her handsomely.

Bessie dreamed of regaining her popularity, and her last recordings show that she was able to convert easily to the newer **swing** style of jazz (see Part 4). These performances were also notable for the talented backup musicians, which included trombonist Jack Teagarden, saxophonist "Chu" Berry, and clarinetist Benny Goodman. However, her transition into the swing era was not destined to continue.

Late on the night of September 26, 1937, after doing a show, Bessie left Memphis, Tennessee, for Darling, Mississippi. Seventy-five miles south of Memphis, her car struck a parked delivery van. Bessie suffered severe injuries, and died at 11:30 the following morning in a black hospital in Clarksdale, Mississippi. Her grave in Sharon Hill, Pennsylvania, remained unmarked until 1970, when Janis Joplin, John Hammond, and a few others bought and emplaced a headstone there.

SUGGESTED LISTENING

Nobody's Blues but Mine. 1925–27. Columbia CGT-31093. (CS)
Bessie Smith: The Collection. Columbia Jazz Masterpieces CK-44441.
Empress of the Blues. Columbia Jazz Masterpieces C2K-47091.

The Blues Continues:
Muddy Waters, B. B. King,
Eric Clapton, and Robert Cray

5

B. B. King

Although interest in traditional blues had begun to decline by 1935, it never died out entirely. The blues provided a framework for several jazz styles that arose in the intervening decades and has had a strong influence on several more in the present. Traditional blues served as the basis for **rhythm and blues** (R&B) in the 1940s and for the rock-and-roll styles of the 1950s, and it remains active in rock groups today. Even recent country-and-western, fusion, and contemporary gospel styles are, in their essence, forms of the blues.

Human misery continues to be the theme of recent blues songs—not the misery caused by the oppression of slavery, but that caused by poverty, discrimination, and unemployment. Even older blues musicians such as T-Bone Walker and Champion Jack Dupree have changed the subject matter of their songs to keep pace with the times.

The blues was given a strong new impetus in the 1950s and 1960s with the development of rock and pop styles, particularly those of soloists such as Chuck Berry and Fats Domino and vocal groups such as the Drifters and the Coasters. Even rock-oriented groups such as Bill Haley & the Comets and country-rock singers such as Elvis Presley largely remolded what were originally blues idioms.

More recent rock performers such as Eric Clapton have acknowledged the importance of the blues to rock music. According to Clapton, rock must periodically recharge its batteries with the blues. Ornette Coleman, who adheres to a jazz style very remote from the rigid structures of blues compositions, admits that the blues has been important to his development; he began his career playing R&B. The gospel rock style of Ray Charles also reflects the influences of the blues—particularly in the personal warmth conveyed in his vocal improvisations.

Besides influencing other jazz styles, traditional blues began to experience a revival in its own right in the 1950s. One of the musicians responsible for the new wave of blues popularity was Muddy Waters.

MUDDY WATERS (McKINLEY MORGANFIELD) (1915–1983)

Born in Rolling Fork, Mississippi, on April 4, 1915, Muddy Waters learned at an early age to play the harmonica and sing. Folklorist Alan Lomax discovered Waters working in the cotton fields and organized his first recordings for the Library of Congress. Waters moved to Chicago in 1943, worked in local clubs, and recorded on the Aristocrat label. He remained in Chicago through the 1950s, leaving long enough in 1958 for a successful concert tour in England.

His early recordings, in which his voice was accompanied by only his guitar and a bass, were typical of rural blues; however, he became a transitional force in the development of the 1960s rock bands. Waters used the blues as a vehicle for his observations about a changing society. His late-1950s recording "Rollin' Stone" inspired Bob Dylan's "Like a Rolling Stone," which in turn led to the naming of the British rock group, as well as the title of a periodical. Although he

Muddy Waters

organized a successful large band, he was not able to make a transition into pop music. The newer styles required aggressive performances, and Waters was not oriented in that direction. Dynamic personalities emerged in the 1960s to replace the less intense blues men: B. B. King, Ray Charles, Aretha Franklin, and James Brown took the jazz-blues-rock world by storm.

B. B. (RILEY B.) KING (b. 1925)

The musician who most influenced rock guitarists is the rhythm-and-blues performer B. B. King. (The initials B. B. stand for his earlier nickname, "Blues Boy.") B. B. has developed an authoritative solo guitar style to match his vocal ability. His guitar (which he calls "Lucille") has become a counterpart to his virile voice. B. B. now finds it difficult to play and sing at the same time, and therefore depends on the call-response technique and well-developed instrumental solos to personalize his style. His bond with his instrument has set an example for many younger rock guitarists. Perhaps his most famous disciple is Eric Clapton, who acknowledges King as the source of many of the melodic ideas used by lead rock guitarists today.

King maintains a strenuous schedule. He tours frequently with his band across the United States and around the world. (His reputation had spread even more widely when his band toured with the Rolling Stones in 1969.) His accomplishments are truly inspiring—a Mississippi farmhand who became the recipient of three honorary doctorates, a National Heritage Fellowship, a National Medal of Art, and five Grammys.

ERIC CLAPTON (b. 1945)

Musicians representing many different regions and backgrounds have adopted and stylistically modified the blues. Eric Clapton, raised by his grandparents in a hamlet thirty miles from postwar London, grew up listening to rock and roll. He only sporadically dabbled in the guitar until he heard recordings of Muddy Waters. Inspired by the blues, Eric immersed himself in study of the instrument, working to create a sound reflecting the spirit of Waters and the "bent notes" of another idol, Texas blues man Freddie King. In 1963 he joined the Yardbirds, an R&B group in London. He soon moved on to work with John Mayall recording the album *Bluesbreakers,* which displayed the virtuosic blues style that has since been a model for guitarists in rock, blues, and even jazz.

The group Cream was formed in 1966 with Jack Bruce (bass) and Ginger Baker (drums) and became the model of the ultimate rock group. Clapton became famous while in this group by playing electric blues solos in the extended blues-rock jams characteristic of the group. Cream's aggressive style also helped plant the seeds for heavy metal groups in the upcoming decades. Along with the powerful and unique guitar style of Jimi Hendrix, Clapton helped open the door to new possibilities for blues-influenced rock guitarists.

After Cream disbanded, Clapton joined Blind Faith (recording an album of the same name) in 1969. This association lasted only a year, after which Clapton left to join Derek and the Dominos. After leaving those groups, Eric recorded a solo album and toured with several different musicians through the late 1970s and early 1980s. He still displays exciting and technically demanding blues-structured melodies in his improvisations. However, the tragedies he experienced in 1990 when four band members were killed in a helicopter crash, and the death of his four-year-old son from a fall in 1991, have sobered his music. In 1993 he was honored at the Grammy Awards, where he received six Grammys, one for his composition "Tears in Heaven," written in memory of his son.

The blues, whether incorporated in country, city, boogie-woogie, R&B, soul, or rock and roll, is a vital force in all the musics born of the American experience. In the case of Eric Clapton, the music comes from England by way of Robert Johnson and Muddy Waters.

Eric Clapton

ROBERT CRAY (b. 1953)

Robert Cray plays and sings music from an unmistakable blues foundation. The subject matter of his compositions and the songs he chooses could be straight from Robert Johnson—cheating, longing, betrayal, infidelity—but his music has shown a gradual transition away from the traditional blues format. His first album, *Who's Been Talkin'*, issued in 1980, presents ten numbers in the usual 12-bar blues harmony arrangement, and Cray plays his guitar with a distinct B. B. King flavor. His later albums (*Strong Persuader*, for example, issued in 1986) are liberally infused with electronic enhancement, horn backups, keyboard wizardry, and eclectic song structure. Cray offers no apology, pointing out that numerous blues traditionalists of the past have ventured into other areas without threatening the survival of the blues.

Robert was born in Georgia, the son of a career soldier, which meant that he, his two brothers, and his two sisters saw much of the world as they were growing up: California, Washington, Pennsylvania, Alabama, Virginia, and Germany. Robert's mother and father collected jazz, blues, and pop records during their

Robert Cray

Photograph by Steve Jennings

travels, so Robert was exposed to music from an early age. He was impressed by the music of Muddy Waters, Miles Davis, and Ray Charles, but it was hearing the Beatles that determined he would make a career of music. His mother bought him a $69 guitar, and he began absorbing and copying the Jimi Hendrix, Steve Cropper, and B. B. King guitar styles, not to mention those of numerous other prominent blues artists.

In the mid-1960s, while in Virginia, Cray formed his first band. In 1971, after bluesman Albert Collins played at Robert's high school graduation in Tacoma, Washington, Cray was so impressed that he became a Collins disciple and studiously practiced to learn his technique. At that time, a Cray schoolmate, bass player Richard Cousins, joined Robert, and the nucleus of the current Robert Cray Band was formed.

Although not an overnight success, Robert and his associates began to get favorable exposure. In 1976 they played on the same bill with Albert Collins; in 1977 Robert appeared in a small role in the movie *Animal House;* and in 1978 record producers Bruce Bromberg and Dennis Walker asked them to do the album *Who's Been Talkin'.* The band received plenty of bookings, 200 to 250 a year, initially up and down the West Coast but eventually across the country. They made more albums and received a W. C. Handy Award in 1984 for the best blues song of the year, *Phone Booth,* and another Handy in 1985 for *False Accusations.*

Cray has achieved star status and favorable recognition from the blues musicians, such as Eric Clapton and Albert Collins, he so long admired. He has been awarded three Grammys and has recognized the responsibilities of his celebrity by adopting a more conservative lifestyle, precipitated, no doubt in part, by his marriage in 1992.

LISTENING GUIDE

"Labor of Love"—1990 (Intro. to Jazz Disc 1, Cut 3)

Vocals and guitar—Robert Cray
Bass—Richard Cousins
Keyboards—Jimmy Pugh
Tenor sax—Andrew Love
Drums and percussion—Kevin Hayes
Guitar—Tim Kaihatsu
Words and music by Tim Kaihatsu

.00	Introduction, tutti rhythm, guitar fill.
.10	First chorus, first phrase (A), organ accompaniment, walking bass, shuffle rhythm from the drums.
.24	Musical repeat (A).
.39	**Bridge,** new chords (8 measures).
.55	The last phrase is only 4 measures.
1.02	Tenor sax solo; traditional blues inflections flavor the solo.
1.32	Bridge, vocal returns.
1.48	Last phrase of the 2nd chorus is again only 4 measures.
1.55	New chorus begins.
2.11	Another 8-measure phrase.
2.24	Ensemble idea from the introduction returns and extends the chorus by 4 measures.
2.32	Guitar solo: Notice the organ, walking bass, and rhythm guitar. The solo chorus continues without a return to the chords of the bridge.
3.36	Fade-out.
3.52	End.

This performance is driven by a shuffle rhythm that has withstood the test of time. It remains one of the most energetic rhythmic patterns of the blues. The structure of the chorus is not typical of a standard blues; however, the chords and the progression still lend themselves to blues melodic patterns and inflections. The result is a reaffirming statement of the cultural strength of the blues. The blues has proven to be the most enduring of all musical styles in both jazz and contemporary musical development.

SUGGESTED LISTENING

Eric Clapton: *Journeyman*. Reprise 26074-2.
B. B. King: *Best of B. B. King*. MCA Records MCAD-31040.
  Live and Well. MCA Records MCAD-31191.
Muddy Waters: *I'm Ready*. Blue Sky ZK-34928.

Ragtime: Scott Joplin

6

Ragtime was one of the most important antecedents of jazz. Like the blues, ragtime was developed by black musicians, but it was more closely tied to the Western European musical tradition than was the blues. It evolved from songs, dances, and marches brought to America by immigrants from Western Europe. Since they were performed almost exclusively on solo piano, ragtime melodies did not—in fact, could not—contain blue notes. Where the blues lent itself to individual interpretation and improvisation, ragtime was formally structured, and its composers intended that it be played exactly as written.

There is some disagreement about the derivation of the word *ragtime*. It may have been a mutation of *jigtime*, the piano dance music that first appeared in the Northeastern United States in the early 1800s; or it might have grown out of the custom of flying a white flag, or "rag," at houses where there was music and dancing. Most likely it is a contraction of *ragged time*, a term used to describe the **syncopation** between the pianist's steady left hand and his roaming, offbeat right hand.

Whatever the source of the term, all rags share certain definite characteristics. First of all, they incorporate several **strains** (melodies or themes). Normally there are four, but three- and five-strain rags are not uncommon. In this regard, rags are closely related to military marches, which also employ multiple themes. In general, ragtime strains are sixteen measures long and are usually played twice: AA BB CC DD.

One of the important jazz qualities of ragtime is its loose, syncopated rhythm. The offbeat right hand places accents all around the heavy beat in the left hand. The **boom-chuck** pattern of a low bass note followed by a chord is its most obvious sound. The left hand maintains this 2/4 boom-chuck pattern throughout the piece, frequently suspending it at the end of the phrases to avoid monotony.

LISTENING GUIDE

Compare the Scott Joplin and Jelly Roll Morton performances of the same composition, "Maple Leaf Rag." Joplin, the composer, performs it as written. Morton, by contrast, adds (and subtracts) a great deal.

Joplin composed the rag in the typical four sections: ABCD. In Joplin's recording, the first melody is restated in the middle of the song. There are, however, four distinct melodies before the song ends. Each melody is 16 measures long, which, when repeated, makes a 32-measure section. The recall of the first and second melodies ties the musical material together. Listen to the different melodies and try to identify when the repeats and recalls occur.

"Maple Leaf Rag"—1916 (SCCJ Disc 1, Cut 1)

Scott Joplin—piano

.00 1st strain (A) (16 measures): The left hand does not play a 2/4 jazz beat all the time.

.15 2/4 jazz beat in left hand rarely appears; the bass line contains a series of short melodic ideas.

.22 Brief repeat of (A) with slight changes.

.37 Brief 2/4 jazz beat.

.45 2nd strain (B) (16 measures): Solid 2/4 jazz beat in left hand.

1.06 Repeat of (B), bass notes in left hand make melodic fills between phrases.

1.29 1st strain (A)—no repeat.

1.34 2/4 jazz beat stops.

1.50 3rd strain (C) (16 measures): 2/4 jazz beat; right hand in upper range with syncopation.

2.12 Repeat of (C), bass-line melody.

2.34 4th strain (D) (16 measures): Same texture as (C).

2.56 Repeat of (D), bass-line melody again.

3.18 End.

Jelly Roll Morton's interpretation of "Maple Leaf Rag" contrasts sharply with that of Scott Joplin. You will notice immediately that Morton introduces many short, improvised melodies that lend the piece a jazzy, blueslike spontaneity. In addition, he often changes the original melodies beyond recognition (although he retains the original harmonies). He also emphasizes the swinging beat, which is not so obvious in Joplin's interpretation. Morton thus transforms Joplin's written composition into a piece of classic New Orleans jazz.

"Maple Leaf Rag"—1938 (SCCJ Disc 1, Cut 2)

Jelly Roll Morton—piano

.00 Introduction: Notice the swinging right-hand 8th notes.

.11 (A) strain (16 measures): Morton adds many inflections to Joplin's melody in the treble and adds still others to the bass part. Syncopation occurs in both hands.

.20 Halts in rhythm (**stop time**).

.34 (B) strain with changes and syncopation.

.55   Repeat of (A) strain with further variations: New left-hand pattern, built on previous 2/4 jazz meter.

1.18   (C) strain: Contains blues elements.

1.38   Another variation of the (C) strain, presenting ideas from other parts of the original composition.

2.00   (D) strain tinged with tango.

2.19   (D) strain again: In full ragtime.

2.40   End.

Morton employs all of Joplin's strains but takes liberties with the formal structure and melody lines. The final product sounds like a theme followed by several variations, which is, in essence, how every good jazz solo should be constructed.

Another reason why the interpretations differ lies in the way the recordings were made. Scott Joplin used piano rolls to preserve his performances, since there were few phonographs at that time. (See the next chapter, on **stride** piano, for an explanation of piano rolls.) For that reason, the rhythm may seem a little stiff in comparison with Morton's live recording.

SCOTT JOPLIN (1868–1917)

The formal nature of ragtime reflects the character of the musician who is universally accepted as its foremost composer: Scott Joplin. The schooled sound of many of Joplin's tunes might suggest that he enjoyed all the privileges and advantages of an upper-class background. Such was not the case. His only advantages were innate musical talent and determination.

Scott Joplin was born on November 24, 1868, somewhere in Bowie County, Texas. His family moved to Texarkana, Texas, when he was about four. He began his musical studies early and showed such promise that his mother, at great sacrifice, bought him a piano. He soon became well known around Texarkana and appeared regularly at social functions and dances.

As a black boy from a laborer's family growing up in the southwest United States shortly after the Civil War, he did not receive much help from society. Schooling was available, but black youngsters were not encouraged to remain in school and most dropped out. However, Joplin realized that education was the way to escape the stereotypical black role. He stayed in school until he was about eighteen and continued studying for years afterward; he even enrolled in the Smith College of Music in Sedalia, Missouri, when he was thirty-five and already an established composer. He expressed his belief in education in his most ambitious work, the opera *Treemonisha*.

Joplin began to compose in his early twenties. His one burning ambition

Scott Joplin

was to achieve respectability for himself and his music. That ambition, however, did not prevent him from performing anywhere he could make money. Since the most lucrative places for black musicians were honky-tonks and brothels, he spent most of his career in them. On the other hand, he was uncompromising about his compositions. He wrote every element carefully and specified exactly how it should be played.

He left Texarkana and became an itinerant musician, wandering throughout the South, the West, and the East for some years. He finally settled in St. Louis around 1890. His first song was published in 1895. In 1897 he moved to Sedalia, Missouri, which was then the center of the ragtime world. There he met John Stark, a white music publisher, and the two men became good friends. In the next fifteen years, Stark published and marketed most of Scott's compositions, even some against his better judgment. He supported and encouraged Joplin during unproductive periods, and paid Scott royalties instead of buying the tunes outright for a small sum, the usual arrangement between black composers and white publishers.

In Sedalia, while working in a well-patronized gambling house and bordello known as the Maple Leaf Club, Scott composed a rag that became a local favorite. (It was inevitable that the club and the rag would share the same name.) In 1899 Stark, who had moved to St. Louis, published "Maple Leaf Rag." It was not immediately successful because it was difficult to play. In spite of its difficulty, however, "Maple Leaf Rag" began to soar in popularity. By the fall of 1900 it was enjoying enormous sales. Stark's publishing house was swamped with orders, and Joplin's bank account prospered.

In Sedalia, Scott became infatuated with Belle Hayden. It was a curious association because Belle had no interest in music; nevertheless, they were married in 1899 or 1900. In 1901 Scott was offered the opportunity to study in St. Louis with Alfred Ernst, the celebrated director of the St. Louis Choral Symphony Society. The move to St. Louis and the loss of their newborn daughter triggered the end of Scott and Belle's already weakened marriage in 1903.

In contrast, the years between 1901 and 1905 were particularly fruitful musically for Joplin. During them he wrote "Sunflower Slow Drag," "Peacherine Rag," and "Augustan Club Waltz," all successes. These were followed by the equally successful "Easy Winners," "A Picture of Her Face," and "Cleopha" (a favorite of John Philip Sousa's). He also wrote "A Breeze from Alabama," "Elite Syncopations," and "The Entertainer" (which achieved renewed popularity when it was resurrected in 1973 for the film *The Sting*). Joplin wrote many more compositions during this period, mostly rags, but also waltzes, ballads, marches, and cakewalks. He also composed a ragtime ballet and an opera, *A Guest of Honor*. He was acclaimed as king of the ragtime writers and alternated between working in St. Louis and touring.

Following a compositionally dry year, he moved to New York City in 1907. New York restimulated his creativity, and he published eight more compositions in that year. In 1908 he published five tunes and, on a visit to Washington, D.C., met Lottie Stokes, who became the second Mrs. Joplin. She accompanied him on his travels, and in his last, unhappy years, she remained devoted and loving.

Joplin's first folk opera, written in 1903, had been a failure, but now in 1909 he became deeply absorbed in writing and producing another, this time in ragtime. In 1910, with Lottie working as a domestic, Scott published only two rags while working furiously on his opera *Treemonisha*. In addition to the score and the choreography, Scott had written the libretto, which told of the triumph of knowledge over ignorance and evil through the education of a black plantation girl.

His involvement with the opera became an obsession. He was determined to make ragtime respectable and to show that black music was worthy of serious admiration. The score was published in 1912, and he secured a commitment to have the opera staged at the Lafayette Theater, but the plan fell through. The Joplins' circumstances gradually deteriorated as they were forced to move to progressively worse neighborhoods. From 1911 to 1913 he published only one rag.

In 1915 he was able to put on one performance of *Treemonisha*. Although he had scored the music for full orchestra, he had to play all the parts on the piano himself because he lacked the money to hire musicians. He was not even able to have scenery made. The critics completely ignored the production.

In his youth Joplin had contracted syphilis; by 1916 the disease, in its third stage, began to ravage his mind and his body. He began to lose his coordination, memory, and rational faculties. He entered a mental hospital in February 1917, and died on April 1. He left behind a legacy of nearly forty rags and some two dozen other works, including marches, waltzes, songs, and two operas. His contribution to American music has only recently received the appreciation it deserves.

SUGGESTED LISTENING

Scott Joplin—1916. Biograph BRC-1006Q. (CS)
King of Ragtime Writers. Biograph BCD-110.

Stride: James P. Johnson and Fats Waller

7

Fats Waller

Ragtime piano music attracted pianists in every part of the country. Some with a creative bent and a well-developed technique liked to add more notes than the written composition required, as we have seen Jelly Roll Morton do in "Maple Leaf Rag." The result was a piano style known as **stride,** and a host of virtuosic ragtime pianists such as James P. Johnson, Willie "The Lion" Smith, Fats Waller, and Art Tatum came forward to display their gifts. Johnson is generally conceded to have fathered the stride style, although he may have been influenced by two New York pianists, Lucky Roberts and Abba Labba. This transformation of ragtime occurred on the East Coast between 1905 and 1910.

The most striking differences stride piano style has from ragtime are its use of improvisation and its faster tempi. A stride composition usually consists of a single melody upon which the right hand embroiders in the treble range. The left hand not only provides a rhythmic and harmonic boom-chuck foundation, but also frequently interjects two, three, or more single-note **motives** in the bass and mid-ranges that complement or even compete with the right hand. The left-hand patterns often carry across bar lines, creating a most exciting melodic syncopation. Listen to "Carolina Shout."

LISTENING GUIDE

"Carolina Shout"—1921 (SCCJ Disc 1, Cut 12)

James P. Johnson—piano

.00   Introduction.
.05   1st theme.
.24   Very similar theme, a little more animated and in the higher register of the piano. Notice how the bass-note activity uses a combination of boom-chuck and walking patterns.
.30   Interesting pattern between the left and right hands.
.44   New theme. Vamplike idea; the bass notes produce the strongest melodic idea here; syncopation between hands.
1.02   Shoutlike chords start each phrase and are answered in the bass.
1.40   New theme.
1.50   Repeat.
1.58   New motive; the bass continues to answer the short melodic statements in the treble.
2.15   Rhythmic chord motive replaces the **shout** motive above.
2.25   Repeat of chord motive (brief).
2.35   Ending.

This example of stride piano uses the three-theme rag "Carolina Shout," and as in the Jelly Roll Morton example of "Maple Leaf Rag," many liberties are taken both melodically and rhythmically. The most interesting rhythmic element of this performance is how Johnson turns the boom-chuck pattern around, confusing the basic 2/4 jazz beat. The performance typically uses motives as the building blocks of the improvisations. Notice how the motives blend into one another, leaving no clear overall melodic structure. Complex rhythmic interactions between his hands are typical of the most notable stride pianists.

JAMES P. JOHNSON (1894–1955)

Johnson was born in New Brunswick, New Jersey. His mother and an Italian music teacher launched the boy's piano career at a very early age with thorough training in classical form and technique. Throughout his development and in later life, this meticulous grounding would be apparent in his robust playing and structurally sophisticated compositions.

The family moved to New York City in 1908, and soon James became deeply involved in the Harlem music scene. In addition to absorbing the examples of Lucky Roberts and Abba Labba (Richard MacLean), Johnson learned much from Eubie Blake, the talented East Coast ragtime pianist who also had an extensive classical background. Johnson did not confine himself to one arena. He could be found at rent parties, dance halls, theaters, and one particularly rough area, the Jungle, in which he not only entertained but also listened to the blues brought north by expatriated southern laborers. This exchange of musical forms could have been one of the most significant events in the history of jazz because it inspired Johnson to combine ragtime with the blues and thereby brought stride into being. It is of interest that Jelly Roll Morton was opening up a similar pathway at about the same time in a different part of the country. Morton is said to have claimed that he invented jazz himself, but, clearly, Johnson could dispute that.

James pursued diverse musical interests throughout his career. In addition to his preeminence in stride, he composed and musically directed several shows, scored the Bessie Smith film *St. Louis Blues,* and, in reflection of his admiration of Scott Joplin's *Treemonisha,* wrote the "opera" *De Organizer.* He maintained a continuing interest in classical music but also composed many popular tunes, some of which, like "If I Could Be with You," "The Charleston," and "Runnin' Wild," became standards. He performed innumerable solo concerts, played in countless bands, and cut a great many records and piano rolls. He remained active in music until 1951, when he suffered a stroke that left him incapacitated until his death in 1955.

   In spite of his full career, James Johnson's importance to the history of jazz has been largely ignored. His concept of uniting the flowing freedom of the blues with the structured discipline of ragtime and the classics was truly inspired. Without it, the progress of jazz would not have occurred as it did. His influence can be heard across the years in the music of Fats Waller, Duke Ellington, Art Tatum, and Thelonious Monk.

FATS WALLER (1904–1943)

By the time he was fifteen, Thomas Wright Waller already weighed over 200 pounds and had acquired the nickname that would stay with him for the rest of his life. He had also discovered the passion that was to be his life's work—music. It would not be his only obsession, however. Food had already become established as a major element in his existence, and drink would soon follow. He was jovial, outgoing, glib, and witty, and he never had to search far for company. His round, pale face, heavy black eyebrows, and enormous, expressive eyes made him a natural clown, and he played the part to the hilt. His antics, however, concealed a deep sensitivity.

   Fats was born on May 21, 1904, into a stable, secure family. His father ruled the household with a firm but benevolent hand, and his mother supplied the children with plenty of love and victuals.

   Fats, a mischievous boy and a quick thinker, could usually talk his way out of punishment for the pranks he loved to play. When six, he became seriously interested in the piano. Naomi, his older sister, would fight his battles for him to keep him from hurting his hands. Fats's brother Bob, seeing the boy's obsession with the piano, engineered the purchase of one for the family.

   Fats studied the violin and the bass as well as the keyboard. The accessibility of the neighborhood church led him to the instrument he came to favor above all others—the organ. In later years he would be the first to demonstrate that the organ could be used in a jazz setting. He dropped out of school in 1918 and got a job playing the pit organ at the Lincoln Theater, accompanying silent films. Later, at many Harlem night spots, he heard and became inspired by the stride piano styles of James P. Johnson and Willie "The Lion" Smith. Johnson had made numerous piano-roll recordings, and Fats used them to learn stride techniques.

   Piano rolls. Piano rolls are long, perforated strips of heavy paper about eighteen inches wide. They are fitted into a mechanical piano and rolled off one spool onto another across a vacuum bar. The perforations in the paper determine which notes are sounded. The piano essentially plays itself when the foot pedals are pumped. The keys move up and down so that one can see as well as hear what notes are being played. Fats would pump a phrase or two, fitting his fingers to the keys as they moved, and then try it on his own. James P. Johnson learned of Fats's efforts and agreed to give him lessons. A lifelong friendship was born.

Fats and his musician friends circulated in what was called the "shout circuit." These were eating, drinking, and dancing parties that were staged at private houses to pay the rent; guests were expected to donate money. Fats's musical and comedic talents kept him in constant demand.

He cut his first records and piano rolls in 1922, played the shout circuit, and toured various Eastern cities. In 1923 his lifestyle proved the undoing of his three-year marriage to his wife, Edith. In 1926 he married Anita Rutherford, whose nature was much more forgiving than was Edith's. This marriage lasted, and the couple had two sons, Maurice, born in 1927, and Ronald, born in 1928.

Fats became the favorite musician of a variety of low-life characters who frequented the night spots where he played. In 1925 Fats was abducted by a couple of mobsters and brought before Al Capone for a private recital.

Fats was a prolific composer. He wrote the score for a black stage show, *Tan Topics,* and the score for the review *Keep Shufflin.* If his funds got low, he would dash off a song and sell it. Fats was a free, independent spirit who treated his obligations lightly. He developed a reputation for being irresponsible and sometimes failed to appear for recording dates and performances. Although his cavalier attitude angered and exasperated promoters, studio personnel, and fellow musicians, he could usually talk his way back into their good graces.

Fats found both a stabilizing influence and a compatible lyricist in Andy Razaf. Together they created the popular "Honeysuckle Rose," with Razaf reading Fats the lyrics over the phone and Fats humming the famous melody back to Razaf.

In 1929 he wrote "Ain't Misbehavin'" and "What Did I Do to Be So Black and Blue?" for the show *Hot Chocolates.* Louis Armstrong sang "Ain't Misbehavin'" in the show, and both the tune and the trumpeter became famous. In 1932 Fats got a year's contract with the very powerful radio station WLW in Cincinnati. He returned to New York in 1933, recorded extensively, and frequently appeared on the stage. The money rolled in in ever-increasing amounts but rolled out at the same rate.

In 1935 Fats appeared in the first of several movies, and in 1936 had to book a long concert tour to pay off back alimony, agents' commissions, union fines, and IRS debts. He accompanied Bessie Smith during her last New York shows. He put a big band together in 1937 to profit from the growing swing market, but his reputation for irresponsibility made U.S. promoters wary. Instead, he made a triumphant tour of Scandinavia and Europe.

In 1942 he appeared at Carnegie Hall and was featured in the film *Stormy Weather;* that same year he also made a strenuous tour of military posts to support the country's war effort.

On December 16, 1943, Fats's lifestyle and a case of bronchial pneumonia caught up with him. He died in a snowbound train in Kansas City. Fortunately he left plenty of evidence of his genius, including 22 piano rolls, 162 published songs, and an additional 163 unpublished. Some of his songs have been credited to other composers; for drink money he sold "I Can't Give You Anything but Love" and "Sunny Side of the Street" to Jimmy McHugh, who became immortalized for them. He participated as soloist, accompanist, **sideman,** and leader in no fewer than 515 recordings. He packed more musical accomplishment into thirty-nine years than most ambitious musicians could expect in twice that time.

LISTENING GUIDE

"Handful of Keys"—1929 (Folkways, vol. 9, Piano II/1 FJ2809)

Fats Waller—piano

.00 Introduction.

.08 1st **chorus** (A) : 2/4 beat in the left hand; (A) is repeated.

.22 **Bridge** section (B) : New chords are introduced.

.30 (A) is repeated.

.37 2nd chorus (A) (A) : The right hand is played one **octave** higher.

.52 Bridge (B) : A new idea appears with the descending scale in the right hand; left hand continues with the 2/4 beat.

.59 Last (A) continues in the upper octave; completes chorus AABA.

1.06 Interlude: The 2/4 beat in the left hand stops.

1.10 A new theme is introduced, beginning with the syncopated pattern in the left hand.

1.26 Improvisation continues.

1.39 The first theme (A) returns, but is played faster and ranges over three octaves.

1.53 The bridge passage introduces another new idea; notice the blue notes.

2.06 The left hand plays a scale in octaves.

2.08 Improvisation: The syncopation in the right hand increases.

2.23 Bridge passage introduces another new idea, spelling out the chord slowly.

2.30 The right hand plays more syncopated chords.

2.35 The ending consists of a syncopated interplay between right and left hands.

Hints of the Modern Pianist

Fats Waller's sensitivity is an infrequently acknowledged facet of his personality. His recording of "I Ain't Got Nobody" demonstrates his ability to play subtly. Waller intersperses the 2/4 bass pattern with a **walking bass,** a ragtime bass, and repeated chord patterns. Although the music is rhythmic, it flows with the serenity and tenderness of a ballad. Listen to the many moods he creates, especially at the very end, where his right and left hands become so independent.

"I Ain't Got Nobody"—1937 (SCCJ Disc 2, Cut 5)

Fats Waller—piano

.00	Introduction: Full chords.
.11	1st chorus; Notice the chords below the melody, and the call-response between the melodies in the left and right hands.
.33	Repeat of melody, same texture; the left-hand melody predominates.
.43	Ragtime bass begins with trills.
.54	New section of melody.
1.11	**Glissando** in right hand.
1.16	A subtle stop-time effect: Left and right hands play the same rhythm.
1.36	Walking-bass line; the melody remains in the right hand; there is a strong swinging feeling overall.
1.45	The right hand plays a long descending scale.
1.53	The walking bass contains descending chords.
2.08	Both hands employ ascending chords.
2.20	Left hand repeats the same chord. The effect is like a simple boogie-woogie (see Chapter 8); notice the blues inflections.
2.36	Ascending and descending glissandos occupy the right hand.
2.42	The ragtime style returns.
2.52	The right hand plays very high in the treble and seems to be rhythmically unrelated to the left hand.
3.06	End.

The **chord-melody** technique, also called *homophony,* became widely used in the 1940s and 1950s. It occurs here in the first part of each chorus. The top notes of the right-hand chords outline the melody, making chords and melody rhythmically identical—a striking contrast to the ragtime pattern. **Dissonant** notes in the chords add flavor to the melody.

SUGGESTED LISTENING

Fats Waller: *Piano Solos (1929–41).* 2-Bluebird AXK2-5518. (CS)

Boogie-Woogie:
Jimmy Yancey
and Meade "Lux" Lewis

8

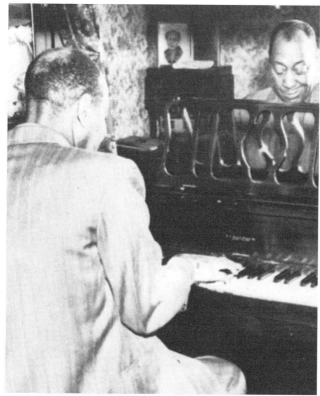

Jimmy Yancey

In the mid- and late 1930s, a closely circumscribed piano style, *boogie-woogie,* became popular. Boogie-woogie is a form of solo piano music based on traditional 8- and 12-bar blues progressions. Energy is derived from the driving pattern of the left hand. There is nothing sophisticated or subtle about this procedure. The few musicians who could complement it with fresh and interesting right-hand melodies and counterrhythms were truly imaginative. Unfortunately, the style was susceptible to counterfeiting by second-class talents; thus, the advent of the boogie-woogie craze also signaled its death sentence.

Boogie is still played today but in altered forms. Rock & roll piano borrowed its rhythmic sound in the 1950s and 1960s, and it is common to hear young rock piano players practicing the blues today with simple boogie-woogie bass patterns.

The two primary identifying elements of the boogie-woogie style are a strong rhythmic pattern in the left hand, usually made up of eight notes or chords per measure, and a right-hand part containing many chords interjected with repeating motivic ideas that are played against the left-hand pattern in a syncopated fashion. The boogie-woogie style can be easily recognized after a few measures by the characteristic repetitive figure in the left hand. This figure, called an **ostinato,** can be simple, complex, or anything in between. In the following examples, the first pattern is very simple, the second is just slightly more complex, but the third would be difficult for even a competent pianist to sustain over several choruses. In any case, it is the tension and release created by the interaction of the left and right hands that spark the excitement.

Boogie-woogie ostinato figures

LISTENING GUIDE

"Honky Tonk Train" is a traditional boogie and uses the first pattern shown in the preceding example. Each chorus contains the three phrases typical of the 12-measure blues. The musical ideas presented in the first two choruses are frequently recalled throughout the performance. Notice the interplay between the unchanging pattern of the left hand and the active chords of the right hand. Each chorus is a new beginning, and as each progresses, the syncopation increases. The many ornaments in the right hand, such as trills and shakes, energize the already thick texture.

"Honky Tonk Train"—1937 (SCCJ Disc 2, Cut 6)

Meade "Lux" Lewis—piano

.00	A short trilled chord is the only introduction.
.02	1st chorus: A 12-measure blues; the melody is based on right-hand chord activity.
.19	2nd chorus: The right hand plays syncopated chords; both hands seem to be independent.
.36	3rd chorus: The right hand starts with trills, then becomes highly syncopated.
.53	4th chorus: A short melodic idea is repeated in the right hand.
1.11	5th chorus: A trill (or shake) occupies a large interval in the right hand.
1.28	6th chorus: A very short ascending melodic motive occurs in the right hand.
1.44	7th chorus: A call-response motive appears in the right hand in which 2 high chords are followed by 2 low chords.
2.01	8th chorus: Notice the independence of hands.
2.19	9th chorus.
2.36	10th chorus: The dynamics become softer; syncopated chords return.
2.57	Ending.

Historians generally agree that boogie-woogie piano grew out of the guitar-accompanied blues performed at dances at black social gatherings. Often two guitarists played, with the second player filling in accompanying chords. Later, pianists at these functions began by imitating the guitar format, the left hand taking the second guitar's part. The transition to piano first took place in

Jimmy Yancey (1894–1951)

The musician who was most influential in promoting the boogie style was Jimmy Yancey. Yancey was born in Chicago in 1894. In his youth he followed the vaudeville circuit as a dancer. He taught himself the piano and specialized in the "fast blues." His followers included a notable group of boogie-woogie pianists such as Crippled Clarence Lofton, Albert Ammons, Pine Top Smith, and Meade "Lux" Lewis. There were a few other good stylists, such as Pete Johnson, Cow Cow Davenport, Speckled Red, and Romeo Nelson, and a handful of skilled imitators, especially Earl "Fatha" Hines, Bob Zurke, and Freddy Slack.

the lumber and turpentine camps of east and south Texas and western Louisiana. Huddie Ledbetter said he heard piano boogie-woogie played in Caddo County, Texas, in 1899. It was called "fast western" or "fast blues" in the beginning and was not known as boogie-woogie until it had migrated to Chicago following World War I.

MEADE "LUX" LEWIS (1905–1964)

Critics agree that one of the best, most inventive, and most exciting boogie-woogie pianists was Meade "Lux" Lewis. He was born in Chicago in 1905, the son of a guitar-playing Pullman porter. An uncle nicknamed him "the Duke of Luxembourg" because he liked to dress up. The name was eventually shortened to "Lux." He did not begin studying music until he was sixteen and then it was the violin; but after hearing Yancey play the blues, he switched to piano. He made enough progress to play in bars and clubs around Chicago and even toured Michigan and Kentucky.

At this time Lewis got the inspiration for the most enduring of all boogie-woogie compositions, "Honky-Tonk Train Blues." He recorded it several times, first for the Paramount Company in 1927; for Parlorphone, Decca, and RCA Victor in 1936; for Blue Note in 1940; and for Clef in 1944.

Lux dropped out of the music world in 1929, a bad year for musicians and the country. He worked on a shovel gang for the WPA (Works Progress Administration) and drove a taxi in Chicago. There he met another taxi driver, Albert Ammons, and the two began playing piano again. In late 1935 John Hammond, who had been searching for Lux for two years, found him playing for tips in a Chicago saloon.[1] Lewis's professional music career was relaunched.

He recorded extensively for the next eight or ten years. Among his more interesting sides was "Celeste Blues," a boogie-woogie piece that he composed and recorded on a small keyboard instrument called a celeste at the RCA Victor

---

[1]For more information on John Hammond's contributions to the jazz world, see Chapter 13.

**Albert Ammons and
Meade "Lux" Lewis**

studio on the same morning he first saw the instrument. He appeared at a swing concert at the Imperial Theater in New York in May 1936 but was largely ignored. He continued playing in New York but soon returned to Chicago, where he went on relief. In December 1938 he was presented at Carnegie Hall in a jazz concert and was the sensation of the evening. He teamed up with Albert Ammons and Pete Johnson afterward in numerous nightclub and recording sessions and coast-to-coast radio network appearances.

He moved to Los Angeles and continued performing in small clubs across the country until June 1964, when, on a return trip from a Minneapolis engagement, he died in a car crash. In the years following the crest of boogie-woogie's popularity, Lux had heard his music maligned as being one-dimensional. It is true that some imitators had turned boogie-woogie into a simple trick for the left hand; in the hands of Lewis, however, it was rich with rhythmic and melodic ideas.

SUGGESTED LISTENING

Meade "Lux" Lewis: *Barrel House Boogie.* RCA Bluebird 8334-2-RB.

New Orleans Dixieland:
Joe "King" Oliver

9

Dixieland is generally believed to have been born in the 1890s in New Orleans, although several areas in the South also contributed to its development.[1] The first black jazz bands were large marching groups that were often called upon to play for funeral processions and for Mardi Gras celebrations. Such bands usually included cornets (or trumpets), clarinets, "tailgate" trombones,[2] tubas, banjos, and drums. Smaller groups were formed later to play in the bars and bordellos of the notorious Storyville district, and it is from them that the Dixieland ensemble as we know it today took shape. Such ensembles included the same horns—cornets, clarinets, and trombones—but the rhythm section might include a string bass and a piano instead of a tuba.

COLLECTIVE IMPROVISATION

The essence of Dixieland style lies in its use of *collective improvisation,* a musical procedure in which the three lead instruments, the horns, improvise **contrapuntal** melodies above the steady beat of the rhythm section. In their **improvisation,** the players follow certain patterns and formulas to produce the pure Dixieland sound. One horn, usually the cornet or the trumpet, might play a primary melody, while the other two improvise independent but related solo melodies above and below it. (Because of their ranges, the clarinet would play the melody above and the trombone would play the one below; the tuba, if there was one, would play the fundamental low note of each chord.) The improvised solo melodies blend together harmonically while each preserves its own independent movement. The beat provided by the rhythm section (banjo, drums, and tuba) is in **flat-four** (4/4) time—that is, each beat in a measure is given the same accent, or amount of stress. Of all the instruments, it is the banjo that imparts the distinctive 4/4 quality to New Orleans jazz rhythm. The drummer also provides strong rhythmic support, as well as sound effects from cowbells, wood blocks, and drum rims.

The musicians of a New Orleans jazz ensemble responded continuously to one another to create a full-textured interplay of uninterrupted sound. Each player knew when to assume the leading role and when to allow someone else to come to the fore. During Dixieland's formative and reigning years, the improvisatory formulas were well known and were studied by all aspiring players. Collective improvisation receded in subsequent jazz styles and did not reappear

---

[1] The term *Dixieland* did not come into use until the 1920s, when white Chicago musicians began to copy southern black music. Inspiration for the term probably originated with a white New Orleans band that, despite its popularity, played inferior jazz: the Original Dixieland Jass [*sic*] Band. This band, ironically, was the first to record New Orleans Jazz, for RCA Victor in 1917.

[2] So called because when the band rode in a wagon, the trombonist had to sit at the rear facing backward to keep his slide from getting in the way of the other musicians.

as a principal element until the era of modern jazz in the 1950s (see Chapter 25). In New Orleans at the turn of the century, however, the improvisatory style flourished in the hands of its originators and early masters, among whom were Buddy Bolden, Bunk Johnson, and Freddie Keppard. It was King Oliver, however, who, having joined Keppard in Chicago, made the first major musical impact on the North.

JOE "KING" OLIVER (1885–1938)

Born on May 11, 1885, in the Garden district of New Orleans, Oliver grew up in a big-city environment. His mother died in 1900, and his half sister Victoria Davis cared for him until he went on his own. His musical career began at age fourteen, when he was persuaded to join a boys' brass band. He worked diligently on the cornet and was playing in marching bands and cabarets as early as 1900. While he was touring with the boys' band in 1901, an injury blinded him in one eye. He was always self-conscious about the disfigurement, but the injury proved no hindrance to his musical development. By 1907 he was in demand as lead cornetist in such bands as the Melrose Brass Band, the Magnolia Band, and the Eagle Band.

While in New Orleans, he was primarily a sideman in bands, and it was in these that he met many of the musicians who would later play for him: Lorenzo Tio Sr., clarinet; Johnny St. Cyr, banjo; and Honoré Dutrey, trombone. Kid Ory's band was the most important in which he played. Ory was the first, in 1917, to proclaim Oliver "King."

During the day, Joe worked as a butler for a family that was sympathetic to his musical aspirations and would let him off whenever he had a chance to play. He was blowing with increasing strength and confidence and began to influence many local players, the most celebrated of whom was the young Louis Armstrong.

Chicago

Oliver's success in New Orleans brought him recognition in such distant cities as Chicago. When Storyville was closed down by the Navy in November 1917, many jazz entertainers lost their jobs; in 1918 Oliver accepted an offer from Bill Johnson in Chicago to join the band in the Royal Gardens Cafe. A year later he took over leadership of the Lawrence Duhé band and in the next two years built an enthusiastic following. In 1921 Kid Ory, who had a band in San Francisco at the time, asked Oliver to come to California. Joe went and remained most of that year on the West Coast playing not only with Ory but also with Jelly Roll Morton's big band in Los Angeles and his own band in Oakland.

King Oliver's Creole Jazz Band, 1923 *Left to right: Baby Dodds, drums; Honoré Dutrey, trombone; King Oliver, cornet; Louis Armstrong, trumpet; Bill Johnson, bass; Johnny Dodds, clarinet; Lil Hardin, piano.*

The Creole Jazz Band

When he returned to Chicago in 1922, he sent for Louis Armstrong to fill out his most famous band, the **Creole** Jazz Band. The reciprocal influence of Oliver and Armstrong created music of astonishing originality. Although Armstrong openly admitted Oliver's influence on him, Oliver undoubtedly was equally affected by the young and creative Armstrong. On stage together they acted as one. In their solo duets the two cornetists played with a sense of ensemble that seemed uncanny. Both possessed technical abilities unmatched by any other horn players. With the added talents of Johnny and Baby Dodds, Honoré Dutrey, and Lil Hardin, the band became the envy of the jazz world. The band made a series of milestone recordings in 1923, the first series of recordings (except for a few recordings by Kid Ory) by a black jazz group. The most memorable side was "Dippermouth Blues."

King Oliver's Creole Jazz Band performed from 9 P.M. to 3 A.M. at the Lincoln Gardens. White musicians would congregate at the cafe after work, usually around midnight, to listen and learn. It seemed that the course of jazz was being directed by Oliver, but despite the band's success, it lasted only two years.

LISTENING GUIDE

"Dippermouth Blues"—1923 (Joe Oliver; SCCJ Disc 1, Cut 5)

King Oliver's Creole Jazz Band
Cornets—King Oliver, Louis Armstrong
Clarinet—Johnny Dodds
Trombone—Honoré Dutrey
Piano—Lil Hardin
Banjo—Bud Scott (and vocal break)
Drums—Baby Dodds

.00   Introduction to an **up-tempo** blues.
.05   Collective improvisation: Muted cornets and trombone; the banjo is the predominant rhythm instrument, while the clarinet plays in the high range.
.21   2nd chorus: Same **texture;** the trombone slides from note to note.
.37   Clarinet solo, stop-time accompaniment; notice the melodic flexibility and blues inflections.
.53   2nd solo chorus: Same stop-time accompaniment.
1.10 Collective improvisation: All horns solo equally, the cornet plays the melody.
1.26 Wa-wa cornet by Joe Oliver; the clarinet plays very softly in the low range.
1.42 2nd solo chorus by the cornet.
1.59 Collective improvisation intensifies; the cornet leads.
2.12 Vocal solo break.
2.14 Collective improvisation.
2.29 Musical **tag,** coda.
2.32 End.

Notice the balanced control of the texture. Every moment is tastefully filled by one or more players, and the resulting network of sound is full and lively. There is no written score; yet, each musician is so sensitive to the group that the ensemble remains unified throughout: The communication is exquisite. Although the recording techniques at the time were not well developed, the exuberant spirit of collective improvisation is quite evident.

The instrumentation is typical of early New Orleans Dixieland, including the two cornet parts. The distinctive sound of the banjo dominates the rhythm section. Lil Hardin on piano and Baby Dodds on drums feed the rhythmic drive but are never obvious, partly due to the early recording process, and to the flat-four strumming on the banjo.

The solos by Dodds and Oliver demonstrate the high level of improvisation that had developed by the 1920s. The clarinet playing is mature both technically and stylistically. Oliver's blues-flavored solo became a model for the many trumpeters soon to burst on the scene. The sophisticated interplay of the soloists within the collective improvisation established this style as one of jazz history's most polyphonically complex.

Money disputes caused the Dodds brothers and Dutrey to quit in 1924. Lil Hardin, now married to Armstrong, was eager to develop a name for Louis, and they, too, soon left Oliver. With those losses Oliver's following began to fade. His personnel kept changing, and the band never again achieved its previous success. By 1925 he was forced to let his musicians go.

To keep working, Oliver, billed as "the world's greatest jazz cornetist," joined Dave Peyton's Symphonic Syncopators. The band worked at the Plantation Cafe for a short time under Peyton's direction, and when Oliver took over leadership, he changed the name to the Dixie Syncopators. The fortunes of the band appeared to improve when Vocalion offered it a contract in 1926 to record a "race" series for the company. Among the recordings, "Snag It," "Sugarfoot Stomp," "Deadman Blues," and "West End Blues" helped bring Oliver his greatest acclaim. The boom was short-lived, however. The night before he was to reopen at the Plantation, following a renovation, the place burned down.

The work that followed entailed traveling to Milwaukee, Detroit, and St. Louis for college dances. Moving to New York, he played at the Savoy Ballroom for two mildly successful weeks. That engagement, however, led to an offer of a long-term contract from the managers of the soon-to-be-opened Cotton Club. Oliver, too proud to take less than what he was accustomed to, turned it down. Duke Ellington accepted the offer and stayed for three very successful years.

Little else turned up, except for a recording contract with the Victor Company. The few offers that appeared were not always accepted. Oliver often regarded even generous terms as unsatisfactory. By 1931 the King had cut his last record for Victor and the band broke up entirely.

He spent the next five years touring the South with bands made up of various musicians, but the response was discouraging. He was victimized by unscrupulous promoters; the number of bus breakdowns and accidents that plagued his bands exceeded credibility. Once, in a West Virginia mountain blizzard, the musicians had to burn the tires from the disabled bus to keep from freezing to death.

Oliver's personal life mirrored his musical disappointments. He suffered from pyorrhea and high blood pressure, and could not afford medical treatment. In 1936 he settled in Savannah. To survive he ran a fruit stand for a short time and finally became a janitor for a pool hall.

Although he had to give up music entirely and lived with sickness and poverty, people who saw him during the last years of his life said his spirit remained positive and his faith unshaken. He died of a cerebral hemorrhage on April 8, 1938. By then swing was king and the grandeur of Oliver's successes had vanished.

Johnny Dodds (1892–1940) and Warren "Baby" Dodds (1898–1959)

Two names that appear again and again in the company of such giants as Louis Armstrong, King Oliver, Jelly Roll Morton, and Kid Ory are those of the Dodds brothers: Johnny, the clarinetist, and Baby, the drummer.

The boys grew up in a family of six brothers in New Orleans. Johnny began his instrumental training on a tin whistle, and Baby started out pounding on tin cans and cigar boxes. An unforgettable thrill in Johnny's life occurred on his seventeenth birthday, when his father returned from a trip with a long, slim surprise package wrapped in brown paper—Johnny's first clarinet. Johnny studied under one of New Orleans's most eminent clarinetists, Lorenzo Tio Jr. Baby began formal drum studies in 1912. At various times, both boys played in the famous New Orleans bands led by Bunk Johnson, Kid Ory, Papa Celestine, and Fate Marable.

*Johnny joined King Oliver in Chicago in 1919, and Baby was reunited with his brother in the Creole Jazz Band in 1921. Both boys left Oliver in 1923 but, for most of the rest of their careers, remained in Chicago playing in a number of small groups and in Johnny's own band. Baby seems to have been a little more adventurous, going to New York a few times and to Europe on one short tour. Johnny went to New York once. Johnny suffered a severe heart attack in 1939 and died the next year. Baby continued **gigging** even after a stroke in 1949 and another in 1950, but he was forced to retire in 1957.*

Hugues Panassie, dean of French jazz critics, considered Johnny one of the two greatest jazz clarinetists ever to have lived. (The other was Jimmy Noone.) Baby was admired not only for the rhythmic force of his drumming but also for his lyric ability to complement and augment soloists. There is no doubt that the brothers left enduring marks on the early pages of jazz.

SUGGESTED LISTENING

King Oliver's Jazz Band, 1923. Smithsonian Collection. 2-LP set.

The Move to Chicago:
Louis Armstrong
and Bix Beiderbecke

10

Earl Hines and
Louis Armstrong

Selections by Louis Armstrong and Bix Beiderbecke have been chosen to illustrate the differences between New Orleans and Chicago-style Dixieland. These recordings highlight the differences between the two styles and testify to the impact these leading musicians had on the future development of jazz.

Armstrong played a hybrid Dixieland style that had evolved from the earlier New Orleans jazz he and his mentor, King Oliver, had grown up with. In the 1920s the Chicago style eventually replaced that sound with a 2/4 jazz beat. More prominent drumming and an active left hand on the piano gave definition to the accents placed on the first and third beats of each measure. The pianist's left hand played a low bass note on the first beat of the measure and an accented chord in the middle keys on the second. The next two beats repeated this procedure, hence the "boom-chuck, boom-chuck" beat.

This two-beat pattern did not originate with Chicago Dixieland; it was integral to ragtime and stride piano music. White musicians who had heard King Oliver's band in Chicago adapted the 2/4 beat to instrumental jazz. The sound of the relocated New Orleans bands electrified Chicago groups, such as the Austin High Gang, which included the MacPartland brothers, Bix Beiderbecke (briefly), Frank Teschemacher, Bud Freeman, and Davey Tough. They adopted New Orleans jazz as their own, eliminated the banjo, added piano and saxophone, and flavored it with the old ragtime beat.

The result was a mixture of two styles. Very often the blur between 2/4 and 4/4 was unintentional. The groups built their performances around individual soloists without considering the stylistic changes that might occur. If a Chicago-style rhythm section was used, the resulting sound would be primarily 2/4 jazz; if a banjo was used instead of the piano, the result would be closer to the New Orleans style. The musicians themselves were quite flexible. Their main concern was with whom they would play, not necessarily which style of jazz was the more important. The differences between the New Orleans and Chicago Dixieland styles are summarized in the following table.

New Orleans vs. Chicago Dixieland Styles

	New Orleans	*Chicago*
Main melody	Trumpets (1 or 2)	Trumpet
Higher melody	Clarinet	Clarinet
Lower melody & chordal notes	Trombone	Trombone, but more soloistic; tenor sax
Strongest rhythm instrument	Banjo, 4/4 beat; drums stay soft	Drums, using heavy afterbeat; pianist's left hand plays 2/4 beat
Fundamental note of chord	Tuba	String bass, using some walking patterns
Solos	Short	Long, sometimes very long
Collective improvisation	Heavy emphasis	Less emphasis, more individual solos

LISTENING GUIDE

New Orleans Style

Perhaps the most celebrated and thoroughly analyzed record of this period is "West End Blues," recorded by Louis Armstrong in June 1928 with the Hot Five. Armstrong begins the King Oliver tune with a trumpet solo that according to many jazz historians redirected the course of jazz. When Armstrong starts the theme proper, the ensemble backs him in Dixieland fashion.

"West End Blues"—1928 (Intro. to Jazz Disc 1, Cut 5)

Trumpet and vocal—Louis Armstrong
Trombone—Fred Robinson
Clarinet—Jimmy Strong
Piano—Earl Hines
Banjo—Mancy Cara
Drums—Zutty Singleton

.00 Double-time (twice as fast as the normal beat) introduction by trumpet (solo **cadenza**).

.16 Flat-four rhythm section; trumpet leads the texture, clarinet and trombone play slower melodies in accompaniment.

.50 Trombone solo, drummer uses wood blocks, banjo continues 4/4 beat, right-hand trills in piano accompaniment.

1.25 Call-response between clarinet and voice; voice improvises double-time melodies like those in the introduction; banjo strums a flat-four beat.

1.58 Piano solo, melodic right hand (double-time).

2.11 Octaves in right hand make melody more forceful.

2.33 All horns play long notes, banjo and piano play a flat-four beat.

2.45 Trumpet solo with double-time melodies over long notes by clarinet and trombone.

2.56 Piano interlude.

3.10 Ending.

Chicago Style

Bix Beiderbecke's recording of "Somebody Stole My Gal," recorded two months earlier than Armstrong's "West End Blues," demonstrates the contrasting styles.

"Somebody Stole My Gal"—1928 (Intro. to Jazz Disc 1, Cut 6)

Cornet—Bix Beiderbecke
Trombone—Bill Rank
Clarinet—Izzy Friedman
Bass sax—Min Leibrook
Piano—Lennie Hayton
Drums—Harry Gale

.00 Introduction: Horns in harmony, **tutti** rhythm (not improvised), orchestra bells in background.

.06 Chicago-style ensemble; collective improvisation; 2/4 jazz beat; all melodies are equal to the texture; bass sax plays bass line and fills.

.35 Cornet leads and the other horns respond at the ends of phrases.

.54 Clarinet solo, accompanied by long notes (possibly not improvised); verse to this song is used as a bridge.

1.12 Piano solo, ragtime style; the right hand is more rhythmic than melodic.

1.30 Cornet solo accompanied by rhythm section.

1.56 The full ensemble plays a very short interlude.

1.58 Trombone solo, rhythm section continues.

2.16 Solo break by trombone.

2.18 Full ensemble improvising.

2.43 Written ending with a return of the orchestra bells, tutti rhythm in horns.

Comparing the Two Styles

The two selections differ noticeably in clarity. The relaxed playing of Armstrong's band is typical of the New Orleans style, whereas the precise playing of Beiderbecke's band typifies the Chicago style. Both cornet players were considered leaders in jazz improvisation as well as in technical virtuosity. The double-time beginning of "West End Blues" foreshadows the phrasing that will be played by jazz trumpeters in later years.

The piano solos are very different stylistically. They share a ragtime flavor, but the hornlike melodies of Earl Hines are prophetic of a new concept in jazz piano. His melodic lines are very similar to those in Armstrong's introduction.

Oddly enough, elements in the *earlier* New Orleans style of "West End Blues," such as the double-time melodies and phrasing techniques, will reappear at the birth of bebop.

LOUIS ARMSTRONG (1901–1971)

". . . Armstrong was the greatest of all jazz revolutionaries,"[1] writes Joachim Berendt in *The Jazz Book*. Few jazz historians would dispute that statement. Between 1925 and 1929, Louis recorded instrumental and vocal solos (with studio groups called the Hot Five and the Hot Seven) that redirected the course of jazz.

Genealogists would be hard put to find the root sources of his genius. Daniel Louis Armstrong claimed to have been born in a New Orleans slum on July 4, 1900, but research discloses the actual date to have been August 4, 1901. His father deserted the family when Louis was five. His mother worked as a domestic and, against discouraging odds, held the rest of the family together.

When he was twelve, Louis celebrated New Year's Eve by firing a few blank cartridges from his stepfather's pistol. He was arrested by the New Orleans police and was put in the Colored Waifs' Home. His confinement lasted a year and a half. A teacher there, Peter Davis, gave Louis a bugle and a cornet, together with lessons on the instruments. Armstrong was an eager pupil and was soon appointed leader of the band. After he was released from the home, he sold papers and worked in a dairy but did little musically for the next three years. Just when it appeared that Louis might be headed nowhere, King Oliver, then playing in Kid Ory's Jazz Band, took the seventeen-year-old boy under his wing. The raw talent that had begun to bloom at the home flourished under Oliver's supervision.

In 1917 the United States Navy shut down Storyville, the red-light district where most New Orleans jazz was heard. As a result, King Oliver left for Chicago and Louis replaced him in Kid Ory's Band.

In 1922 Louis joined King Oliver's Creole Jazz Band in Chicago. The pianist, Lil Hardin, was a classically trained musician who saw Armstrong's immense potential. Despite some initial resistance on his part, she forced him to extend himself in formal study, and his musical development accelerated. Their close professional association stimulated a personal bond that led to their marriage in 1924. This was his second marriage (his first, when he was eighteen, had lasted only three years).

Now began the most productive period of his life. For the next six years, he played with several bands, mostly in Chicago and New York, but also on tours across the country. It was also during this time that the historically significant Hot Five and Hot Seven records were made, including the "West End Blues." (Although the piece lasts only three minutes and eleven seconds, its historical impact has been incalculable.) Oddly, Armstrong did not seem to realize what he had done. In his autobiography, *Swing That Music,* published in 1936, Armstrong virtually dismissed the entire period from 1926 to 1930.

---

[1]Joachim Berendt, *The Jazz Book* (Westport, Conn.: Lawrence Hill and Co., 1975), p. 58.

The Swing Period

Many jazz scholars dismiss Armstrong's career after 1930. They feel that he had already made his contribution to music history and thereafter was content to be merely an entertainer. It is true that his latter-day image is that of a gravel-voiced, laughing stage personality. Nevertheless, he took his responsibilities to his public seriously and provided the highest-quality music.

From 1931 on, Armstrong became a world figure. He traveled to England and the Continent, where his reception was tumultuous. He was featured in the movie *Pennies from Heaven* in 1936 and later appeared in several more films. During that time and until 1947, he led what was to become the traditional swing band: piano, bass, drums and guitar, four trumpets, three trombones, and four or five saxes. The material he turned out was slick and predictable. It may have been commercial, but Louis's trumpet was still the most exciting voice in jazz.

The Post-Swing Period

In 1947 Armstrong returned to a Chicago Dixieland format. His smaller band sparked an increase in musical freedom and quality, of which its 1948 rendition of "Ain't Misbehavin'" is a fine example. Together with "Hello Dolly" and "Sleepy Time Down South," this was one of Louis's theme songs. He had introduced the Fats Waller number in the Broadway review *Hot Chocolates* in 1929.

In the following years, Louis remained before the public in varying degrees of prominence. He traveled widely and was welcomed enthusiastically wherever he played. He became known as a "musical ambassador," an unofficial title nonetheless endorsed by the United States government. Louis was apolitical and seldom revealed any strong feelings about racial discrimination, but he must have had them nevertheless. Several younger black musicians accused him of "Uncle Tomism" because of that attitude. He did occasionally express his views on the subject, however; he turned down a State Department tour in 1957 saying, "The way they are treating my people in the South the government can go to hell."[2]

When Armstrong died on July 6, 1971, there was a great outpouring not only from the musical and entertainment communities but from the public at large. Although there might have been a general shortage of appreciation for the artist, there was no lack of affection for the man. Toward the end of his life, Armstrong was said to have become bitter. No doubt he had made a lot of money, and his name was as well known as that of any musician in history, but the quality of recognition he received was not up to the magnitude of his accomplishments.

[2]Ibid., p. 61.

BIX BEIDERBECKE (1903–1931)

Leon Bismarck Beiderbecke's upper-middle-class parents hoped he would follow in his father's respectable business footsteps in Davenport, Iowa, but even as a child Bix indicated he was really interested only in music. He was picking out tunes on the family piano when he could barely reach the keyboard.

He had absolute pitch and infallible tonal memory. It was a gift, however, that carried a penalty he would later regret having to pay. He did not have to learn to read music to be able to play. His first, and only, piano teacher gave up in disgust when it became evident that when Bix had him demonstrate a passage, Bix was memorizing. The cat was out of the bag when Bix could not keep from embellishing the melody or "improving" the harmonic setting. He did, of course, learn to read passably, but even near the end of his career he was dropped from the Casa Loma Orchestra for, among other reasons, not being able to read well enough.

Davenport is on the Mississippi and was a stopping place for the paddle-wheel excursion boats that brought New Orleans jazz upriver. In 1919 Bix was introduced to the first Original Dixieland Jazz Band records, heard and met Louis Armstrong on one of the boats, fell in love with jazz, bought a used cornet, and taught himself to play.

The fact that he learned without lessons is significant. Valve combinations to produce certain notes on brass instruments are interchangeable with alternate fingerings. Conservatory-trained musicians rarely use alternates; Bix used them extensively. Some analysts believe his technical deviations contributed to the unique tone Bix got from his horn.

From 1919 to 1923 Bix served his apprenticeship as a dance-band cornetist. His parents had finally given up on his formal education when he was expelled from Lake Forest, a military academy near Chicago, to which they had sent him in 1922. His aversion to school, however, was not the sign of a limited intellect, for Bix loved to read and converse on many subjects. The academy's location afforded Bix a number of chances to slip off to Chicago to hear and even to sit in with a number of New Orleans expatriates. Unfortunately, since this was during Prohibition and most jazz was played in speakeasies, Bix began the drinking that would ultimately lead to his destruction.

Nineteen twenty-three was the year Bix matured musically. He rose from competent sideman to sought-after soloist. It was also when he began emerging as an innovator. He developed a tone and an attack that imparted a clear, singing quality to his instrument. He played in the midrange of his horn, but even so he fashioned soaring, lyrical melodic lines that found unexpected **harmonic extensions** and startling **intervallic** leaps. He had always been a student of harmonies; he loved the synergism of stacked intervals and could hear and analyze complex harmonies. In trumpet sections playing scored arrangements, he could hear notes of the harmony left vacant and instantly play

Wolverine Orchestra, 1924. *Left to right: Vic Moore, drums; George Johnson, tenor sax; Jimmy Hartwell, clarinet, alto sax; Dick Voynow, piano, leader; Bix Beiderbecke, cornet; Al Gande, trombone; Min Leibrook, tuba; Bob Gillette, banjo.*

them even though he was not reading. He would challenge musicians to play any ten-note cluster on the piano and would bet that he could identify every note. He never lost.

In 1923 he formed a band called the Wolverines, which gained almost instant popularity in the Northeast and the Midwest. In 1924 they recorded sixteen sides for Gennett Studios. Sales were brisk. Among the numbers was Hoagy Carmichael's "Riverboat Shuffle," which Bix subsequently also recorded with other bands. Bix had met Carmichael when the Wolverines played a dance at Indiana University, and the two remained close friends.

By this time it was evident that Bix could not handle alcohol. Alcoholism sometimes incapacitated him; nevertheless, the years between 1924 and 1929 saw his artistry and reputation continue to grow. In late 1924 he joined the Jean Goldkette organization and began a long professional association with saxophonist Frank Trumbauer. He was surrounded by jazz talent: trombonists Bill Rank, Miff Mole, and Tommy Dorsey; cornetist Red Nichols; clarinetists Jimmy Dorsey, Pee Wee Russell, and Benny Goodman; sax player Adrian Rollini; guitarist Eddie Lang; violinist Joe Venuti. Of all these, Bix had risen to a position of preeminence in the opinion of the public and musicians alike as the most exciting white jazz soloist.

In this period of American history, the color line was harshly drawn. White musicians played together in public while black artists remained within their own orbit. The mark that Bix was leaving in jazz history was separated from the one Louis Armstrong was making. That Armstrong's was the more far reaching and significant has never been disputed, but Bix's contribution was important because it was creative and established a following that can still be heard. The two men's paths crossed from time to time. They admired one another; each one listened to and drew from the imagination of the other.

In October 1927 Bix and Trumbauer joined "The King of Jazz," Paul Whiteman, who conducted the most successful "symphonic jazz" orchestra of the period. It featured three trumpets, one cornet, four trombones, eight reeds, six violins, a banjo, a tuba, a string bass, two pianos, drums, two vocal trios, four arrangers, and a librarian. The roster included Henry Busse, Tommy and Jimmy Dorsey, Matty Malneck, Bing Crosby, Harry Barris and Al Rinker, and composer-arranger Ferde Grofé. The music was only distantly related to jazz, but Whiteman recognized the contribution jazz artists could make to the orchestra, and he paid top dollar.

Some historians have speculated that Bix hated having to play in such a structured, pretentious organization, but it seems likely that given his love of classical music and sophisticated harmony, Bix found the arrangements, such as those written by Grofé, perfectly suited as settings for his jewellike solos. Besides, Whiteman grew to love and protect the shy, gentlemanly, but troubled artist, and Bix found comfort in that security. Until October 1929 Bix played exclusively with the Whiteman orchestra, participating in no fewer than eighty-five recording sessions as well as countless radio broadcasts and concerts. In addition to his cornet solos, Bix was often featured at the piano to play, among others, his own composition, *In a Mist,* an impressionistic, Debussy-like piece.

In January 1929 Bix suffered an alcoholic seizure that incapacitated him for over a month. He rejoined Whiteman in March and apparently remained dry for several months, but by August he was drinking again. He began missing rehearsals and appearances, and in September Whiteman sent him home to Davenport for an extended rest.

Bix moved to New York City in February 1931. His last engagements were played in bands that contained musicians who would be giants of the coming swing era—the Dorsey brothers, Benny Goodman, Gene Krupa, Bunny Berigan, Glenn Miller, Carl Kress, Jack and Charlie Teagarden, Will Bradley, Bud Freeman, Joe Sullivan, Artie Shaw, Eddie Miller, Ray Bauduc, Lenny Hayton, Glen Gray—but except for occasional flashes, he was not the dominating force he once had been.

On August 6, 1931, Bix suffered a seizure that was too much for his ravaged system. He was buried in Davenport on August 11.

SUGGESTED LISTENING

Louis Armstrong: *New Orleans.* Folkways Vol. 3 FJ2803.

Chicago No. 1. Folkways Vol. 5 FJ2805.

Chicago No. 2. Folkways Vol. 6 FJ2806.

Swing That Music. MCA Records MCAC 1312. (CS)

Satchmo's Collectors Items. MCA Records MCAC 1322. (CS)

Bix Beiderbecke: *Singing the Blues.* Columbia Jazz Masterpieces CK45450.

At the Jazz Band Ball. Columbia Jazz Masterpieces CK46175.

The Smithsonian Collection of Classic Jazz.

Jelly Roll Morton

11

Jelly Roll Morton

Jelly Roll Morton was responsible for introducing many innovations, not the least of which was the infusion of Latin rhythms into ragtime-blues jazz. He undoubtedly was the first to bring a composer-arranger's orderliness to jazz music. Although swing was to eventually leave him in its wake, it owed him a debt of gratitude for demonstrating what careful **notation** could do.

Morton's arrangements alone set him apart from the many other New Orleans musicians. Most bands relied upon the excitement of collective improvisation during most of a performance. Morton heightened the contrasts in each composition by writing fresh ideas for ensemble passages and accompaniment behind the soloists.

LISTENING GUIDE

"Dead Man Blues" and "Black Bottom Stomp" are excellent examples of Jelly Roll Morton in his triple role of performer-composer-arranger. Note the varying textures within each composition. Morton arranged distinctive sections to contrast with the choruses of collective improvisation. Notice how each chorus presents a new and refreshing sound.

"Dead Man Blues"—1926 (SCCJ Disc 1, Cut 7)

Piano—Jelly Roll Morton
Trombone—Edward "Kid" Ory
Trumpet—George Mitchell
Clarinet (solo)—Omer Simeon
Clarinet—Barney Bigard
Clarinet—Darnell Howard
Banjo—Johnny St. Cyr
Bass—John Lindsay
Drums—Andrew Hilaire

.00 Introduction: Funeral march.
.14 Slow Dixie beat, 4/4: Collective improvisation.
.37 Clarinet solo with piano accompaniment in ragtime style.
.58 Trombone leads into the trumpet solo with piano accompaniment.
1.23 2nd chorus: Trumpet solo.
1.30 Banjo and piano play a modified stop time in the background.
1.45 Clarinet trio plays tutti rhythm; the rest of the band plays sharp accents.
2.07 Repeat of clarinet trio, with a trombone solo in the background.

2.29   Collective improvisation; trombone continues its melodic solo.
2.52   Coda: Clarinet trio, followed by a sharp accent from the band.
2.56   End.

The most striking sound in "Dead Man Blues" is the unexpected clarinet trio. Dixieland bands rarely had more than one clarinet, and Morton had to bring in two additional clarinets especially for this arrangement. The trombone solo over the repeated clarinet trio was also a new concept in Dixieland arrangements. Morton also had the rest of the band accent the syncopated beat.

"Black Bottom Stomp" offers an even more elaborate arrangement. Morton had amazing control over what was to be played. Only after listening to this selection several times is it possible to identify when the band is improvising and when it is performing from notation. The most obvious notated spots occur at the ends of solos when all the horns play the same rhythmic idea leading into collective improvisation.

"Black Bottom Stomp"—1926 (SCCJ Disc 1, Cut 6)

Piano—Jelly Roll Morton
Trumpet—George Mitchell
Trombone—Edward "Kid" Ory
Clarinet—Omer Simeon
Banjo—Johnny St. Cyr
Bass—John Lindsay
Drums—Andrew Hilaire

.00   The introduction is highly arranged.
.07   The first statement of the theme is also arranged.
.22   Trumpet call.
.26   Band responds.
.30   Trumpet call, stop time.
.33   Band responds.
.37   The clarinet solos while the piano plays the same melody in the background.
.41   Clarinet improvisation.
.49   Phrase repeats.
.56   Collective improvisation.
1.02   An arranged phrase ending.
1.15   Clarinet solo in low register.
1.21   Solo break.
1.31   An arranged fill for the entire band, with accented chords.

1.33	Piano solo in stride style.
1.52	Muted trumpet solo, stop-time accompaniment.
2.10	Banjo solo, accompanied by bass and drums; chorus begins with stop time, and then the bass walks, that is, plays a note of the chord on each beat.
2.29	Collective improvisation; rhythm section fades into the background.
2.35	Short cymbal solo break.
2.48	Accent on 2nd and 4th beats by the drummer, producing a 2/4 jazz beat.
2.54	Trombone solo break.
3.05	Tag or coda.
3.09	End.

JELLY ROLL MORTON (1885–1941)

Jelly Roll Morton was born Ferdinand La Menthe in 1885 or 1890 near New Orleans. His father, an itinerant trombone player and carpenter, deserted his family when the boy was very young. Although Jelly Roll claims to have taken the name of his stepfather to avoid being called "Frenchy," he may also have wanted to disown his real father. In his youth, he experimented with drums, trombone, harmonica, violin, and guitar, but finally settled on the piano. He received a considerable amount of formal classical training, and that background proved valuable in later years.

Jelly Roll went to live with his great-grandmother when his mother died. Schooling interested him less than playing piano and making music in the Storyville district of New Orleans. When his great-grandmother, a strict Catholic Creole, learned where he was spending his time, she threw him out. He was fifteen.

For the next twenty-odd years, he was constantly on the move. In addition to what he could pick up by playing the piano, he made money pool hustling, bell hopping, pimping, tailoring, peddling, and card sharking. He joined minstrel shows, managed nightclubs, and promoted boxing matches. He carried a gun, was arrested by mistake in Mississippi for a mail-train robbery, and escaped from a chain gang. He was an inveterate braggart.

Jelly Roll's long, light-skinned face reflected his French Creole ancestry, but his black Creole parentage relegated him to a limbo existence between black and white. He distrusted blacks and was not accepted by whites.

In 1923 Morton moved to Chicago, where he stayed for five years. It was his

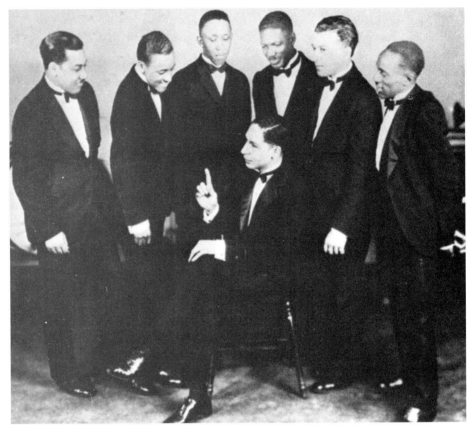

Jelly Roll Morton's Red Hot Peppers, 1926. *Left to right: Omer Simeon, clarinet; Andrew Hilaire, drums; Johnny Lindsay, bass; Jelly Roll Morton, piano; Johnny St. Cyr, banjo; Edward "Kid" Ory, trombone; George Mitchell, trumpet.*

best period. He headed and performed with numerous bands in addition to leading the Red Hot Peppers.

The Red Hot Peppers

The jazz band known as Jelly Roll Morton and His Red Hot Peppers was formed in 1926 to meet a commitment made to the Victor Recording Company. The first session was held on September 15 in Chicago with musicians assembled by Jelly Roll just for the recordings. Over the following four years, Morton reassembled studio bands under the same name thirteen more times. Before their contract lapsed, they cut fifty-seven very successful sides.

The group's instrumentation and personnel were never firmly organized.

Jelly Roll recruited musicians he felt could best bring each of his compositions and arrangements to life. The band assembled for the first date did, however, constitute a sort of basic cadre. It contained a clarinet, a trumpet, and a trombone, and a rhythm section consisting of piano, bass, drums, and banjo. In the second session, on September 21, 1926, Jelly Roll added two clarinets, and in the third session two violins.

Walter and Lester Melrose, the music publishers, were largely responsible for the high quality not only of the recordings but also of the musical performances. They spared no expense in securing the best equipment, and they paid the musicians five dollars apiece to rehearse, an unheard-of extravagance.

Several rehearsals were necessary if Jelly Roll's meticulously detailed arrangements were to be successful. He insisted that every written ensemble part be followed precisely.

An extraordinary number of musicians played in the Red Hot Peppers at one time or another. Morton's direction provided excellent training for future stardom. Duke Ellington's band welcomed many Morton alumni: trumpeters Bubber Miley, Arthur Wetzel, and Freddy Jenkins; trombonists Joe Nanton, Charlie Irvis, Wilber De Paris, and Sandy Williams; clarinetist Barney Bigard; saxophonists Johnny Hodges and Russell Procope; bassist Wellman Braud.

Morton moved to New York in 1928 and continued to cut Red Hot Peppers records with new musicians. The records sold well, but the first stirrings of swing were beginning to be heard and it would not be long before New Orleans jazz would go into a decline. In 1929 and 1930 the band went on the road. Jelly Roll made all the bookings himself. He bought a large bus for the band and had his name and "The Red Hot Peppers" painted on the side, but he rode separately in his Lincoln with his wife, Mabel. By 1930, however, the band began to lose its popularity.

Jelly Roll fell upon hard times after 1930. He had been in the habit of carrying a roll of thousand-dollar bills, and he had owned a number of diamonds, some mounted on his gold belt buckle and garters (one was embedded in a front tooth). He lost all his assets when a business venture failed. All he had to show for his years of prosperity was a hole in his tooth where the diamond had been.

His health declined and he was able to find little work. He blamed his condition, among other things, on a voodoo spell cast on him by a West Indian former associate. In 1935 he moved to Washington, D.C., and managed a sleazy upstairs club.

In 1938 Alan Lomax (the same folklorist who had discovered Leadbelly) tracked Jelly Roll down and brought him to a recording studio for the Library of Congress. Over a two-month period, Morton cut twelve long-play albums of original and traditional compositions. Besides playing the piano and singing, he provided a spoken commentary on his life and the lives of early jazz musicians. The albums sparked a Jelly Roll Morton revival. He returned to New York, where he remained until late 1940, recording thirty-three more pieces.

In November 1940 Morton went to Los Angeles hoping to secure some diamonds from his godmother's estate. When he got there they were gone. His life lost direction and purpose after that, and he spent the next eight months in Southern California, moving around aimlessly as his health deteriorated. He died on July 10, 1941, in a Los Angeles hospital.

SUGGESTED LISTENING

Jelly Roll Morton and His Red Hot Peppers. RCA Bluebird 6588-2-RB.

Leading Dixieland Soloists

Sidney Bechet

SIDNEY BECHET (1897–1959)

Before the electronic manipulation of natural sounds became commonplace in jazz, a horn player achieved individuality of **timbre** through technique or by choosing an uncommon instrument. Sidney Bechet employed both measures. He perfected a florid, European tone with a wide **vibrato,** on both the clarinet and the very difficult soprano saxophone.

Sidney was born in New Orleans in 1897, the seventh child of Omar and Josephine Bechet. His father, a shoemaker and sometime trumpet player, kept musical instruments in the house, and his mother used to take the children to the opera. Although the whole family was musical, Sidney showed special talent. At the age of six, he started clarinet lessons with New Orleans's foremost teacher, George Baquet, and soon was playing in bands. By his teens he had played with all the New Orleans greats: Bunk Johnson, King Oliver, Louis Armstrong, and Freddie Keppard, for whom he had a special regard.

Oddly, he could not read music then and never perfected the skill, but in his case it did not matter. He became a master of his instruments, first the clarinet and later the soprano sax. According to the jazz historian Martin Williams, "There seems to me no question that he was the greatest New Orleans **reed** man."[1] Certainly his name stands in the company of Jelly Roll Morton and Louis Armstrong. Although Bechet never reached Armstrong's stature in America, he was a star of the first magnitude in France, where he lived a good part of his life.

He first went to Europe in 1919 with the Will Marion Cook orchestra, a large, Paul Whiteman–type organization. Cook featured Bechet on clarinet solos, and Bechet was immediately acclaimed a virtuoso. However, a brush with the law in England resulted in his deportation to the United States. He landed in New York, where he joined a show featuring Bessie Smith. It was then that he began playing the soprano saxophone; thereafter, the name Bechet became synonymous with that instrument.

In 1924 he briefly joined Duke Ellington's band but soon left to go back to Europe. In 1928, in Paris, he got into a shooting scrape and spent eleven months in jail. After being released, he went to Berlin and then returned to New York.

He joined Ellington again in 1932, at which time he tutored Johnny Hodges. The resulting Hodges alto saxophone sound became an indispensable ingredient of the Ellington band. Bechet, ever restless, left to form a number of his own bands, and with them he made several successful records.

During the Depression, he and trumpeter Tommy Ladnier kept poverty at bay by operating the Southern Tailor Shop in Harlem. The back bedroom was the site of many **jam sessions,** which were attended by the elite of the New York jazz world. Ladnier's death in 1939 was a heavy blow to Bechet, but wartime ac-

---

[1]Martin Williams, *Jazz Masters of New Orleans* (Jersey City, N.J.: Da Capo Press, 1978), p. 136.

tivity and prosperity were adding vitality to the swing movement, and Bechet threw himself fully into his career. "Musicianers," to use Bechet's term, found plenty of work.

After the war Bechet moved to Brooklyn, where he opened a music school. In 1951, however, he moved to France permanently. There he married his third wife, Elizabeth Zeigler, a German woman. The event was considered sufficiently noteworthy to be given several pages in *Life* magazine. He bought an imposing residence near Paris, kept a mistress, by whom he had a son, and played and recorded both in Europe and in America until his death in 1959.

The personal magnetism possessed by all great performers is evident in their music. Bechet's personal strength was particularly expressed in his strong tone and powerful melodic lines.

One of his best compositions, "Blue Horizon," was recorded by the Blue Note Jazzmen in December 1944 for the Blue Note Record Company. Although he plays clarinet in this session, his virtuosity shines clearly.

LISTENING GUIDE

"Blue Horizon"—1944 (SCCJ Disc 1, Cut 11)

Clarinet—Sidney Bechet
Trumpet—Sidney De Paris
Trombone—Vic Dickenson
Piano—Art Hodes
Bass—George "Pops" Foster
Drums—Manzie Johnson

.00	Slow blues tempo; the snare drum is played with brushes; the clarinet plays in the low register with a wide vibrato; the piano can be heard in the background.
.42	2nd chorus: The trombone responds to the clarinet.
1.25	3rd chorus: A new melodic idea using large intervals is introduced; other horns provide a slow Dixie-like texture.
2.08	4th chorus: The piano plays a tremolo; the clarinet moves to a higher register.
2.53	5th chorus: Blue notes are emphasized in the solo.
3.35	6th chorus: The clarinet plays in the extreme high register; a heavy, driving beat is supplied by the drums and piano; the trombone continues responding; this is the most climactic chorus.
4.13	Ending.
4.20	End.

EDWARD "KID" ORY (1886–1973)

Before the turn of the century at La Place, Louisiana, a Creole boy of Negro, French, Spanish, and Indian ancestry organized a band with some of his friends. Their instruments consisted of homemade cigar-box contraptions, and a chair served as a drum, but they managed to pick up small change playing on the street. When they had saved up enough, they bought legitimate instruments. Kid Ory chose the trombone. By the time he was thirteen, he was promoting picnics that, for fifteen cents, featured dance music and offered beer and salad.

Ory was musically gifted; although he was not an innovator, he was an important stylist and a catalyst to others in his bands. He was a superior organizer and musical leader in New Orleans just as jazz began to flower. This combination of circumstances and personal qualities favored Ory in his youth and throughout his long life. He played with trumpeter Buddy Bolden; in his own bands he employed King Oliver, Mutt Carey, Johnny Dodds, Jimmy Noone, Sidney Bechet, George Lewis, and Louis Armstrong at one time or another.

After World War I, when many New Orleans jazz musicians migrated to Chicago and other Northern cities, Ory moved to Los Angeles. He remained on the West Coast, mostly in Los Angeles and San Francisco, for five years. He was largely responsible for planting the enduring Dixieland sound in San Francisco

Kid Ory's Creole Jazz Band, 1919–20. *Left to right: Minor Ram Hall, drums; Edward "Kid" Ory, trombone; Papa Mutt Carey, trumpet; Ed Garland, bass, piano; Wade Whaley, clarinet.*

that was later nurtured by musicians such as trumpeters Lou Watters and Bob Scobey, banjoist Clancy Hayes, and trombonist Turk Murphy.

Ory moved to Chicago in 1924. During his five-year stay, he played with Jelly Roll Morton, Louis Russell, Johnny Dodds, King Oliver, Dave Peyton, and the celebrated Louis Armstrong Hot Five and Hot Seven.

Back in Los Angeles in 1929, Ory played locally for a couple of years and then retired to a chicken farm. In the early 1940s, at the age of fifty-five, he was persuaded to come out of retirement. In 1944 he played on an Orson Welles radio program that included a short segment of early New Orleans music. The program received such an enthusiastic response that Welles made it a regular feature. Ory became the leader of the group. They made a number of successful records, and in 1945 *Time* magazine featured an article entitled "The Kid Comes Back." Ory found himself at the forefront of a nationwide New Orleans music revival.

Kid Ory appeared in several movies, including *New Orleans* in 1946, *Crossfire* in 1947, *Mahogany Magic* in 1950, and *The Benny Goodman Story* in 1955. He made two European tours in the 1950s and returned permanently to Los Angeles in 1961. After three more active years, he gradually retired; and in 1973, at the age of eighty-seven, he quietly passed away.

Kid Ory can be heard in the Smithsonian Collection with Jelly Roll Morton in "Granpa's Spells," "Dead Man Blues," and "Black Bottom Stomp," and with Louis Armstrong in "Struttin' with Some Barbeque" and "Hotter Than That." Ory was a well-rounded musician. He had studied harmony and counterpoint and was proficient on the trumpet, clarinet, piano, banjo, bass, drums, guitar, and saxophone; however, it was his trombone playing that helped define the Dixieland sound.

SUGGESTED LISTENING

Louis Armstrong and Earl Hines—1928. Smithsonian Collection, R002.
Sidney Bechet—The Victor Sessions/Master Takes. RCA Bluebird 2402-2-RB.

SUPPLEMENTAL LISTENING GUIDE FOR PART 3

"Struttin' with Some Barbeque"—1927 (Louis Armstrong; SCCJ Disc 1, Cut 15)

> *Cornet—Louis Armstrong*
> *Trombone—Kid Ory*
> *Clarinet—Johnny Dodds*

Piano—Lil Armstrong
Banjo—Johnny St. Cyr

.00   Introduction, the verse of the song; cornet takes lead, all others accompany with collective improvisation.
.14   Beginning of the main melody, the chorus, or principal strain.
.34   2nd chorus.
.52   Banjo fill.
.54   Clarinet solo, low register, melody is structured around main chordal notes; banjo plays a flat-four pattern.
1.11 Solo break.
1.13 Trombone solo; flat-four banjo with accents on 2nd and 4th beats of each measure; the piano plays only on the accented beats.
1.30 Solo break for the trombone.
1.33 Cornet solo with the chords on only the 2nd and 4th beats of each measure (stop time), a difficult feeling to solo over.
1.50 Double-time fill (solo break).
2.03 Cornet plays a ragtime melody pattern.
2.10 Syncopated tutti rhythm.
2.15 Collective improvisation over a flat-four banjo part.
2.33 Banjo fill.
2.45 Syncopated tutti rhythm returns and becomes softer until the ending.
2.59 End.

The overall structure of this selection is especially interesting. Less time is spent on collective improvisation and more with ensemble accompaniments to solos. Notice how these accompaniments reinforce the offbeats of each measure, and for the cornet solo the texture is stripped down to the second and fourth beats alone. The collective improvisation that follows seems even more energetic by comparison. The total package ends with yet another unison rhythmic idea, further expanding the levels of contrasts.

"I Gotta Right to Sing the Blues"—1933 (Louis Armstrong; SCCJ Disc 1, Cut 20)

Trumpets—Louis Armstrong (and vocal), Elmer Whitlock, Zilmer Randolph
Trombone—Keg Johnson
Alto sax and clarinet—Scoville Brown, George Oldham
Tenor sax and clarinet—"Budd" Johnson
Piano—Teddy Wilson
Banjo and guitar—Mike McKendrick

Bass—Bill Oldham
Drums—Yank Porter

.00   Introduction, tutti.
.04   Piano finishes the introduction.
.08   Vocal melody while a small Dixieland ensemble plays accompaniment, flat-four rhythm beat.
.34   Stop-time effect with the 1st and 3rd beats being sung and the 2nd and 4th beats being played by the band.
.42   Return of the collective improvisation texture.
1.12   Piano fill.
1.16   Trumpet lead accompanied by a tutti ensemble typical of big-band arrangements, piano fills.
1.44   Trumpet solo, four-beat rhythm section, sax soli accompaniment (long notes forming chords.)
2.12   Stop-time effect returns followed by trumpet solo and sax soli.
2.52   End.

This selection has both small-group collective improvisation and big-band ensemble sections. In both cases, the authority with which Armstrong plays is continually evident. His vocal and trumpet solo work are stylistically commanding. The four-beat rhythm section sets off Armstrong's lay-back and expressive melodic techniques. In this period, Armstrong ended almost every number with a spectacular climb to a screaming high note. In this case, the ascent to the B-flat above the staff is hardly in keeping with the theme of the song but provides the expected Armstrong signature.

"Riverboat Shuffle"—1927 (Bix Beiderbecke; SCCJ Disc 1, Cut 22)

Cornet—Bix Beiderbecke
Trombone—Bill Rank
Clarinet and baritone sax—Don Murray
C-melody sax—Frankie Trumbauer
Alto sax—Ernest "Red" Ingle
Piano—Itzy Riskin
Banjo and guitar—Eddie Lang
Drums—Chaunsey Morehouse

.00   Introduction, tutti statements followed by a guitar solo fill.
.06   Repeat idea.
.12   Collective improvisation.
.17   Tutti statement and guitar fill returns.

.23 Collective improvisational statement answered by the guitar (2 times).

.34 Collective improvisational statement answered by the piano.

.40 Once again but answered by the clarinet.

.55 Cornet lead-in and solo, 4/4 rhythmic drive with accents on 2 and 4 by the piano.

1.14 Solo break.

1.32 Tutti lead-in.

1.34 Ensemble (tutti) statement, trombone answers (same texture as the beginning). Statements repeat with a brief interlude of collective improvisation.

1.52 Clarinet solo.

2.08 Solo break.

2.28 Collective improvisational statements followed by solo fills from the cornet, then the C-melody sax, and finally the guitar.

2.50 Solo break by the C-melody sax.

2.56 Ending (collective improvisation).

3.06 End.

The texture of this performance is a product of short tutti statements or collective improvisational statements followed by solo answers or fills without accompaniment. This piece opens and closes with this device. The solos in the middle are similarly separated. The solos themselves drive straight ahead, interrupted only by solo breaks. The result is a well-manicured arrangement with refreshing textural contrasts. Compare the lyric quality of Bix Beiderbecke with that of Armstrong.

"Singin' the Blues"—1927 (Bix Beiderbecke; SCCJ Disc 1, Cut 21)

Cornet—Bix Beiderbecke
C-melody sax—Frankie Trumbauer
Trombone—Bill Rank
Clarinet and alto sax—Jimmy Dorsey
Piano—Itzy Riskin
Guitar—Eddie Lang
Drums—Chaunsey Morehouse

.00 Introduction, all horns in duet.

.06 Solo C-melody sax, 2/4 beat established by the guitar playing melody, bass line, and fills.

.35 Repeat of 1st section.

.59 Solo break, double-time.

1.04   Cornet solo, guitar accompanies in similar manner.
1.27   Solo break, double-time.
2.00   Collective improvisation, first contribution of the drums.
2.14   Clarinet solo, guitar again supplies chords and bass line.
2.25   Solo break for the clarinet.
2.30   Cornet assumes the lead in a collective improvisation.
2.45   Solo break for the guitar.
2.57   End.

This selection is unique in that the rhythm, harmony, and bass line are the sole responsibility of the guitar. This sound is especially surprising because of the growing absence of guitar in bands at this time, due mostly to its soft volume compared with other instruments. The solos, however, float above this rhythmic foundation with equal freedom.

Swing: Benny Goodman and Fletcher Henderson

13

The swing era is largely associated with the big bands that played in large ball-rooms for multitudes of dancers and jitterbugs. The "jive" swung hard and the ballads were "mellow"; such expressions of the day described hot jazz and tender love songs. In the 1930s the nation was on the brink of a world war and was in the throes of a severe economic depression. Swing provided an escape from those political and social pressures. Jazz crossed a barrier and entered the world of popular music, but it did so with some sacrifice. The music became more structured, since ensemble playing was emphasized at the expense of improvisation. Two kinds of big bands existed within the swing classification: white bands that played arrangements intended for popular-music audiences, and black bands that emphasized improvisation and a more driving beat. Both, however, shared in the harvest of popularity sown by swing.

Terms Specific to Big Bands

A number of terms came into use with the advent of the big bands. Three in particular are important to the discussion of big-band arrangements: **tutti, soli,** and **shout chorus.** During a tutti, all brass and reed sections play together to create a solid unified texture. During a soli, all the members in *one* section play the same musical material—for example, all the saxes playing together accompanied only by the rhythm section. A shout chorus integrates the soli activities of the various sections at the climax of an arrangement. The most common arrangement is for the saxes to state a melody while the trumpets play short rhythmic chords (shouts). The trombones either join the trumpets in the shouts or supply a countermelody to the saxes. This exciting interplay usually occurs near the end of an arrangement. The shout chorus serves the same function in a big band as collective improvisation does in Dixieland; that is, an exciting climax after individual solos.

Benny Goodman's theme song, "Let's Dance," demonstrates how tutti, soli, and shout choruses are used. Notice the highly organized manner in which the sections perform. The call-response is calculated, and the accompaniments to the solos are always soli. Throughout the arrangement, the brass section is contrasted with the sax section. The tutti sections are used strategically to articulate musical climaxes. This recording shows how important solos were to Goodman. The two in this recording are quite long compared with those played in the average white society band.

LISTENING GUIDE

"Let's Dance"—composed 1934 (Intro. to Jazz Disc 1, cut 7)

Arranger—Bassman-Henderson
Clarinet—Benny Goodman

Trumpets—Jimmy Maxwell, Ziggy Elman, Johnny Martel
Trombones—Red Ballard, Vernon Brown, Ted Veseley
Saxes—Toots Mondello, Buff Estes, Bus Bussey, Jerry Jerome
Piano—Fletcher Henderson
Guitar—Arnold Covey
Bass—Artie Bernstein
Drums—Nick Fatool

.00 The melody is in the sax section; muted trumpets play background.
.19 Repeat, with one soft piano fill.
.37 Clarinet solo, sax section accompanies.
.56 Brass section accompanies, no saxes.
1.06 Sax section replaces brass.
1.13 Tutti fill by entire band.
1.15 Alto sax solo, accompanied by rhythm section.
1.34 Tutti band in background.
1.44 Just rhythm section again as accompaniment.
1.50 Tutti chorus (all the horns play the same rhythm but different notes).
2.00 Saxes and brass are woven into a shout chorus.
2.11 Clarinet solo accompanied by sax section.
2.21 Tutti—shout: The drummer plays a strong 2/4 beat.
2.28 Clarinet tag.
2.30 Band ends with one note.

THE STRUCTURE OF THE BIG BANDS

The size of the big bands varied considerably, but the basic structure was relatively consistent and remains the same today.

Sections

The *saxophone section* has from three to five members. Various saxophones are usually available—alto, tenor, and baritone, and sometimes soprano. In addition to this combination, the players often **double** (play a second instrument) on clarinet or flute.

The *trombone section* normally has three or four members. The section can alter its sound through the use of various mutes inserted in the bells of the instruments.

The *trumpet section* consists of three or four members. Several different mutes are likewise available to this section.

The *rhythm section* is made up of the piano, the string bass, and drums. Although seldom used today, the rhythm guitar was an important instrument in swing-era bands. (Count Basie, however, continued to use a swing-era-style guitarist.) The banjo is rarely, if ever, used.

Roles in the Horn Sections

Bands are organized by sections. The leader of each **horn** section plays the most important and demanding melodic part. Section members are expected to use the same inflections and interpretation as their leader. The second-chair player is usually responsible for the improvised solos, although any member may solo from time to time.

Roles in the Rhythm Section

The rhythm section has no particular leader unless one of the members is the leader of the band. This section is less restricted than any other. The pianist is free to add melodic ideas between phrases, and the bassist and the drummer may also be allowed to fill passages or add accents. When the drummer accentuates a musical idea in the band, he is said to be "kicking" the band. **Kicks** range from subtle strokes on the snare drum to violent crashes of the bass drum and the cymbal together. The string bassist may have a written part or may be instructed to **two-beat** or **walk.** A two-beat pattern is similar to the tuba part of a Dixieland band, which has a note on the first and third beat of each measure. The walking pattern implies a note on each beat of the measure.

In many ways, the interplay between sections is similar to that of early jazz groups. Sections rather than individuals employ the call-response techniques found in blues and Dixieland, but the fills are written out. Because several musicians play at the same time, written music is necessary to avoid chaos. If a band of eighteen members tried to improvise collectively, the texture would be too thick to be intelligible.

The freedom of the early jazz groups almost disappeared in the big bands. Individual musicians were required to play the written music and could improvise only when the arrangement called for it. Those who could read but not improvise found places in the sections. There were few places for jazz musicians who wanted to improvise but could not read music. Musicians who could both read and improvise were in great demand. Swing-era soloists who could add a measure of personality to the structured arrangements sometimes became celebrities, and some became famous enough to form their own bands.

The Arranger

The big bands were so organized that individual players had very little influence over how the band sounded. Musical decisions were made by the arranger before the band ever performed. For example, Fletcher Henderson,

Edgar Sampson, and a few other arrangers created the sound that made Benny Goodman the "King of Swing." Henderson also wrote for his own band, giving it its own distinctive sound. The mark of a premier arranger was the ability to analyze a band's potential and write scores to make it shine. Such musicians commanded top pay.

Showmanship

The informality of early jazz had no place in the big bands. To compete with society dance bands like those of Eddie Duchin and Guy Lombardo, swing bands took to wearing flashy satin tuxedos, their music stands sported sparkling logos, the bass drum was decorated with a logo and the drummer's initials, sections stood to soli or shout, and the trumpeters swung their derby mutes in eye-catching arcs. Band members indulged in novelty numbers in which one or more might come forward to sing a comic or ribald vocal. It was good theater and drew in the customers, but big bands had their problems too. The number of musicians alone caused many bands to give up, and the boredom of section playing often caused discontent. In addition, big-band showmanship often prevented the instrumentalists from sharing the limelight. The most popular personalities besides the leaders were generally the vocalists. Instrumentalists felt slighted by the public whenever a mediocre vocalist received ovations while a brilliant jazz soloist went unnoticed. Nevertheless, showmanship became a permanent part of the big-band picture. In the early 1940s a rebellion against such swing conventions helped foster the development of bebop.

FLETCHER H. HENDERSON (1898–1952)

Born in Cuthbert, Georgia, the son of a school principal, Fletcher grew up in a well-to-do family. His mother gave him piano lessons, and his formal schooling continued to his graduation from Atlanta University. He played dance dates around home as he was growing up, and in 1920, when he went to New York City, ostensibly to attend Columbia University, he got a job as a song demonstrator for a music company instead.

In 1921 he formed a blues-oriented band to accompany Ethel Waters, with whom he toured for a year, but not before receiving approval from his parents, who disdained such unrefined music. He also accompanied Bessie Smith, but he never was considered any better than just adequate in that role.

In 1923 Henderson formed a new band, the heart of which was Don Redman, a brilliant, conservatory-trained multi-instrumentalist, who rewrote the stock arrangements of popular songs. Redman was a visionary who could infuse the stodgy, pedestrian voicings with the rhythm and exuberance of the New Orleans–style black bands. Redman remained with Henderson until 1927. The list of musicians who played in the band during that time, and thereafter, contains the names of most of the stars of that era. Just a few were Louis Armstrong, Joe Smith, Tommy Ladnier, Coleman Hawkins, Buster Bailey, Fats Waller, John Kirby, Chu Berry, Sid Catlett, Cootie Williams, and, later, Art Blakey, Dexter Gordon, and Vic Dickenson.

After Redman's departure, the band drifted somewhat aimlessly until Benny Carter took over his chair, not only as saxophonist, but also as arranger. Fletcher's brother Horace also contributed a number of first-class arrangements. It was not until 1933 that Fletcher Henderson himself began writing arrangements. At the urging of impresario John Hammond, Benny Goodman began using Henderson's arrangements, and these, as much as any other factor, were responsible for the Goodman orchestra's success. Belatedly, Henderson has recently been recognized for his historic contribution to the creation of swing.

Henderson was a strange paradox. He was self-effacing, even retiring. It has been said that his wife, who sometimes played trumpet in the band, dominated him; yet, he assembled and managed orchestras populated by some of the most inflated egos in music. He is remembered primarily for his arrangements, but for ten years he depended on other arrangers to define and develop his bands. It might be inferred that he was just lucky, a person in the right place at the right time, but there was much more to him than that. His mind heard the sound combinations that would elevate dance music to a new plateau. Benny Goodman believed he, Goodman, would have had a fine orchestra without Henderson but that with him it became a great orchestra.

From 1935 to 1949, Henderson went back and forth a number of times from being Goodman's chief arranger to fronting his own band (with Goodman's and John Hammond's backing), but his bands never met with much success. In 1950 Fletcher suffered a stroke, and in 1952, after two heart attacks, he succumbed in a Harlem hospital. Perhaps more than anyone else, Fletcher Henderson was instrumental in infusing, to the extent possible, black jazz into white popular music. He was responsible for one of the truly significant advances in American music.

LISTENING GUIDE

"Wrappin' It Up"—1934 (Fletcher Henderson; SCCJ Disc 2, Cut 2)

Arranger—Fletcher Henderson
Trumpets—Russell Smith, Irving Randolph, Henry "Red" Allen
Trombones—Keg Johnson, Claude Jones
Alto sax and clarinet—Buster Bailey, Hilton Jefferson, Russell Procope
Tenor sax—Ben Webster

Piano—Horace Henderson
Guitar—Lawrence Lucie
String bass—Elmer James
Drums—Walter Johnson

.00 Introduction, brass play a tutti statement and saxes/clarinet supply short answers.
.09 Beginning of 1st chorus, full ensemble, sax soli plays the melody, with short brass punches filling in openings, 4-beat rhythm section.
.28 Tutti, all wind instruments play the same rhythm but different notes.
.47 Jefferson alto sax solo, smooth lyric tone, soft brass accompaniment (long notes).
1.16 Brass section and soloist play the same rhythm (very brief).
1.24 Brass section lead-in.
1.26 Red Allen trumpet solo, sax soli supplies accompaniment.
1.34 Return to a full tutti.
1.43 Trumpet solo returns with the sax soli.
2.03 Tutti and clarinet soli (call-response) similar to the introduction.
2.12 Bailey clarinet solo.
2.22 Sax soli, very active melodic line with large interval skips.
2.30 Tutti ending.
2.40 End.

The heart of this recording is Fletcher Henderson's arrangement. If finding the formula for making a big band swing can be attributed to anyone, it would have to be Henderson (together with Don Redman). His arrangements, as is evident here, provide ample space for the strong soloists in his band as well as exciting interplays between the brass and saxophone sections.

BENNY GOODMAN (1909–1986)

The Benny Goodman orchestra clearly showed that a big band could attain a high level of artistry. Goodman's band demonstrated his musical and organizational talents.

Benny Goodman's training and upbringing produced one of history's most accomplished jazz musicians. He was one of the swing era's best clarinetists and also one of its most successful band leaders. Goodman was a perfectionist. His dominance over his band is legendary. The "Goodman ray," an icy stare, was leveled at any musician who did not perform at Goodman's required level of excellence. This drive for perfection coupled with a keen business sense assured Goodman his goal of producing the most marketable music of the day.

Benjamin David Goodman was born on May 30, 1909, into a very poor Jewish family in the Chicago ghetto; he was the eighth of eleven children. His father eked out a living as a tailor after emigrating from Russia. The family lived in an unheated basement during the cold Chicago winters. Benny learned quickly that he had to take advantage of every situation. When he was ten, his father enrolled him and his brothers Harry and Freddy in a synagogue music program, where they were lent instruments and given lessons. Harry was given a tuba, Freddy was given a trumpet, and Benny, being the smallest, was given a clarinet. When the synagogue ran out of money, the boys were placed in a boys' band at Hull House (a social-service institution in Chicago). Benny made good progress and began to listen to and imitate popular performers. His precocious musical abilities were quickly evident. Still ten years old, he made his professional debut for five dollars in a vaudeville theater. During the next two years, Benny studied with Franz Schoeppe, whom Benny considered his greatest teacher. Schoeppe was a classical musician and shaped Benny's technique according to the strictest traditional standards. Although Schoeppe did not consider jazz very important, he had two other leading jazz clarinetists as students, Buster Bailey and Jimmie Noone.

Goodman's growing ability made it possible for him to quit high school after one year and work in a dance hall four nights a week. This experience led to a job in the Ben Pollack band (one of the first white big bands). He joined the band in Venice, California, in 1925. Glenn Miller also joined at that time, and Benny would later room with Miller while working in New York. Benny worked on and off with the Pollack band until 1928.

In 1928 he decided to leave Pollack and work in New York. Because of his personal contacts in studios and theaters, he made more money as an on-call musician than he would have if he had taken steady work with a band. He joined the Red Nichols band in 1929, and in 1931, using some Nichols personnel, Benny led his first band in the revue *Free for All.*

At this time John Hammond started to take an active part in Goodman's life. Hammond, the scion of a wealthy New York family and a jazz enthusiast, was influential in promoting the careers of many great jazz performers, such as Billie Holiday and Count Basie. He discovered a number of the talented instrumentalists who helped spark Goodman's band, among whom were Teddy Wilson, Lionel Hampton, Fletcher Henderson, Charlie Christian, and Gene Krupa. John Hammond's contribution to Goodman's success cannot be overstated. If Hammond was convinced that a musician had potential, he would force him into Goodman's world. On one occasion, Hammond brought guitarist Charlie Christian to a recording date, but Goodman showed no inclination to listen to Christian. Bassist Artie Bernstein and Lionel Hampton decided to help Christian and spirited him into the session. Goodman, to avoid embarrassment, let Christian play and quickly recognized his ability. After this incident, Christian became a regular member of one of the famous small groups that Goodman organized. For his part, Goodman was aware of Hammond's importance and consulted him on most business decisions.

Guided by Hammond, Goodman formed his most famous band in 1934. His first big break came when he was hired late in that year to appear on a New York radio network show called *Let's Dance*. The band played the last hour of a three-hour, late-evening dance-band show that was broadcast coast to coast. It gave Goodman national exposure. The contract lasted for twenty-six weeks, and although it did not produce instant success, it put Goodman well past the first rung of the ladder. The best musicians were hired for this show. Hammond was instrumental in engaging drummer Gene Krupa to add sparkle to an already exciting band. He also helped secure a large number of Fletcher Henderson arrangements, as much to help out Henderson, who needed the money, as to aid Goodman. It was a providential partnership.

The years following saw Goodman rise to the top of the popular music world. In the late 1930s his band drew large and enthusiastic audiences to dance halls and theater concerts. The most memorable was the first jazz concert ever held in Carnegie Hall, the bastion of classical music in New York City.

One of the Goodman band's subtler but important accomplishments was

Benny Goodman Sextet, 1941. *Left to right: George Auld, tenor sax; Benny Goodman, clarinet, leader; Charlie Christian, guitar; Artie Bernstein, bass; Cootie Williams, trumpet.*

the racial integration of jazz performers. Goodman did not hesitate to use any great black musician he needed. Although he was pressured to maintain a strict line between his band and black bands, Goodman (and Hammond) insisted that Lionel Hampton and Teddy Wilson appear every time the band performed. The musicians seemed less concerned with the color barrier than the promoters, whose major concern was ticket sales. This integration had two important results. First, it created a new mixture of black and white musical concepts. Hard-driving, solo-oriented swing was combined with the deliberate and refined music of the white society bands. Second, the band's sound pleased both black and white audiences. Goodman's small groups also delivered an exciting mixture of musical ideas. Besides his own mastery of the clarinet, the stimulation of Christian's guitar, Hampton's vibes, and Wilson's piano brought forth some of Benny's best performances.

Small Groups from the Swing Era

Small groups exposed jazz talents that were often hidden in big bands. Historians and critics generally believe jazz progressed only in small-group settings and not in the more popular big-band format. The best soloists from big bands were often featured in small groups that played between sets, adding contrast to the evening and giving the musicians some artistic freedom. These small groups often became successful in their own right. Benny Goodman's Trio, Quartet, and Sextet; Artie Shaw's Gramercy Five; Bob Crosby's Bob Cats; and Tommy Dorsey's Clambake Seven are notable examples of groups that made many records under their own names. One such group had members from two great bands—Count Basie's and Benny Goodman's. "I Found a New Baby" boasts a typical cross-section of talent. Although the players came from different bands, they all spoke a common swing language. The arrangement is highly organized. The accompaniment figures behind the solos are carefully worked out, a typical big-band characteristic. Collective improvisation appears only once, at the very end, and provides a glimpse of this music's Dixieland heritage.

LISTENING GUIDE

"I Found a New Baby"—1941 (SCCJ Disc 2, Cut 23)

Clarinet—Benny Goodman
Trumpet—Cootie Williams
Tenor sax—George Auld
Piano—Count Basie
Guitar—Charlie Christian

Bass—Artie Bernstein
Drums—Jo Jones

.00   The introduction begins with a motive that will be used through-
       out the piece; piano fills.

.06   1st chorus (A): The clarinet has the melody; the other horns play
       softly in the background, using the motive of the introduction;
       the guitar strums on each beat; the drums play a swing pattern.

.15   Repeat of (A): The clarinet plays in a relaxed style.

.25   Bridge (B).

.34   Last statement of (A), end of the 1st chorus.

.44   Guitar solo: The single-line melody is representative of a modern
       guitar style.

1.22   Piano solo, accompanied by horns playing the introduction mo-
       tive.

1.31   A dialogue in which the piano echoes the motive played by the
       horns.

1.40   Another dialogue, in which the clarinet echoes the piano motive.

1.57   Muted trumpet solo; horns play softly in background.

2.16   Tenor sax solo; drums became louder; the sound is big and ag-
       gressive.

2.35   Interlude featuring the drums.

2.43   A collective improvisation ends the performance. The form of
       each chorus is AABA.

2.53   End.

Goodman after the Swing Era

In spite of his dedication to jazz, Goodman did not abandon the classics. After 1935 he played in chamber groups and was a soloist with major symphonies. He performed with leading string quartets (the Budapest Quartet and the New York Quartet) and commissioned works from major composers such as Béla Bartók, Paul Hindemith, and Aaron Copland. At the same time, he continued to lead his swing band on a full-time schedule.

The end of World War II signaled the end of all but a few big bands. Stan Kenton and Woody Herman, Duke Ellington and Count Basie hung on; but by the end of 1946 most of the rest, including the Goodman band, had broken up. Benny, however, did not fade from sight. He continued to appear at festivals, in classical and jazz concerts, and in TV specials. He assembled small groups and big bands for particular occasions and for concert tours. In 1956 he took a group on a Far East tour, during which he played a much-publicized duet with the king of Thailand, and in 1958 he took a band to Europe. His most impressive international success was the 1962 tour of Russia sponsored by the State Department.

The 1980s brought a resurgence of big-band popularity. While Woody Herman, through frequent personnel turnover, pumped youth and musical currency into his bands, Goodman elected to stay with what he understood and liked best, and his bands were somewhat anachronistic. They mostly played the same music that had created such wild enthusiasm in the 1930s, albeit employing the best musicians available, disciplined to play with all the customary Goodman precision. Despite its dated repertoire, his band did not lack for bookings. As late as June 7, 1986, Benny and the band played an engagement at Wolf Trap, dedicating that concert, as he had several previously, to the memory of Fletcher Henderson. He appeared to be healthy and played with youthful vigor and intensity, so it was a shock when he was discovered dead of cardiac arrest on June 13 in his New York apartment.

A number of jazz historians imply that because Benny got rich from jazz, he committed some kind of moral or artistic faux pas. The fact is, however, that Goodman was a towering musician and one of the most influential artists in the history of jazz.

SUGGESTED LISTENING

Benny Goodman: *This Is Benny Goodman.* RCA Bluebird PK-6040 and PK-5120. (CS)

Fletcher Henderson: *Hocus Pocus: Fletcher Henderson and His Orchestra, 1927–36.* RCA Bluebird 9904-2-RB.

Duke Ellington

14

Duke Ellington,
Band, 1932

Anyone's personal selection of the best in any field is sure to invite rebuttal from others. Almost any knowledgeable jazz student can make a convincing case for other jazz greats, but Ellington has such an imposing array of qualifications that he clearly stands out among his peers. His genius was most apparent in the distinctive, inventive sounds he drew from his principal instrument, his orchestra. He played the piano very well, but his gift lay in the inspiration he shared with the musicians in the band. Duke heard the essential, individual qualities in each of his instrumentalists and vocalists and wove those qualities together into a unique musical fabric. He composed and arranged for particular instrumental voices—not just for a trumpet, but for Cootie Williams's trumpet, or Rex Stewart's cornet. Unlike leaders who insisted on a uniform sound within sections, Duke encouraged individuality. His instrumentation was standard: three trumpets, three trombones, five reeds, piano, drums, bass, and guitar; but the sounds he created were unique. Ellington thought of musical textures in terms of colors (he was originally an artist and had won and declined an art scholarship from the NAACP in 1917). He perceived each of his musicians as a specific hue on his palette, and he mixed them in startling and exhilarating combinations.

ELLINGTON THE COMPOSER

Ellington composed on the run—in taxis, trains, or hotel rooms. He was often still working on a new **tune** as he walked into a rehearsal. He would pass around scraps of paper; as the band read a composition for the first time, various members would give him suggestions for changes. If Ellington agreed with a modification, it would be penciled in. If a thought occurred to him midway through a rehearsal, he would call out to a musician, "Do a little something in here." As a result, the band book (folio of scores) was not easily understood by new musicians, and it usually took them six months to catch on.

In sheer quantity of music, Duke ranks with such prolific composers as Joseph Haydn, who wrote 104 symphonies, 83 quartets, 14 masses, and numerous shorter works. Ellington copyrighted 952 compositions, including 3 sacred concerts, 21 suites, 3 shows, 3 movie scores, and a ballet.

DUKE'S MUSICIANS

Duke received unprecedented loyalty and tenure from his musicians. He often let some of his musicians take advantage of him, but they all loved him and, for the honor of serving in his organization, put up with year after year of torturing one-night stands. Several made the orchestra not only their careers but also their lives. Trombonist Joe Nanton's death at age forty-four ended a twenty-year membership in the band. Alto saxophonist Johnny Hodges, excluding a five-year absence, was in his fortieth year with Duke when he died. Billy Strayhorn,

Ellington's alter ego and intellectual companion, died at age fifty-one after twenty-nine years of service with the band. Saxophonist Harry Carney, one of Ellington's faithful friends, had spent forty years in the orchestra when Duke died, and then died himself six months later. Russell Procope, the clarinetist, stayed twenty-eight years; trumpeter-violinist Ray Nance, twenty-three; drummer Sonny Greer, thirty-two; saxophonist Otto Hardwick, twenty-seven; and trombonist Lawrence Brown, thirty-five.

Ellington returned their loyalty, not only personally, but also monetarily. In 1951, after depleting his personal reserves to pay his musicians, he sought a manager to organize his finances. The prospective efficiency expert wanted Duke to pay the band the industrywide average of $2,500 a week, but Ellington refused to lower it below the $4,500 he had decided was fair. His musicians were consistently the highest paid in the business. He wanted to keep the same musicians to ensure consistent musical results. The high pay was, of course, one reason band members stayed on so long, but Ellington's personality and the band's eminence throughout the world were likewise great incentives.

Relationships between Duke and the musicians were not always serene. Duke usually handled a confrontation with patient understanding and waited until the matter cooled. Sometimes he merely turned off communication. Trumpeter Clark Terry tells of a time when the band was riding a bus through the mountains. Bassist Oscar Pettiford, who had never found much favor with Duke because of his (Pettiford's) boppist leanings, started raging at Duke about money. Ellington referred him to road manager Al Celley, and when Pettiford persisted in the tirade, Duke simply closed his eyes and went to sleep.[1] His forebearance was not unlimited, however; in fact, when someone finally angered him, as Sonny Greer did in 1951 by a remark Duke interpreted as an insult to his mother, he never forgot it. Greer had been with Ellington since 1919, but after their parting Duke had little to do with him. At a 1972 concert, the emcee noticed Sonny, then nearly seventy, watching in the wings. He introduced him, and amid wild applause Sonny clambered up behind the drum set. Duke stood by impassively until Greer realized that the band would not play as long as he sat there.[2]

DUKE'S EARLY YEARS

Edward Kennedy Ellington was born in Washington, D.C., on April 19, 1899. "Uncle Ed," as everyone called his father, made a comfortable living and provided well for the family. He exerted a strong influence on his son with his cul-

[1] Stanley Dance, *The World of Duke Ellington* (New York: Scribner's, 1970), p. 188.

[2] Derek Jewell, *Duke* (New York: W. W. Norton & Co., Inc., 1977), p. 208. Printed by permission of W. W. Norton & Co. and Hamish Hamilton Ltd. Published in the United Kingdom by Elm Tree Books Ltd.

tured comportment and elegant English. His mother ran the household and raised Duke in a proper Christian atmosphere. As a result, Duke had a self-assured, outgoing personality with a certain regal air even as a boy. A friend nicknamed him "Duke" when they were still in grade school.[3]

Duke began studying the piano as the result of being hit accidentally with a baseball bat. His mother witnessed the incident and decided to have him study music to encourage less hazardous activities. She paid a Mrs. Clinkscales for lessons several times a week, which he skipped as often as he attended. Although he was more interested in baseball and art at the time, he was an apt music student. When asked to play at a party, he found, to his delight, that pianists attracted girls. After that, he paid much more attention to music.

While in high school, he began to get calls to play at dances. He formed a small band of his own; when it dawned on him that part of the fee went to an agent for booking the job, he advertised as an agent himself and began making a great deal of money. He owned his first Cadillac and a house on Sherman Avenue before he was twenty.

In 1922 Ellington tried to break into the New York music scene with a small group consisting of drummer Sonny Greer and saxophonist Otto Hardwick, but he did not find the money plentiful enough and returned briefly to Washington. In 1923 he tried New York again, having added trumpeter Arthur Whetsol and guitarist Elmer Snowden to the band. The band was well received, and the musicians moved to New York permanently. Hired by the Kentucky Club, they stayed four and a half years. During this time, the band gradually stopped sounding like an imitation of the Fletcher Henderson orchestra and began taking on its own character. When South Carolina trumpeter Bubber Miley joined in 1925, he injected a guttural, muted "jungle" sound into the music. This sound became one of the band's themes for the remainder of its existence.

In 1926, while still at the Kentucky Club, Duke began to sell compositions to a small-time impresario, Irving Mills. The relationship blossomed and Mills became Ellington's manager. Being white, he could engineer Duke's band into bookings it might otherwise have been denied. Furthermore, he arranged for their first recordings, and it was not long until the band was heard, under various names, on several labels: "Duke Ellington" on Victor, the "Jungle Band" on Brunswick, the "Washingtonians" on Harmony, and several others.[4] The Ellington-Mills collaboration lasted until 1940. Mills's name appeared as co-composer on many of Ellington's records, although it is doubtful that Mills ever wrote a note. Mills received 45 percent of the proceeds while he was Duke's manager.

In 1927 Duke left the Kentucky Club for the Cotton Club, Harlem's top nightclub during the Prohibition era. In 1930 Duke and his wife, Edna, whom

[3] Duke Ellington, *Music Is My Mistress* (Garden City, N.Y.: Doubleday, 1973), p. 20.
[4] Ibid., p. 73.

he had married when he was nineteen, were divorced, and Ellington brought his parents, his sister, Ruth, and his son, Mercer, to New York. In 1930 Duke's career began to take off. He appeared in the movie *Check and Doublecheck* and onstage in New York when he was not playing at the Cotton Club. He had begun writing music early in the 1920s, and his output grew steadily in the 1930s. At first Duke's music was primarily instrumental or served as accompaniment to singers in the floor shows. When the band needed a vocalist, Duke called on Sonny Greer. But in 1931 Ellington brought Ivy Anderson into the organization, and until she left in 1942, her voice was as much a part of its special sound as any instrument. Meanwhile, Ellington gradually increased the size of the orchestra from nine pieces during the Kentucky Club days to the blue-chip fifteen-piece orchestra of the 1930s. Johnny Hodges, whose alto sax was the standard by which all others would be judged until Charlie Parker, had joined in 1928. Bubber Miley, who was dying of tuberculosis, was replaced in 1929 by one of

Duke Ellington Band, 1934. *Left to right, back row: Joe Nanton, trombone; Juan Tizol, trombone; Lawrence Brown, trombone; Arthur Whetsol, trumpet; Fred Guy, guitar. Middle row: Barney Bigard, clarinet and sax; Marshall Royal, alto sax; Johnny Hodges, alto sax; Harry Carney, saxes; Wellman Braud, bass. Front row: Sonny Greer, drums; Ellington, leader, piano; Freddy Jenkins, trumpet.*

jazz's all-time great trumpeters, Cootie Williams. Trombonist Juan Tizol came in 1929 and Lawrence Brown in 1932. The band attracted virtuoso talent like a magnet: saxophonist Ben Webster, cornetist Rex Stewart, and bassist Jimmy Blanton. In the midst of all these temperamental egos, Duke was able to keep the band functioning as a team. His was a genius at leadership as well as music.

His reputation abroad, particularly in England and France, grew considerably. His recordings had been distributed widely in Europe and had been received with much enthusiasm, although this fact was not known to Duke until word of it was brought back by Otto Hardwick, who had toured Europe in 1929. His first trip abroad was a seven-week series of concerts in Europe in 1933. He did return to Europe in 1939, and then not again until 1948.

Billy Strayhorn

In 1939 Ellington entered into an association with composer-arranger-pianist Billy Strayhorn (1915–1967) that became the closest personal and intellectual partnership in the history of jazz. "Swee Pea," as Strayhorn came to be called, was a shy, bookish, twenty-three-year-old when he submitted a tune, "Lush Life," for Ellington's consideration. It has since become a permanent fixture in the literature of jazz. Duke immediately recognized how closely attuned to each other he and Billy were and welcomed him into the organization. Strayhorn wrote a number of beautiful tunes for the band: "Something to Live For," "After All," "Raincheck," "Daydream," "Passion Flower," and the band's theme song, "Take the 'A' Train." He and Duke wrote "Satin Doll" together, and many more. The two men absorbed each other's musical and philosophical ideas. Billy played piano with the band frequently. On records it is impossible to distinguish his playing from Duke's without resorting to the liner notes.

Significant personnel turnovers occurred in the 1940s and 1950s. First, Cootie Williams left to join Benny Goodman in 1940. Some thought he had betrayed Duke, but Ellington was magnanimous; he even helped Cootie negotiate a favorable contract with Goodman. He let Cootie know his chair would be open, and in fact Cootie did rejoin the band in 1962. Duke replaced Williams almost immediately with trumpeter-violinist-vocalist Ray Nance. In 1942 Jimmy Blanton died of tuberculosis and Barney Bigard left. Ben Webster left in 1943, Rex Stewart and Juan Tizol in 1944, and Otto Hardwick in 1945. Joe Nanton died in 1946. Johnny Hodges, Lawrence Brown, and Sonny Greer all departed in 1951. But the band was not diminished in any way by their replacements: trumpeters Cat Anderson and Clark Terry, alto saxophonist Willie Smith, drummer Louis Bellson, trombonists Tyree Glenn and Tizol (who had rejoined), clarinetist Russell Procope, and perhaps the most important, tenor saxophonist Paul Gonsalves.

Throughout this period, Duke was turning out some of his most memorable compositions. He wrote and staged a full-length show, *Jump for Joy*, and appeared in two films. But by 1950, big-band popularity had slipped badly, and

Johnny Hodges

Ellington had become a less visible force in jazz. The decline had been gradual but relentless—that is, until the night of July 7, 1956, at the Newport Jazz Festival. The band had been scheduled as the last attraction, behind a lineup of contemporary artists. Ellington did a couple of his recent compositions, and since it was close to midnight, some of the crowd of 10,000 began to leave. Duke announced as his final number his 1937 composition "Diminuendo and Crescendo in Blue." Paul Gonsalves led off with a fiery solo; with the band swinging behind, he built chorus upon driving chorus. People in the act of leaving rushed back to their seats. The auditorium went wild. Shouts of "More! More!" rang out, and Gonsalves responded with twenty-eight choruses. Duke was back on top; his picture appeared on the cover of *Time*. Later, if asked his age, he would say he was born in July 1956.

The 1960s found Duke probing musical areas and concepts that differed from his earlier works. He wrote a number of suites with African, Far Eastern, Middle Eastern, and West Indian themes. He played and recorded not only with traditionalists like Louis Armstrong and Count Basie but also with new-wave musicians like Max Roach, Charlie Mingus, and John Coltrane. His mind was open to fresh thoughts, and he acknowledged the validity of honest musical exploration.

Duke became more and more obsessed with music in later life and allowed nothing to interfere with it. Two years before he died, he was diagnosed as having lung cancer, but he made no effort to reduce his schedule. He toured Africa and Europe, and conducted his Third Sacred Concert in Westminster Abbey in 1973.

Duke's continuing religious faith gave him the strength to face his hectic life. His faith joined with his music in the last years of his life. He wrote three sacred concerts, the first being premiered in San Francisco's Grace Cathedral in 1965. The second was first heard in New York in 1968 and featured the Swedish soprano Alice Babs, with her breathtaking range and tonal purity. The third premiered at Westminster Abbey.

Ellington's headlong rush slowed down only in the last three months of his life. Even in his hospital room, furnished with a piano, he worked on his opera, *Queenie Pie.* On May 24, 1974, Duke died in New York within a week of the deaths of Paul Gonsalves and Tyree Glenn.

Duke was in every respect a world figure. He received 119 awards, decorations, and citations from nations, states, cities, and societies around the globe. Seventy-six times he and his band were voted the top jazz organization by various periodicals in the United States and abroad. Fifteen colleges and universities conferred honorary degrees upon him. Through it all, he balanced graceful nobility with honest humility. His genius commanded respect more than envy and affection more than awe.

LISTENING GUIDE

Two examples of the classic Ellington sound, "In a Mellotone" and "Ko-ko," were recorded by the same personnel in 1940. They demonstrate Ellington's diverse composing and arranging skills. They also illustrate the responsibility Ellington placed on his musicians. He featured more of the musicians in his band than any other leader in history. He and Strayhorn wrote concerto-like pieces for several band members: "Passion Flower" for Johnny Hodges, "Boy Meets Horn" for Rex Stewart, and "Concerto for Cootie" for Williams. Notice the controlled use of inflections in each selection. The most obvious come from the brass section, which employed the many mutes available to them. The most expressive device is the *plunger* (often in combination with a straight mute). Used with either trumpet or trombone, it is manipulated in the bell of the horn to produce a variety of effects that have the voicelike quality of blues singers. These inflections are used extensively by black bands and give even the most refined of them a bluesy quality.

"In a Mellotone" features Cootie Williams and Johnny Hodges. Williams builds his solo around the increasingly active sax section, so that the result sounds like a spontaneous dialogue. The sax section, however, was restricted to the written score, and the soloist had the responsibility of working around the arrangement. Likewise, Hodges uses a solo break as a major articulation in his solo. Following the solo break, the band in tutti plays the melody as Hodges continues with fills. The soloists build excitement by taking advantage of what they know is going to happen in the arrangement.

"In a Mellotone"—1940 (SCCJ Disc 3, Cut 7)

Piano—Duke Ellington
Trumpets—Wallace Jones, Cootie Williams
Cornet—Rex Stewart
Trombones—Joe Nanton, Lawrence Brown
Valve trombone—Juan Tizol
Clarinet and tenor sax—Barney Bigard
Alto sax—Otto Hardwick, Johnny Hodges
Tenor sax—Ben Webster
Baritone sax—Harry Carney
Guitar—Fred Guy
Bass—Jimmy Blanton
Drums—Sonny Greer

.00   Piano introduction, bass fills.
.12   Saxes play melody in unison, fills by trombones in soli, rhythm section activity is bass and brushes on the snare drum.
.42   2nd chorus: Same scoring.
1.09   Piano interlude.
1.14   Cootie Williams (trumpet solo) uses the straight mute and the plunger, saxes fill in soli; a balanced dialogue is established.
1.45   Growl in solo.
1.56   More growls in solo, saxes are more active.
2.11   Tutti (same rhythm, different notes).
2.21   Johnny Hodges (alto sax solo) uses double-time phrasing; the piano plays accompaniment for the first time.
2.37   Brass section plays long notes in accompaniment.
2.40   Solo break in double time.
2.45   Solo remains in double time.
2.58   Tutti band plays the melody, solo fills by the alto sax.
3.15   End.

"Ko-ko" features two trombonists, Juan Tizol and Joe Nanton; Tizol plays the melody for the first chorus, and Nanton solos with a straight mute and plunger for the next two choruses. The trombone section backing Nanton creates the "wa-wa" effect by opening and closing the bells of their horns with plungers.

Ellington, in his solo, plays clusters of dissonant notes interspersed with short scales. During his solo the band is in full swing. Rarely does a band play so complicated a backup to a piano solo. The resulting thick texture leads into Jimmy Blanton's animated **walking-bass** solo. The fills are arranged shouts for the entire band, a startling contrast. Ellington was one of the first big-band leaders to use the string bass as a solo instrument. As a result, Jimmy Blanton became the first well-known big-band bass soloist.

"Ko-ko" is a minor blues composition with futuristic harmonic ideas. Ellington's intriguing melody and unusual arrangement were bold departures in 1940.

"Ko-ko"—1940 (SCCJ Disc 3, Cut 4)

Same personnel as "In a Mellotone"

.00	Introduction, baritone sax plays a low note, trombones play short chords in the background.
.12	Muted trombone plays the melody, sax soli fills (call-response).
.32	Trombone solo (with straight mute and plunger), trombone section plays short chords using an open-and-closed bell technique, piano plays sharp chords as fills.
.50	Another solo chorus for the trombone.
1.08	Sax section plays in unison, trombone section continues punches, piano solos use dissonant chords and angular scales.
1.27	Tutti chorus: Every section is playing complementary ideas, which produces a very thick texture.
1.45	Tutti lead-in to the bass solo.
1.48	Bass solo fill (walking pattern).
1.57	Tutti fill.
2.04	Shout chorus, saxes play the melody, the brass section plays long, loud, dissonant chords.
2.22	Fade, baritone sax returns to long low notes.
2.36	Ending.
2.41	End.

INNOVATIONS OF THE ELLINGTON BAND

The strength of the musicians in the band, especially through the 1930s and 1940s, gave definition to the total ensemble. Many arrangements were a collective effort. By building arrangements around the players, the band developed new organizational concepts for the soloists and the ensemble alike. For example, in "Concerto for Cootie" Ellington used a concerto format inspired by classical music. Another important musical design developed with the three sacred concerts. These forms, while new to jazz, retained the fundamental Ellington sound. Recordings of the sacred concerts demonstrate the personal and emotional qualities implicit in Ellington's solo playing. The piano weaves the movements together with delicately improvised interludes.

Several styles developed by the Ellington band became permanent features. The styles were nurtured by the open atmosphere of the organization. The "jungle style," a trumpet and trombone technique marked by throat growls, was first introduced by Bubber Miley and later carried on by Cootie Williams and Joe Nanton. Cuban, or Latin, jazz established a foothold with the recording of "Caravan," written and played by the Puerto Rican trombonist Juan Tizol.

Ellington was a great overseer who led his band into new creative worlds. His musicianship was superior to, and unthreatened by, anyone else's in the band. His musicians respected him and combined forces with him to create an ensemble greater than the sum of its parts, a collaboration of outstanding soloists, composers, and arrangers. The band is a monument in jazz history. It had a driving swing built upon a strong blues heritage. Ellington often ended concerts by having the audience snap their fingers in unison while he explained what it meant to be "cool." As he left the stage with the band still swinging, he would say, "One can be as cool as one wishes." From Duke Ellington, the statement seemed believable.

SUGGESTED LISTENING

At Newport (1956). Columbia CK 40587
The Great Times (with Billy Strayhorn). Riverside OJCCD 108-2.

Count Basie, Billie Holiday, and Lester Young

15

Count Basie

WILLIAM "COUNT" BASIE (1904–1984)

Although Harlem lies only thirty miles north of Red Bank, New Jersey, where Bill Basie was born, he waited almost eighteen years to make the trip. In that time he became a better-than-adequate pianist under the tutelage of his mother, a domestic servant, and a German lady named Holloway, who charged twenty-five cents a lesson. Originally, Basie wanted to be a drummer, but his boyhood friend, Sonny Greer, demonstrated how much more there was for him to learn, so Basie turned to the piano. The two boys left Red Bank about the same time, Greer going to Washington, D.C., where he started a lifelong association with the Duke Ellington band, and Basie to New York City.

In Harlem, Basie happened upon Fats Waller playing at the Lincoln Theater. Although Waller was only five months older than Basie, he was already an established stride pianist. Basie attached himself to Fats, who soon taught him the style and, more important, how to swing.

Basie's piano style is the key to the contagious swing generated by his bands. It has always been the significant element of the rhythm sections that supported his bands. In the beginning he employed both hands fully, typical of most stride performers. As time passed, however, he retreated from flamboyant stride techniques and began to use brief right-hand figures to intensify the rhythm. His style not only became the fingerprint of the Basie band, it also stimulated confident, driving swing from his musicians. The band he had from 1936 to 1942 contained one of the most admired rhythm sections of all time: Besides Basie on piano, Walter Page played bass, Jo Jones drums, and Freddie Green guitar. From time to time, critics have tried to identify the key element. Some favor Page, others Jones, but there was no singly dispensable ingredient. Basie established balance within the section by confining his playing mostly to his right hand. The result is an almost transparent texture punctuated by short melodic quips from Basie.

Disc 2 of the *Smithsonian Collection of Classic Jazz* carries three numbers recorded by Basie in 1938 and 1939: "Doggin' Around," "Taxi War Dance," and "Lester Leaps In." Although these numbers obviously focus on tenor saxophonist Lester Young, they also show the way the typical Basie rhythm section unifies and drives the band. The contribution of Freddie Green's four-to-the-bar unamplified guitar is very important. It set the standard for big-band rhythm guitar. Green, incidentally, remained with Basie for nearly fifty years.

Of the many soloists who developed while in the Basie band, Lester Young was probably the most important because of his advanced, lyrical sense of melody and unusual tone. Young's phrasing was sophisticated, yet sounded simple. His melodic lines found new avenues through common chord progressions. His tone sounded more like a husky flute than the full-throated reed instrument popularized by Coleman Hawkins.

LISTENING GUIDE

"Taxi War Dance"—1939 (Lester Young, Count Basie; SCCJ Disc 2, Cut 21)

Arranger—Buck Clayton
Alto sax—Earle Warren, Jack Washington
Tenor sax—Buddy Tate, Lester Young
Trumpets—Buck Clayton, Ed Lewis, Harry Edison, Shad Collins
Trombones—Dickie Wells, Benny Morton, Dan Minor
Piano—Count Basie
Guitar—Freddie Green
Bass—Walter Page
Drums—Jo Jones

.00	Introduction: Piano plays a boogie pattern, short brass punches.
.08	Tenor solo (Lester Young), guitar plays 4/4 jazz beat, piano **comps.**
.27	Bridge section uses new chords.
.45	The boogie pattern with brass punches returns.
.47	Trombone solo (Dickie Wells), same rhythm section activity.
1.23	4-measure dialogue that begins with full band shout.
1.28	4 measures of tenor solo (Buddy Tate).
1.32	4 measures of full band.
1.36	4 measures of tenor sax (Tate).
1.41	8 measures of piano solo: Bridge section, modern swing melody, left hand does not play 2/4 jazz beat.
1.51	Shout chorus interchange with soloist returns.
2.00	Piano boogie pattern (full band).
2.04	Tenor solo (Young), followed by full band and tenor solo again.
2.17	Piano solo: 8-measure bridge section.
2.26	4-measure shout followed by a 4-measure tenor solo (Young).
2.35	Ending: 2 measures of piano, 2 measures of tenor (Tate), 2 measures of bass, 2 measures of drums.
2.45	Shout ending.

This arrangement has many short openings for soloistic comments. The intensity of the full band comes in short, four-measure statements that are bridged by the solos. This selection also has two longer solos, first by Lester Young and then by Dickie Wells. Notice how the sophisticated phrasing of Young's opening solo makes it difficult to hear the normal phrasing of the chorus by the rhythm section. Also of interest is the rapid change in texture from a full, shouting big band to solo and back again. Basie's bands have always displayed startling contrasts in volume and density.

Basie developed and hired many stars. Hershel Evans played tenor sax in the warm, romantic, Coleman Hawkins tradition; he ranked, until his early death in 1939, as virtually Hawkins's equal, as did Ben Webster. The list of players who have worked for Basie reads like a Who's Who of saxophone immortals: Chu Berry, Don Byas, Buddy Tate, Illinois Jacquet, Paul Gonsalves, Paul Quinichette, Wardell Gray, Georgie Auld, Frank Foster, and Frank Wess.

Trumpeters Oran "Hot Lips" Page, Harry "Sweets" Edison, Clark Terry, Thad Jones, and Buck Clayton all played with Basie. Long before Miles Davis, Clayton took the metallic, constricted tone of the Harmon mute out of the commercial dance band and used it to play pure jazz.

Alto saxophone players Earle Warren and Marshall Royal, as well as trombonists Dickie Wells, Benny Morton, Vic Dickenson, and J. J. Johnson, further illustrate the range of talent in the Basie organization. Great soloists were everywhere in the band. The Basie band never relied on one virtuoso; many distinctive voices added variety and personal inflections.

It took Basie a longer time to become a band leader than it does most who attain such stardom. After his apprenticeship with Fats Waller, he jobbed around Harlem and then went on the road for several years as accompanist and sideman on the TOBA circuit. At one point in the early 1930s, his show was stranded in Kansas City. There he joined the Bennie Moten band. Most of its members formed the nucleus of the first Basie band after Moten died unexpectedly in 1935.

In 1936, after hearing Basie on a small Kansas City radio station, John Hammond arranged to bring the band to New York. The settings and delivery of the Basie band changed somewhat over the years. In the swing era, big bands played for dances. After 1945 the few bands that survived mostly played concerts, which on the one hand provided greater latitude in tempo and complexity of arrangements, but on the other placed a greater premium on polish. Basie's band remained in the vanguard over the years.

Basie's life was characterized by continuity and a levelheaded pursuit of his goals. In 1931 he met fifteen-year-old Catherine Morgan, who was dancing in an act called the Whitman Sisters (she was known as Princess Aloha). The attraction between them endured through an eleven-year courtship and beyond. Their daughter Diane was born in 1944, and the couple adopted three more children. Catherine died in April 1983, three months before their forty-first wedding anniversary.

Basie admitted he was rather wild when he was younger; but in 1950, when he discovered that his managers and agents were prospering while he was getting deeper in debt, he quickly settled down. He had always been a good band organizer—he would not hire any musician who was heavily addicted to drugs or who was temperamentally disruptive; however, he was not, until his enlightenment, a good money manager. After recognizing the need to be frugal, he became very careful with his income. Musicians loved being in his band but had to bargain forcefully to negotiate a raise.

In later years Basie learned to pace himself and make accommodations for stress. He gave up alcohol and cigarettes in 1960. Despite a heart attack in 1977, and spinal arthritis, which restricted him to a motorized wheelchair, he continued to travel with the band until his hospitalization in February 1984. The spark that powered one of the best swing bands in history was quenched April 26, 1984, in Hollywood, California, when Bill Basie died.

BILLIE HOLIDAY (1915?–1959)

To be blamed for the death of one's grandmother when six years old, to be raped at the age of ten, to be locked in a room with the body of a dead girl as a punishment when only twelve, and to spend some years as both a call girl and a street prostitute is not the ideal training for a singer. That, however, was Billie Holiday's early life; yet, her love of music and her ambition drove her to perform and succeed. Her style, fashioned after Bessie Smith's, paved the way for future jazz singers. Besides the blues, she excelled at interpreting jazz standards, imbuing them with the **lay back** and inflections of the blues. Her musical prowess set her above the many other big-band singers. She was sought after by both white and black bands.

Eleanora Fagan Gough was born in Baltimore in either 1912 or 1915 (the date is still in question)—to parents who were in their early and mid-teens. Her father, Clarence Holiday (the source of the name Gough is not clear), left when Eleanora was a baby. Not much later, her mother, Sally Fagan, moved to New York City, leaving the child with relatives who were anything but loving. To earn money, Eleanora ran errands for a Baltimore brothel and in 1927 moved to New York, where for the next three years she made a living as a prostitute.

One evening in 1930, inspired by a love of singing, she persuaded a night-club owner to let her try some songs with the house band. The first night, she made fifty-seven dollars from money tossed onto the stage by the patrons. From that point, using the name Billie Holiday (because of her admiration for screen star Billie Dove), she obtained jobs on and around 133rd Street in Harlem.

At one of these engagements, John Hammond, the rich and tireless entrepreneur of jazz (see Chapter 13), discovered her and recognized her star quality. In 1933 Hammond organized her first recording session with Benny Goodman. It was not until July 1935, however, that Billie's records found popular acceptance. Over the next six years, she recorded over eighty numbers with small bands organized specially for the jukebox market. These bands were assembled by pianist Teddy Wilson and included, at one time or another, Benny Goodman, trumpeters Roy Eldridge and Buck Clayton, tenor saxophonists Ben Webster and Lester Young, bassist John Kirby, guitarist John Trueheart, and drummer Cozy Cole. Billie received thirty dollars for the first of these sessions. The three seemingly ordinary tunes, "What a Little Moonlight Can Do," "Miss Brown to You," and "I Wished on the Moon," all became hits.

Billie Holiday

Billie suffered many ups and downs during her career. She lost jobs in New York and Chicago because her song selections were "too slow" or "not what the customers wanted." Bar crowds usually wanted fast songs with an occasional slow song, not the other way around. Slow songs, however, best displayed Billie's style. In these, she communicated personal and highly emotional moods to her audiences.

LISTENING GUIDE

The recording "He's Funny That Way" is typical of many swing-era arrangements written for big bands and small combos alike. There are only two choruses, each thirty-two measures long, with just a brief, improvised introduction by Lester Young on tenor saxophone. As Holiday sings, Young continues a musical dialogue throughout most of the recording. Young's subtle improvisation complemented Holiday's singing. The similarity to the recording of "St. Louis Blues" by Bessie Smith with Louis Armstrong (see page 22) is obvious.

Throughout the song, the guitarist plays one chord on each beat, a practice that was widely followed during the swing era.

Billie Holiday's singing is best described as "laid back." Her distinctive style was founded in her ability to stay behind the beat in a consistently relaxed manner. Although she admired and emulated Bessie Smith, she did not have Bessie's large voice. Holiday's singing was distinguished by a sense of sincerity. In spite of her relaxed and simple manner, she intuitively fashioned a most sophisticated vocal style.

"He's Funny That Way"—1937 (SCCJ Disc 2, Cut 10)

Vocal—Billie Holiday
Trumpet—Buck Clayton
Clarinet—Buster Bailey
Tenor sax—Lester Young
Piano—Claude Thorhill
Guitar—Freddie Green
Bass—Walter Page
Drums—Jo Jones

.00   Introduction: Tenor sax solo.
.09   Vocal begins, dialogue with sax; a guitar chord is played on every beat, the piano plays very few notes, the sax plays fills; notice the lay back.
.46   Bridge (middle section): The sax stops playing, the piano plays fills, replacing the improvisation of Young.
1.05 Last section of chorus: The sax enters with improvisation again.
1.23 Muted trumpet solo: The sax plays long notes in the background, the guitar continues with a chord on each beat, the solo is supported by active brush work on the snare drum.
2.01 Vocal enters at bridge, tenor sax plays in background, piano is more obvious, guitar is softer.
2.20 Last section of 2nd chorus.
2.33 Trumpet and clarinet enter, establishing a final cadence.
2.38 End.

Billie joined the Count Basie band in March 1937 and established a life-long friendship with Basie's tenor player, Lester Young. Whenever Lester was with her, she was at her best. However, Basie found her too independent and temperamental and let her go in February 1938. She immediately joined the Artie Shaw band, which was booked on a tour through the South. She was the first black singer to tour the South with a white band. Billie later admitted this experience filled her with anxiety. She left Shaw the same year, again with less than cordial feelings.

In 1939 she introduced two songs, "Strange Fruit" and "God Bless the Child." These are powerful sociological statements that, in retrospect, helped project her tragic image. In the late 1930s and early 1940s, as Holiday became better established and more musically sophisticated, her personal life was beginning to take on those tragic proportions recounted in biographies and the movie *Lady Sings the Blues*. Always a heavy smoker, a user of marijuana, and an excessive eater, Billie became more involved with hard drugs. During her first marriage (in 1941 to Johnnie Monroe), she started taking opium; during her second (to trumpeter Joe Guy), she became a heroin addict.

Despite her addictions, Holiday was singing well and earning as much as a thousand dollars a week. But the pace was too fast. She began to lose ground and became more and more unreliable. In 1945 Billie and Joe Guy formed a band to go on tour. Unfortunately, since neither of them had any organizational ability, the group disbanded in six months. Nevertheless, Billie's vocal talent carried her through this failure and the many others that were to come. Her following was constantly increasing. She gave a triumphant solo concert in New York's Town Hall in 1946, and in the same year appeared in a feature-length film, *New Orleans,* with a most impressive cast: Louis Armstrong, Kid Ory, Barney Bigard, Meade "Lux" Lewis, Red Norvo, and Woody Herman.

She continued to have drug problems, even though her career was improving. In 1947 she was arrested on a narcotics charge and, pleading guilty, served eight months in prison. When released, she immediately gave a sell-out concert at Carnegie Hall. Despite her narcotics conviction, she obtained a cabaret card allowing her to perform once again in New York nightclubs.

At age thirty-six she tried a third marriage, this time to Louis McKay, who like Monroe and Guy, was unstable and abusive. The injuries he inflicted on her forced her to cancel some of her performances.

Somehow her career survived these setbacks—at least for a time. In 1954 she made a successful tour of Europe and had a spectacular reunion with Lester Young at Newport. It was her last display of musical strength. In 1956 she was arrested again on a narcotics charge and entered a clinic. Her recovery was only temporary. After her release, she had some bright performances, but her self-destructive lifestyle led to the inevitable. Her condition deteriorated and she died on July 17, 1959.

LESTER "PRES" YOUNG (1909–1959)

Until he was ten, Young lived with his family in Mississippi and Louisiana. After that, they moved to Memphis and Minneapolis. His father formed a family band with Lester, brother Lee, and sister Irma, and they appeared at tent shows in the Midwest and the Southwest. He played drums then, but sometime before he was eighteen, when he left the family band, Lester switched to saxophone. He played in a number of bands, including those of Bennie Moten and King Oliver,

Lester Young–Count Basie Band, 1940. *Left to right: Lester Young, tenor sax; Ed Lewis, trumpet; Count Basie, piano; Jo Jones, drums.*

and in 1934 he went with Count Basie. He left to briefly replace Coleman Hawkins in Fletcher Henderson's band, but when he refused to become a Hawkins clone, he left Henderson by mutual agreement and returned in 1936 to Basie, with whom he flourished and with whom over the next eight years he produced some of the most influential jazz to come out of that, or any other, period.

In September 1944, when he was thirty-five, the Army drafted Lester Young, even though he declared his dependence on alcohol and soft drugs.

Pres (short for "President")—as Billie Holiday had named him—had always been sensitive to the injustices of life. He was hurt by discrimination and other wrongs, but he was temperamentally incapable of plotting revenge, so he used whatever substances he could to ease the pain. He was gentle and gentlemanly, courteous and considerate, and when others were otherwise, he withdrew into himself. He never spoke ill of people but apparently never forgot a wrong.

Lester was original in other ways. He wore distinctive clothes—ankle-length coats and porkpie hats—and he spoke in a private language that took a while to understand. When he played his saxophone, he sometimes held it sideways like a flute. But above all, Pres was a music maker. He was more than a first-rate musician who could play faster or higher, for example, or improve on the ideas and embellishments of others. He created music. His creations were eminently melodic and logical. His recorded solos still inspire wonder.

Five months after his induction into the Army, Lester was found to be in possession of forbidden substances. A general court-martial convicted and dishonorably discharged him and sentenced him to a year in prison. In the Fort Gordon, Georgia, stockade he was, thankfully, allowed to play music with fellow prisoner guitarist Fred Lacy and with Sgt. Gil Evans, the pianist-arranger who was stationed at nearby Oliver General Hospital. After ten months, he was released.

Lester returned, of course, to professional music. He spent most of his remaining thirteen years with one troupe or another of Norman Granz's Jazz at the Philharmonic, but his life and career followed a downward slide. His habits and addictions, not to mention his painfully deteriorating teeth, took a gradual toll physically and emotionally. He died without realizing what a gigantic influence he had had in the evolution of his music.

SUGGESTED LISTENING

Billie Holiday: *The Quintessential Billie Holiday.* 8 vols. Columbia CK-40646, CK-40790, CK-44048, CK-44252, CK-44423, CK-45449, CK-46180, CK-47030.
Count Basie: *The Best of Count Basie.* MCA Records MCA 2-4050E. (CS)
Lester Young: *Lester Swings.* VERVE VE-2-2516. 2 LPs.

Swing in Transition

16

Coleman Hawkins and Don Byas

The explosion of musical enthusiasm that accompanied the swing era propelled a great many jazz musicians into prominence. The number of nationally known orchestras expanded rapidly, and the names of leaders and sidemen alike became widely recognized. Big bands played dance music that ranged from jazz to commercial. The balance between these two musical directions varied considerably from band to band. On the jazz end of the spectrum were bands like Duke Ellington's, Jimmie Lunceford's, and Count Basie's. On the commercial end were bands like Guy Lombardo's and Jan Garber's. In between were the Dorsey brothers, Glen Gray, Artie Shaw, Will Bradley, Glenn Miller, and Woody Herman, all of whom leaned heavily toward jazz; Sammy Kaye and Kay Kaiser favored more commercial music.

For musicians, jobs were relatively plentiful, with a place and an audience for almost any musical taste. Musicians who lacked the skill to solo but were disciplined readers could find anonymity and a degree of security as section members in commercial bands. Likewise, for those with the gift to solo, there were a great many stages on which to perform.

Certain bands seemed to cultivate their own stars. Foremost, of course, was the Duke Ellington orchestra, but another that featured an unusually large number of front-rank soloists was the Dixieland-flavored Bob Crosby band. Drummer Ray Bauduc, bassist Bob Haggart, pianist Bob Zurke, trumpeter Billy Butterfield, cornetist Yank Lawson, saxophonist Eddie Miller, and the portly clarinetist Irving Fazola all recorded solos that remain as fresh and delightful as on the day they were made.[1]

Some stars ascended on their own: trumpeter Roy Eldridge, violinist Joe Venuti, the gypsy guitarist Django Reinhardt, vibraphonist Red Norvo, cornetist Bobby Hackett, and possibly the most influential, tenor saxophonist Coleman Hawkins.

The musical polarity between performers during the swing era was amazing. The following discussions of Coleman Hawkins and Mary Lou Williams should help to expose the depth and diversity exhibited by swing-era soloists.

COLEMAN HAWKINS (1904–1969)

Hawkins, a native of St. Joseph, Missouri, was born on November 21, 1904. His musical training on the piano began at the age of five. He also studied cello and turned to the tenor saxophone when he was nine. "Bean," as Hawkins was later nicknamed, attended Washburn College in Topeka, Kansas, leaving when he was eighteen to tour with Mamie Smith's Jazz Hounds. Mamie was a blues singer with a reputation nearly as formidable as Bessie Smith's (they were not related).

[1]Specific examples are the Bauduc-Haggart "Big Noise from Winnetka," Zurke's "Little Rock Getaway," Butterfield's "What's New?" Lawson's "Dog Town Blues," Miller's "Call Me a Taxi" (with the Bob Cats), and Fazola's beautiful "My Inspiration."

When the band reached New York, Coleman left to join Fletcher Henderson and made his first recording with "Smack" (Henderson's nickname) in 1923. The association lasted eleven years, during which time Hawkins achieved fame as a tenor saxophonist, the first on this instrument to do so.

In 1934 Hawkins left Henderson to go to Europe, where he was highly successful, staying until 1939. He returned and formed a nine-piece band that recorded what was certainly the zenith of swing tenor saxophone improvisation, "Body and Soul." His rich, warm tone and gentle vibrato wove clusters of sixteenth- and eighth-note phrases all around the original slow melody. The solo was brilliant and it has endured. Words have been put to this improvisation and it has been sung by several artists. As recently as 1980, the vocal group Manhattan Transfer recorded it note for note.

LISTENING GUIDE

"Body and Soul"—1939 (SCCJ Disc 2, Cut 8)

Tenor sax—Coleman Hawkins
Trumpets—Tommy Lindsay, Joe Guy
Trombone—Earl Hardy
Alto saxes—Jackie Fields, Eustis Moore
Piano—Gene Rodgers
Bass—William Oscar Smith
Drums—Arthur Herbert

.00   4-bar piano introduction sets mood and tempo.

.08   Hawkins starts the 1st 8-bar (A) section, adding some embellishments but remaining close to the composed melody, drummer using brushes, piano and bass playing a slow 2/4 jazz beat.

.32   The second (A) section finds Hawkins departing further from the melody, building his solo on arpeggios (chord notes played consecutively).

.50   The 8-bar bridge (section B) starts; a new melodic line that passes through two harmonic modulations. Hawkins continues to embroider with 8th- and 16th-note flurries.

1.11   Return to (A) section to complete the song. The intensity of Hawkins's improvisation grows, clearly building toward the next chorus.

1.31   The 2nd chorus begins with Hawkins extending the melodic range and intensity. Horn background enters for the first time with long-note harmonies.

1.52 Hawkins heightens the excitement of the 2nd 8-bar (A) section with more pronounced intervallic leaps but continues to confine his improvisation to an octave and a half in the midrange of his instrument.

2.12 At the bridge the background horns drop out. Hawkins explores the harmonic changes with clusters of spiraling, separated motives. In the last bar of the bridge, Hawkins serves notice of the final section.

2.32 The background horns return. Three times in the next 4 bars, 2- and 3-note statements are gathered and thrust higher and higher out of their midrange confinement to a climax, and then the melody subsides in the next 3 bars.

2.50 The last bar is played as an unaccompanied coda cadenza.

2.53 The band returns for a final chord.

2.59 End.

Hawkins continued to work regularly through the 1940s, the 1950s, and most of the 1960s. He toured and recorded in the United States and abroad. He never let his interest in style stagnate. He greatly admired Dizzy Gillespie and Charlie Parker and assembled an all-star band for the first recorded bebop session. Leonard Feather has noted that if some of his 1940s recorded solos are played at a faster speed, the quicker tempo and higher pitch make them sound remarkably like Charlie Parker on alto sax.[2]

Hawkins played with almost every jazz artist of his time, was honored as the foremost tenor sax player in numerous polls from 1939 to 1959, and was a perennial all-star. He died in 1969 in New York City, his status reduced by then to that of a revered but supplanted leader. In the view of many observers, however, Hawkins's stature as a developer of style and master of his instrument has never been equaled—Lester Young, Ben Webster, Stan Getz, John Coltrane, and Sonny Rollins notwithstanding.

TEDDY WILSON (1912–1986)

In June 1936 Benny Goodman went to a party at Mildred Bailey's house in New York. Mildred, one of the few truly fine white jazz vocalists, had invited a number of musicians. One of them was Teddy Wilson, who had been talked into playing the piano. By chance, Goodman had brought his clarinet, and the two

[2]Reprinted from *The Encyclopedia of Jazz in the Seventies* by Leonard Feather and Ira Gitler, copyright 1976, by permission of the publisher, Horizon Press, New York.

began running over some songs. The other guests were overwhelmed by the obvious chemistry. They prevailed upon the two to record some tunes, and a few days later, together with drummer Gene Krupa, the Goodman Trio was born. Wilson joined the Goodman band full-time, but playing in a white band before a live audience required special arrangements. Goodman used a white pianist when the full band was on the stand. Teddy played as a soloist between sets, and when the trio performed, it was treated as a stage show.

The public took a long time accepting the idea of black and white musicians playing together, but throughout the ordeals of discrimination, Teddy Wilson maintained his dignity and serenity. He and the Trio represent an identifiable benchmark in the struggle to eliminate the color barrier.

Wilson was born in Austin, Texas. When he was six, his parents, both teachers, moved the family to Tuskegee, Alabama. He studied piano, violin, clarinet, and oboe and attended Tuskegee College as a music major. When he was eighteen he began his professional career. Over the years, he played with the cream of jazz musicians. For a short time, after leaving Goodman in 1939, he fronted his own big band, but his strength was in small combos. He was a marvelous accompanist. Not only was he in demand by Mildred Bailey, but Billie Holiday also insisted on his backing for her most memorable records, and he was eagerly sought by Ella Fitzgerald, Sarah Vaughan, Lena Horne, and many others. His style was a refinement of Fats Waller's and Earl Hines's. He devised subtle harmonies and played with a restraint that gave the impression of leisurely control even during up-tempo numbers.

In the years after leaving Goodman, Wilson pursued a full career as studio musician, soloist with numerous bands in concert, teacher at The Juilliard School and the Metropolitan Music Academy, and featured artist at many festivals. On a number of occasions, he rejoined Goodman for reunion concerts. In spite of a three-year fight with cancer, Teddy Wilson played his special music almost to the time of his death. He was a quiet, gentle man who let his music do the speaking.

LISTENING GUIDE

"Body and Soul"—1935 (SCCJ Disc 2, Cut 7)

Clarinet—Benny Goodman
Piano—Teddy Wilson
Drums—Gene Krupa

.00   The piece begins with the melody, no introduction. The clarinet plays the melody with very little melodic manipulation.

.41 First solo by Wilson. This is the bridge section; however, the melody is replaced by an improvisation.

1.01 This is the last section of the AABA form, with the clarinet playing the melody again.

1.20 Wilson solos now over the (AA) section of the chorus, borrowing only a small amount of melodic material from the song.

2.00 Goodman plays the bridge section, this time staying with the written melody.

2.21 Wilson improvises over the last (A) section of the chorus.

2.43 Back to the bridge with the clarinet adhering to the written melody.

3.02 The last (A) section is played. Goodman starts with an improvised idea but quickly returns to the familiar melody.

3.18 Ending.

This performance is a balance of soloing between Goodman and Wilson. They trade off solos throughout. Because there was no bass player, Teddy Wilson had to supply the bass and chord accompaniment. Notice his lively technique at the beginning of his first solo. He possessed a musically fertile mind, especially for melody. Gene Krupa, known historically for his powerful and aggressive drumming, plays a subtle dancelike pattern throughout with little kicks and fills.

DAVID ROY ELDRIDGE (1911–1989)

Roy Eldridge grew up in north Pittsburgh in a family consisting of an older brother, his mother, who played piano, and his contractor-businessman father. He never attained a height of much over five feet, but the feisty, emotional, competitive nature that characterized his school years—which ended in the ninth grade—made him the equal of giants.

He took up drums at the age of six and trumpet a couple of years later. He had a wonderful ear; he learned Coleman Hawkins's tenor sax solo from the Fletcher Henderson record of "The Stampede" (Disc 2 of SCCJ), and on the strength of that, he was offered a job. He did not learn to read music until 1928, two years after joining the Horace Henderson band.

"Little Jazz," as Otto Hardwick named Eldridge, loved the challenge of cutting contests, wherein musicians would try to outdo each other in after-hours jam sessions. He searched for technique and concept that would carry him beyond his peers. He absorbed elements of the trumpet/cornet styles of Rex Stewart, Red Nichols, Jabbo Smith, and, of course, Louis Armstrong, superimposing those ideas on the long, flowing saxophone phrases of Coleman

Photo © Joe Alper

Roy Eldridge

Hawkins and Benny Carter. He increased speed and expanded range and infused his solos with fervor and emotion. He played with a case-hardened, rough-
textured tone that ranged from explosive and fiery to melancholy. In his
day—the mid-1930s to the early 1940s—he was the advance scout. He was the
bridge that carried the music from Louis Armstrong to Dizzy Gillespie's bebop.

Besides leading his own bands, both big and small, at different times,
Eldridge played in a number of bands: Boyd Raeburn's, McKinney's Cotton
Pickers, Fletcher and Horace Henderson's, Johnny Neal's Midnite Ramblers,
Elmer Snowdon's, Charlie Johnson's, Teddy Hill's, and Count Basie's; and the
white bands led by Gene Krupa, Artie Shaw, and Benny Goodman. It was with
Krupa and Shaw that he probably received his widest recognition, at least with
white listeners. He was not happy in that setting, however, since he never ac-
cepted the discrimination that confronted him off the bandstand.

With Krupa he recorded a landmark version of "Rockin' Chair" that ranks
among the all-time great trumpet solos.

Eldridge stopped playing professionally after 1979 following a heart attack. He moved to a suburb of New York with his wife, Vi, whom he had married
in 1936, and their only child, Carole. He told visitors he did not miss the music.
He gave away his piano and left the drum set given him by Gene Krupa un-

touched in his basement. He died in February 1989, three weeks after the death of his wife. Time and the music had long since moved ahead, but students of jazz will remember that until the winter night in 1942 when Dizzy Gillespie finally cut him at Minton's Playhouse, Little Jazz was king.

MARY LOU WILLIAMS (1910–1981)

Mary Lou Williams's career spanned six decades and encompassed every significant style in jazz history. Not only did she live through ragtime, Dixieland, boogie-woogie, swing, bebop, third stream, and avant-garde, but she was also an active participant in and contributor to each style. Duke Ellington referred to her music as "always contemporary—always a little ahead."[3]

Mary Elfrieda Winn, born May 8, 1910, in Atlanta, Georgia, demonstrated that she had the ear of a prodigy by picking out tunes on the piano at the age of three. Because her mother felt that her own piano schooling, which was based on reading music, had robbed her of a musical ear, she refused to teach Mary Lou to play the piano in the traditional way. Instead, she invited professional musicians into their home so that Mary Lou could listen to them play; and so at an early age she heard ragtime, boogie-woogie, and the blues.

In 1922, at the age of twelve, Mary Lou substituted for the pianist in the show *Hits and Bits*. She quickly learned the musical score by ear, and her mother permitted her to complete the tour with the show. In 1925 *Hits and Bits* folded, and Mary Lou joined the Synco Jazzers, where she met John Williams. They were married in 1926. Also during that year, Mary Lou spent a week as pianist for Duke Ellington's Washingtonians.

John Williams and the Synco Jazzers were booked into the Pink Rose Ballroom in Memphis, Tennessee, in the spring of 1927; but later that year, John left to join Terrence Holder, and Mary Lou became the leader of the band. By 1929 the Terrence Holder Band was under new leadership—that of Andy Kirk. Kansas City was its home base, and Miss Williams joined her husband there. When asked to play with the Kirk band on a recording contract, she played the book with no trouble, adding a sound to the band that the promoter demanded on all future recordings.

Miss Williams began to work more and more with the Kirk band, contributing some of her own compositions and arrangements to their book. Her first score, done in 1929, was "Messa Stomp." By 1931 Mary Lou Williams had joined Kirk's Twelve Clouds of Joy as a full-time pianist and chief arranger. The association was to continue until 1942. Mary Lou's contribution to the success of the Kirk band was significant. Her fellow sidemen paid tribute to her during this time with the composition "The Lady Who Swings the Band."

[3]Peter O'Brien, "Mary Lou Williams—the Asch Recordings, 1944–47," *liner notes* (New York: Folkways Records and Service Corp., 1977).

Mary Lou Williams

The swing decade had found Mary Lou Williams at the center of the jazz world. Her Harlem address became a haven of creativity for many of the younger musicians. She encouraged their experimentation. They brought their work to her to be critiqued, and many of their compositions germinated at these all-night sessions. Among the innovators who were regular visitors to Mary Lou's Hamilton Terrace apartment were Dizzy Gillespie, Bud Powell, Thelonious Monk, Tadd Dameron, Erroll Garner, Mel Tormé, Sarah Vaughan, Miles Davis, Charlie Parker, Oscar Pettiford, and even Benny Goodman.

Nineteen forty-four marked the beginning of a four-year period during which Mary Lou was resident musician at both Cafe Society clubs in New York. During this period, she wrote her *Zodiac Suite*, a musical interpretation in twelve parts of the twelve signs of the zodiac. It premiered in 1945. In 1946 Williams scored three sections of the suite for the New York Philharmonic. Its performance at Carnegie Hall that same year marked the first time a jazz musician had performed with a symphony orchestra.

Miss Williams played briefly with Benny Goodman in 1948 and lived for a while in California. The musical climate was changing in the United States in the early 1950s, and she headed for Europe to spend most of her time in London and Paris. She found popular and financial success during those years in Europe, even having a club named for her in Paris: Chez Mary Lou.

In 1955, for unexplained reasons, Mary Lou dropped out of the music scene. For almost three years, Miss Williams devoted all her time to prayer, religion, and charity work. She returned to the world of jazz by accepting an invitation from Dizzy Gillespie to join him in performing her *Zodiac Suite* at the Newport Jazz Festival in 1957.

During the 1960s, Williams composed three jazz masses, including *Mary Lou's Mass.* She recorded her cantata *Hymn to St. Martin de Porres: Black Christ of the Andes* in 1964.

Her later years netted her some of the recognition that she so richly deserved. A street was named for her in Kansas City. She was the recipient of seven honorary degrees. In 1978 she was invited by President Jimmy Carter to be one of the featured artists at his White House Jazz Party. In 1977 Miss Williams became artist-in-residence and professor of music at Duke University—a post that she held until cancer ended her life in May 1981.

Miss Williams contributed more than 350 compositions to the jazz repertoire. She wrote and arranged for many of the big bands of the swing era, including those of Tommy Dorsey, Glen Gray, Louis Armstrong, Duke Ellington, Benny Goodman, and Jimmie Lunceford.

To Mary Lou, jazz was love. As she told her students at Duke University, "You got to put some love in it. Jazz is love. You have to lay into it and let it flow."[4]

SUGGESTED LISTENING

The recording of "Libra," which is found in the Folkways collection of jazz (FJ 2809), volume 9, is a solo piano performance of one movement from Williams's *Zodiac Suite.* This selection represents a mixture of classical and jazz ideas. The year 1945 seems early for such a rich and sonorous chord structure. The absence of a heavy beat gives the music an impressionistic sound atypical of the swing era.

[4]Quote from Barbara Rowes, "From Duke Ellington to Duke University, Mary Lou Williams Tells the World: 'Jazz Is Love,'" *PEOPLE Weekly,* May 12, 1980, Time Inc., pp. 73–74.

VOCALISTS

The swing era was characterized by another phenomenon: the arrival of the band vocalist. Previously, jazz singers—mostly blues artists like Bessie Smith—were the feature attraction. Instrumentalists who appeared on the same stage were merely backup accompanists. When swing arrived, band leaders realized it would be necessary to balance the fast-tempo instrumental numbers with easy, swinging ballads. They also realized that a singer's visual attractiveness would enhance the band's marketability. Consequently, a generation of pretty girls who could sing on key and memorize lyrics appeared onstage: Martha Tilton, Helen Ward, Helen Forrest, Marian Hutton, Jo Stafford, and Peggy Lee. There was a contingent of handsome men as well: Bob and Ray Eberle, Dick Haymes, and Frank Sinatra. Some of them were capable of singing jazz well. There were also a few exceptional jazz vocalists, such as Ella Fitzgerald, Jack Teagarden, Jimmy Rushing, and Sarah Vaughan.

Ella Fitzgerald

ELLA FITZGERALD (b. 1918)

Ella has been the model for vocal clarity, flexibility, and invention since her beginning with the Chick Webb band after having been discovered in an amateur contest at Harlem's Apollo Theater in 1934. Her bell-like quality added definition to her fluid, improvised melodies. Her use of **melodic extensions** and large intervals produces acrobaticlike melodies to the standard songs she uses from the swing era. She recorded for Decca Records for twenty years while working in small clubs as a solo act or with small rhythm sections. She finally began recording for Norman Granz in 1955. Her greatest exposure was orchestrated by Granz in concerts for JATP (Jazz at the Philharmonic) as early as 1946. In later years she worked with both Duke Ellington and Count Basie, setting new standards for jazz singing in the big-band format. Her talents explode when teamed with pianists like Oscar Peterson or Tommy Flanagan; they offer the musical space and communication that spark the improvisational dialogue for which Ella is known. Since the 1970s she has been in great demand, singing with symphony orchestras throughout the country. Ella has interpreted the most popular songwriters, focusing again and again on the songs of Cole Porter and George Gershwin. Her **scat singing** is a frequent model examined by students of vocal jazz today.

LISTENING GUIDE

"You'd Be So Nice to Come Home To"—1964 (SCCJ Disc 2, Cut 12)

Vocal—Ella Fitzgerald
Trumpet—Roy Eldridge
Piano—Tommy Flanagan
Bass—Bill Yancey
Drums—Gus Johnson

.00   Piano starts the introduction, muted trumpet and bass play a unison line that continues into the first vocal chorus.
.10   Melody is sung adhering to the written melody.
.20   The bass and trumpet break from the unison pattern. The bass walks and the trumpet improvises fills.
.30   Ella swings the melodic line a little harder.
.47   Improvisational ending to the chorus leads into the trumpet solo.
.52   Trumpet solos and Ella fills.

.56   Ella enters with the words but with a new improvised melody.

1.11   A short trumpet solo again with vocal fill.

1.16   Ella takes the lead again.

1.32   She uses repetition of the words to build a hard-swinging rhythmic line.

1.38   Throat growls.

1.52   Her hardest-swinging melody here leads her improvisation into
the ending.

2.15   The trumpet and bass play the unison line underneath the vocal
improvisation, concluding the chorus.

2.43   End.

The performance highlights the improvisation skills of both Roy Eldridge
and Ella Fitzgerald. Ella's flexibility and pitch accuracy make her one of jazz's
most interesting vocalists. She has a genius for creating swinging melodic
lines using either the words of the song or scat syllables. Her melodic invention while improvising is especially evident in the last chorus of this performance. She communicates with Roy Eldridge in this performance as an equal
instrument of melody and expression.

SARAH VAUGHAN (1924–1990)

Sarah, like Ella, was discovered in a talent contest at the Apollo Theater in New
York's Harlem in 1942. Her vocal training had begun in the church, but after
she joined the Earl Hines band in 1943, she became friends with fellow band
members Charlie Parker and Dizzy Gillespie and fell under the spell of bebop.
The phrasing and intervallic surprises of the style became part of her vocal persona and would be evident in whatever she sang.

In 1944 Sarah, Parker, and Gillespie joined Billy Eckstine's band, and in
1945 she went on her own. In addition to her concert schedules, she began a
recording association with Columbia that lasted until 1953; after that, she
joined Mercury Records. Her repertoire covered the spectrum from pop ballads to jazz to Brazilian songs, all of which she delivered with impeccable interpretation.

Sarah Vaughan

LISTENING GUIDE

"My Funny Valentine"—1973 (SCCJ Disc 4, Cut 5)

Vocal—Sarah Vaughan
Piano—Carl Schroeder

.00 Piano introduction is very slow and sets up a very expressive mood.

.18 Sarah enters in a rich lower range. The pianist weaves musical responses around the words but leaves Sarah's voice isolated and expressive.

.55 Interesting phrase ending that leads into the next without break (great breath control).

1.37 Bridge; notice the slight increase in tempo.

2.24   Notice the use of repeated words to create a more rhythmic texture.

2.49   Sarah begins to use a higher range.

3.08   She will soon widen the range even more with dramatic changes from high to low range on a single syllable.

3.34   An expressive melodic line starts on her low range and soars to her upper range. The melodic line is modified considerably from the original melody of the song.

3.55   A long note is held while the pianist improvises freely in accompaniment.

4.06   The pianist continues an active accompaniment while Sarah returns to a more strict statement of the melody.

4.24   Sarah uses a very small voice, further personalizing the words.

4.53   Ending begins with a repeat of the last line of text.

5.23   Sarah uses the extreme lower part of her range to end the song.

5.48   End

Notice the exquisite sharing of musical space by the pianist and the vocalist. The piano fills every moment when the vocal phrase cadences or has a long sustained note. Sarah and the pianist anticipate each other's every move.

This selection is a showcase for Sarah's extraordinary expressive ability to stylize a song. Notice the changes in timbre, volume, and range. It is this flexibility that gave her such a hypnotic power over her audiences, especially in interpreting ballads.

Sarah commanded an astonishing two-and-a-half-octave range, through which she sang with complete assurance and fullness of timbre. As she grew older, her voice became deeper and, if anything, richer, losing none of its range. She sang comfortably in a variety of settings—big bands, trios, symphonic ensembles—and was never anything but wonderful. She came to be called "the Divine Sarah," and when she died at her Hidden Hills, California, home at the age of sixty-six, there were many who felt the most beautiful and thrilling voice in jazz, or out of it for that matter, had been lost.

SUGGESTED LISTENING

Bob Crosby: *The Best of Bob Crosby*. MCA Records 2-MCA 4083E. Out of print.

Roy Eldridge: *Earl Hines with Roy Eldridge: At the Village Vanguard*. XANADU 106.

Ella Fitzgerald: *The Duke Ellington Song Book*. VERVE 837035-2. 3 CDs.
From Spirituals to Swing. Vanguard Records VCD 2-47/48.
The Great Dance Band Era. Available through *Reader's Digest*.
Coleman Hawkins: *Body and Soul*. RCA Bluebird 5717-2-RB.
      The Hawk Flies. Fantasy (Orig. Jazz Classics) OJCC D-027-2
Sarah Vaughan: *The George Gershwin Song Book*. Emarcy Jazz Series 822526-4. 2-LP set.
Mary Lou Williams: *Zodiac Suite*. Folkways 32844.

A complete list of all the important swing-era bands would be beyond the scope of this text. Names mentioned only in passing deserve much fuller treatment. Some we have had to slight were veritable giants: Jimmie Lunceford, Andy Kirk, Benny Carter, the Dorseys, Harry James, Chick Webb, and more, many more. The fact that there were so many is one indication of the significance of this period in music.

SUPPLEMENTAL LISTENING GUIDE FOR PART 4

"Lester Leaps In"—1939 (Lester Young, Count Basie; SCCJ Disc 2, Cut 22)

Tenor sax—Lester Young
Trumpet—Buck Clayton
Trombone—Dickie Wells
Piano—Count Basie
Guitar—Freddy Green
Bass—Walter Page
Drums—Jo Jones

.00   Piano introduction is a late swing style, walking bass and soft drums.
.03   Muted trumpet, trombone and tenor sax (melody) play a harmonized melody built on a **riff** idea, 8 measures repeated (AA).
.18   Bridge (B), new chords and piano solo.
.27   Last 8 measures of chorus (A).
.35   Tenor sax solo, sparse comping on piano.
.51   Bridge.
1.06   2nd chorus, new melodic ideas, dialogue between piano and sax.
1.14   Stop time, tenor sax solo.
1.22   Bridge (B).
1.30   A new stop-time rhythm.

1.38   3rd chorus, piano and sax trade 4-measure solos.
2.09   Tutti statement followed by a 4-measure tenor solo.
2.17   Tutti statement followed by a piano solo.
2.26   This texture continues; notice the clear and sparse solo ideas of the pianist (Basie)—they are typical of his piano style.
3.04   Last tutti statement followed by a collective improvisational ending reminiscent of Dixieland.
3.12   End.

This performance demonstrates Lester Young's lyrical style in combination with Basie's brilliant simplicity and solid rhythmic foundation. Both musicians were instrumental in the conceptual development of soloists for years to come. Because of Young's strong melodic sense, he is generally considered the first of the modern soloists in the ancestry leading to John Coltrane and Sonny Rollins.

"Rockin' Chair"—1941 (Roy Eldridge; SCCJ Disc 2, Cut 16)

Trumpets—Roy Eldridge, Graham Young, Torg Halten, Norman Murphy
Trombones—Babe Wagner, Jay Kelliher, John Grassi
Alto saxes—Mascagni Ruffo, Sam Listengart
Tenor saxes—Sam Musiker, Walter Bates
Piano—Milton Raskin
Guitar—Ray Biondi
Bass—Buddy Bistien
Drums—Gene Krupa

.00   Introduction, trumpet cadenza over a sustained chord in the winds; this is repeated 3 more times.
.21   The main melody begins, walking bass, active brush work on the snare drum; this texture remains the same for three 8-measure phrases.
1.41   Tutti leads into the new full-band texture.
1.46   The trumpet plays above the entire band, which plays in tutti.
2.09   Trumpet lays back and rides over the full ensemble.
2.22   Solo break, which is free in rhythm like a cadenza.
2.30   Piano arpeggio.
2.33   Call-response (solo) between trumpet and clarinet.
2.54   Ending chord.

This blues-flavored Hoagy Carmichael song provided a fitting showcase for Roy Eldridge's dramatic improvisation. The choruses build to a hair-raising climax and demonstrate his ability to outpower the full band accompaniment. Power trumpet playing reached its zenith during the swing era, when soloists such as Harry James, Ziggy Elman, Snooky Young, and Cootie Williams had to make themselves heard and understood over large and often loud big bands, often without the aid of a microphone.

Piano Styles in Transition: "Fatha" Hines, Art Tatum, and Erroll Garner

17

Earl Hines and the Grand Terrace Chorus Girls

Providing, as it does, the three properties of percussion, melody, and harmony, the piano gives a musician the ability to express concepts without the need to convey ideas to supporting players. It is little wonder, then, that many of the advances within a musical genre are found in the works of pianists. The general direction of evolving styles has always been toward greater complexity, and this holds true in jazz. Sophistication notwithstanding, the fundamental need of dissonance and resolution, tension and release, is a constant that is evident in each succeeding pianist's style, even, as we shall see, in the very different music of Cecil Taylor.

Three pianists whose music traced the evolutionary line were Earl "Fatha" Hines, Art Tatum, and Erroll Garner. Preceding them were James P. Johnson and Fats Waller, who, among others, furnished them a starting point along the never-ending line of change. Of the three, Art Tatum's music was probably the most awe-inspiring, a dazzling leap forward, but the contributions of Hines and Garner were every bit as important.

Like their predecessors, the pianists Hines, Tatum, and Garner created new points of departure from which their followers, Oscar Peterson (the Tatum disciple), Bill Evans, Keith Jarrett, and Cecil Taylor, and so many others, took off either directly or at a distance. No one musician can be selected as most important, but those musicians who merely copy owe those with the gift of creativity a great debt.

EARL KENNETH "FATHA" HINES (1905–1983)

Earl "Fatha" Hines's life and career encompassed virtually the entire history of jazz. He was playing professionally during World War I and continued to book occasional concert tours until his death in April 1983. His piano style is easily recognizable. It reflects his early classical training and decades of ardent listening to many kinds of music with a highly discerning ear. He was a proficient reader of musical notation long before most jazz players knew much about written notes.

His musical taste did not solidify and stop at any certain point. Many authorities believe his most important contributions to jazz were the solos he recorded on piano rolls in 1928, but he never stopped exploring and growing. In the 1940s, for example, his band provided a training arena for bebop innovators such as Charlie Parker and Dizzy Gillespie. He also experimented in the 1940s with a large orchestra, adding violins, cellos, and a harp.

Hines was born in Duquesne, near Pittsburgh, Pennsylvania, on December 28, 1905. As might be expected, his father was a musician, and his stepmother—his biological mother died when Earl was three—exerted an influence on him with her church organ playing. He exhibited such a remarkable musical memory that his father bought a piano. He progressed so rapidly under his first teacher that he graduated to an uncompromisingly strict German maestro, Herr Von Holz. Hines was grateful for the training. His ability to **sight-read** and **transpose** any music brought him many jobs.

Hines moved to Chicago around 1923 and thereafter considered it his home. When he arrived, Chicago was the hub of Prohibition-era criminal activity, and the nightclub circuit was where the gangsters did their socializing. He often witnessed acts of violence and corruption but quickly learned when to keep it to himself.

In 1928, besides starting his eleven-year stint at the Grand Terrace Ballroom, Hines embarked on a twelve-year common-law marriage with Kathryn Perry, a violinist and vocalist. His agreement with the Grand Terrace did not prevent him from appearing with the band elsewhere. His concert tours and network broadcasts from the Grand Terrace brought him national and eventually international fame.

Hines's marriage to Janie Moses in 1947 produced two daughters, Janear and Tosca, of whom he was very proud. He was proud also, with justification, of the worldwide respect in which he was held. He pointed to his having been received by Pope Paul VI in 1966, having been included in the famous Duke Ellington White House birthday party in 1969, and having been included in the state dinner for the president of France in 1976. Such recognition did not put him out of touch with reality, however. He was a firm believer in the work ethic, and he knew that the unfair aspects had to be dealt with; but his philosophy was always that although discrimination, for example, is deplorable, to allow oneself to become embittered is self-defeating. The broad smile that almost always lit his face was genuine.

His Music

Although Hines created a piano style based on ragtime and stride formulas, his mystical imagination flavored everything he played. In "Fifty-seven Varieties" he states a tuneful melody in the opening measures but never returns to it. The 32-measure structure of each chorus is, therefore, related only harmonically. Each musical idea grows from what precedes it. The interrelation of melodic ideas creates a logical flow because each element relates to the mood established in the first 8 measures. The inventiveness of his style is most evident in the clever rhythmic interplay between the two hands. Despite the rhythmic complexity, no listener would doubt that it swings.

The technical characteristics of the Hines style include hornlike melodies, forceful octave melodies, and inventive rhythmic textures. Doubling a melody in octaves makes it clearly audible above the ensemble. His solo recordings, and those he made with Louis Armstrong, demonstrate his use of the piano as a strong melodic instrument. He also employs fluid, single-note solos such as the one heard in "West End Blues" (see Chapter 10). His active left hand, which is obviously capable of complicated stride figures, sometimes simply repeats a chord as if it were a banjo establishing a strong dance rhythm. This lively chordal repetition in the left hand characterizes the happy rhythmic Hines style. Inventive ideas grow from the very first measures of "Fifty-seven Varieties."

LISTENING GUIDE

"Fifty-seven Varieties"—1928 (Intro. to Jazz Disc 1, Cut 8)

Earl Hines—piano

.00 A tuneful 8-measure melody (A) is introduced; the left hand plays a ragtime pattern.

.08 An 8-measure phrase complements the first.

.17 A repeat of the first 16 measures.

.33 A new melody and new chords are presented in two 8-measure phrases.

.48 Last section, again 16 measures.

1.04 Interlude: A new rhythmic feeling is introduced and seems to freeze momentarily. The original rhythm and mood are soon reestablished.

1.32 The first complex interplay occurs between right and left hands.

1.36 A phrase descends from the high treble in the right hand; the chords are from the (B) section.

1.44 The phrase descends again from the high treble; notice the interplay between left and right hands.

1.59 A sharp dissonance appears in the melody and is immediately followed by a similar dissonance.

2.05 Another complex interplay occurs.

2.15 Another interplay.

2.29 The right hand plays a **shout** (repeated chord).

2.51 A complicated rhythmic interplay blurs the ending of the phrase.

3.01 A final rhythmic interplay sets up the concluding phrase.

3.07 End.

Art Tatum

ART TATUM (1910–1956)

In any given field of artistic endeavor, there are invariably those individuals who, through exceptional skill and generous twists of fate, tower over their colleagues and exert an influence that endures long after them. In the field of jazz, there stands one such individual, with a style so revolutionary and a technique so awesome that it defies imitation. Indeed, Art Tatum remains a definitive jazz virtuoso, a distinction that is rare in music history.

Tatum's legendary ability was marked by fast, hornlike melodies and clever chord substitutions, executed with an ease and an elegance that no other player could approach. However, it was his phenomenal speed that set him apart from all other pianists. One of Tatum's first recorded solos, "Tiger Rag," is taken at a constant tempo of 370 beats per minute. Even more astonishing is the 1949 concert recording "I Know that You Know," which is taken at 450 beats per minute, a rate that at times hovers around 1,000 notes a minute. This command of the keyboard amazed classical musicians as much as it did the local players. The legendary virtuoso Vladimir Horowitz is reported to have said that he would give anything to have the facility of Tatum's left hand. American composer George Gershwin was taken by the Tatum style as well; for his part, Tatum preferred American songs, particularly those written by Gershwin.

Art Tatum was born in Toledo, Ohio, in 1910. He had cataracts on both eyes at birth and underwent a series of operations as a child that restored some sight in his right eye but could not save his left eye. As a result, he was able to pick out colors and objects only by holding them close to his face. After an early and unsuccessful attempt at age thirteen to learn the violin, he took up the piano and by his early teens was playing at local parties. Tatum's first professional break came around 1927, when he was hired as staff pianist at radio station WSPD in Toledo. He was given his own fifteen-minute show, which was eventually broadcast nationwide on the parent network.

In 1932 Tatum accepted a job as accompanist to Adelaide Hall, a well-known cabaret singer of the time, and was off to New York. In New York, he challenged the center of the competitive jazz world. He thrived on "cutting contests," musical duels that pit the skills of two musicians before enthusiastic and often biased audiences. Word-of-mouth reputation spurred face-to-face confrontations between established players and upstart rookies in jam-packed, smoke-filled Fifty-second Street nightclubs. Many of these encounters took place in after-hours clubs, establishments that remained open after the legal closing time. The music played there in the early morning hours was the music the musicians themselves chose. It was there that new frontiers were explored, and it was there, in those East Side cabarets and bars, that Art Tatum took the jazz world by storm. His mastery of every known keyboard style, from stride to boogie-woogie, devastated other pianists; they refused to play whenever he was in the house.

LISTENING GUIDE

Listen to the changing moods Tatum creates in "Willow Weep for Me." He starts a walking bass several times but fades it out immediately, usually into virtuoso runs up and down the piano. In bars 1–4 and 9–12 of the second chorus, he drops the original melody entirely, substituting a basic blues theme instead. At the end of the recording, he displays his phenomenal technique with very fast scales up and down the entire keyboard.

The arrangement consists of only two 32-measure choruses. Tatum's genius sparkles here, and he shapes his performance for dramatic effect. He uses the repeating **vamp** at the beginning to tie the various musical textures together. The intensity of the piece mounts until it reaches a delicate and flashing **coda** (the final musical statement) that ends the composition.

"Willow Weep for Me"—1949 (SCCJ Disc 2, Cut 13)

Art Tatum—piano

.00 Introduction: Vamp.
.09 Melody with embellishments (A) : Notice the chords at the end of the phrase.
.23 Vamp from the introduction.
.27 Melody repeats (A) with variations.
.41 Vamp.
.46 New minor key melodic section (B), ragtime bass, lush chords follow.
.56 Left-hand runs start a series of fast scales.
1.07 Repeat of (A), last part of 1st chorus.
1.22 Vamp.
1.27 2nd chorus begins (A), 1st 4 bars a blues theme.
1.39 Ragtime bass returns (very brief).
1.49 Repeat of (A), variations on the blues idea.
2.00 Ragtime bass (briefly).
2.11 (B) section.
2.22 Fast technique begins, scales in the left hand—stop time in the right hand.
2.32 Last section (A).
2.41 Coda; tempo accelerates.
2.53 End.

"Sophisticated Lady" (Intro. to Jazz Disc 1, Cut 4)

Art Tatum—piano

.00 The song begins with the opening theme (A).
.16 Beginning of the second phrase (second A); the left hand continues with the 2/4 ragtime pattern.
.32 Bridge (B); notice the falling melodic motive.
.49 Last phrase completing the AABA form.
1.00 Double-time melodic ideas begin to enter the improvisation.
1.15 Notice the unison melodic lines in both hands. The improvisation moves into the extreme upper section of the piano range.
1.34 Syncopated statement of the main melody (A).
1.47 Highly embellished improvisation ends this phase and leads into the next.
2.07 Fast melodic lines descending from the upper range. Notice how the left hand moves in and out of a 2/4 pattern to complicated melodic patterns.

> 2.37   The right hand plays the melody with a chordal harmonization.
> 3.04   The texture thins and the tempo relaxes.
> 3.13   End.
>
> Tatum uses a composition by Duke Ellington to create a brilliant improvisation. This performance is a dazzling display of technique, with long fluid melodic lines and rich chordal voicings.

Tatum guarded his personal life and kept silent about it. He communicated infrequently even with his best friends. He organized his life around his music. He often played for several hours without stopping (one session supposedly lasted two days with only brief intermissions). The small after-hours clubs that were an important part of the 1930s jazz scene were also an important part of Tatum's life because in them he was free to play whatever he chose whenever he felt like it.

Tatum led his own band for a couple of years in Chicago, but the organization never gained much notoriety. In 1943 he led a trio with Slam Stewart on bass and Tiny Grimes on guitar. (Everett Barksdale later became the guitarist.) He stayed with the trio for the remainder of his career, but fans remember Tatum primarily for his solo piano recordings. In 1954 failing health restricted his activities considerably. Two years later he died of a kidney ailment.

More than a quarter century after his death, musicians rediscovering Tatum confess that he left a void no pianist has yet been able to fill. Although he excelled in every jazz piano style, especially stride, his greatest gift was his ability to improvise. He could make the most common popular song an intensely harmonic and melodic composition. In addition to being one of history's greatest technicians, he was one of the finest conceptual musicians in jazz.

ERROLL GARNER (1921–1977)

Historians are justifiably wary about using the word *genius*. With Erroll Garner, however, it applies. When he was two and a half, he could replay music he had heard on the family Victrola, using both hands. He never learned to read notation. It would, for that matter, have been nothing but a distraction to him. His mind and ear effortlessly originated wonders of harmony, melody, and time that other musicians would need painstaking study to comprehend. He could play different rhythms with each hand, permitting them to diverge and wander, then bring them together at the last moment. He composed complete songs in his head, sometimes in the middle of a set on the bandstand—Eddie Calhoun, his long-time bass accompanist, had to watch Erroll's left hand like a hawk. "Misty" came to him during an airplane trip. His music came forth fully matured and polished. He could walk into a recording studio, sit down, and dash off an entire album without rehearsal or retake.

Erroll was a gentle and generous man, happy and outgoing. At the piano, he let the music possess him, rocking in rhythm and punctuating phrases with audible, guttural growls. He was a joy to watch as well as to hear. He earned world adulation but never assumed the star mantle. A few pianists have learned to parody some fragments of Erroll's style, but none has presumed to try to adopt it all. There is hardly a jazz musician, however, who has not gained from his inventiveness. He was one of a kind. When he died in Los Angeles on New Year's Day, 1977, of cardiac arrest, he vacated a place in jazz that has not been refilled, but echoes of his genius can be heard from the keyboard of almost every modern jazz pianist.

LISTENING GUIDE

"Fantasy on 'Frankie and Johnny'"—1947 (SCCJ Disc 3, Cut 20)

Erroll Garner—piano

.00	Introduction (quite long) begins with slow chords.
.10	A rhythmic pattern appears in the left hand.
.17	Each hand plays an independent pattern (counterpoint).
.25	A vamplike left-hand pattern and chords in the right hand lead into the verse.
.43	The melody of the song first appears in the upper register with a boom-chuck pattern (stride) in the left hand.
.53	Tight chords around the melody finish this section.
1.04	Return to the stride texture; notice the dissonances in the right hand around the melody.
1.19	Interlude.
1.37	Next chorus uses the boom-chuck pattern with blues inflections ornamenting the right-hand melody, very laid-back right hand.
1.59	Modulation (the key is moved one half step higher to increase excitement).
2.09	Independent scale ideas in both hands (counterpoint).
2.19	Another modulation up one key area; notice the independence of each hand; chords are used as fills.
2.35	Ending.
2.52	End.

When a composition is called a fantasy, the structure of the music is usually very free. The introduction is a clear example of this freedom. The entire arrangement is fluid in that the various textures seem to flow effortlessly from style to style. Garner's use of chords in the right hand in addition to the melody creates clusters of sound with enjoyable dissonances added to flavor an otherwise simple melody. "Frankie and Johnny" is a 12-bar blues. When presented as an instrumental without its wry and pungent lyrics, it poses a challenge to sustain interest, a condition Garner is more than equal to.

SUGGESTED LISTENING

Art Tatum: *Solos*. MCA Records MCAD-42327.
   Art Tatum: Piano Starts Here. Columbia PCT-9655E. (CS)
Erroll Garner: *Concert by the Sea*. Columbia Jazz Masterpieces CK-40589.

The Bebop Revolution: Charlie Parker and Dizzy Gillespie

18

Dizzy Gillespie

Only rarely has a musical era paralleled the career of one individual. Bebop was one of those rarities. It is linked to Charlie Parker, who presided at its beginning and during its rise to preeminence. During his lifetime, the bebop style reached its highest level, and although it has been superseded by newer styles, its effects continue to be felt. Bebop was developed by and for virtuosos. There are many theories explaining why: Instrumentalists were seeking improvisational freedoms that they couldn't find in the big bands; black musicians were reasserting their jazz supremacy; jazz was maturing. No matter what the reason, in the early 1940s bebop established a foothold that traditional jazz musicians and critics could not dislodge. It drew small audiences to after-hours clubs, primarily in New York's Harlem. Only a few musicians were capable of performing it well. The sophisticated chord structures, irregular melodies, and flashing speed left uninitiated listeners befuddled. It was far from the commercial music scene and required a certain amount of study on the part of performers and listeners alike.

THE BEBOP STYLE

The bebop style produced four significant changes in musicians' attitudes toward jazz and its performance: (1) It required a greater understanding of jazz theory and called for virtuoso technique; (2) it introduced complex instrumental melodies and phrases to replace the simpler melodies of the big-band era; (3) it introduced increasingly complicated chords and rhythms to the rhythm section; (4) it developed a cult of serious musicians who approached music intellectually as well as emotionally.

Technique

Jazz improvisation shifted from ornamenting an original melody to organizing new patterns of fast, active melodic lines. The patterns often ended with an abrupt two-note figure that suggested the word "be-bop" or "re-bop." Bebop musicians developed theoretical relationships between distended chords and esoteric scales. Their theories justified the use of notes that were previously considered too dissonant. These notes are called **melodic extensions** because they are not among the primary notes of the chords. Furthermore, extensions were added to chords by the pianist to add harmonic color.

New Melodies

Within the new melodic patterns of bebop, important notes—usually the top notes of a melodic line—were accented. This series of accented notes outlined a slower melody. Bebop melodies were not as tuneful as those of the big-band era, and the phrasing overlapped the chords in angular leaps and bounds.

LISTENING GUIDE

"I Can't Get Started"—1945 (SCCJ Disc 3, Cut 10)

Trumpet—Dizzy Gillespie
Trombone—Trummy Young
Tenor sax—Don Byas
Piano—Clyde Hart
Bass—Oscar Pettiford
Drums—Shelly Manne

.00   Introduction using chords from the last phrase of the song, tenor sax and trombone play long chord tones, the bass stays around a 4-to-the-measure beat, the drummer brushes in a slow swing pattern.

.30   The 1st 8-measure section of the song begins, the trumpet creates a melodic variation using the shape and most of the original notes of the Vernon Duke song. Tenor sax and trombone play a unison countermelody.

.58   Notice the melodic extensions that end the phrases.

1.05   The countermelody returns with a repeat of the (A) section more freely improvised.

1.39   Bridge (B), new countermelody, the original melody becomes more obscure.

2.12   Last (A) section, again with the countermelody played by tenor sax and trombone in unison.

2.47   The chorus is extended into an ending, similar to the introduction.

2.55   Short solo break (trumpet).

3.00   Ending.

The fast melodic lines so often associated with bebop are less prominent in this performance; however, typical bebop embellishments are obvious. The many melodic extensions in the solo are typical of bebop. The countermelody is less angular and could very easily be associated with more traditional melodic structures found in swing or later in West Coast accompaniments.

The Rhythm Section

The rhythm section, as usual, carried the weight of harmony and rhythm. The discovery of new ways to play familiar chords increased the pianist's chord vocabulary. The bass player walked more often and much faster than before. The drummer added complicated patterns, filling in the regular beat. The changes the drummer made are perhaps the easiest to hear. Just as big-band drumming was more aggressive than that of Dixieland, bebop drumming increased in complexity through the use of **polyrhythm.** As the term implies, two or more contrasting rhythms are played at the same time. The conflict of different rhythms blurs and disguises the regular beat. In "Un Poco Loco" (New World Records, 271), Max Roach plays a complicated pattern in which he accompanies the solos with explosive punctuations, called **bombs,** on the snare or bass drum in conjunction with cymbal crashes. The bombs and cymbal splashes dominate the sound of the rhythm section and often the entire ensemble.

AABA Form

Most bebop performances were weighted heavily with solos with a minimum of arrangement. The rigidly arranged compositions of the big-band era were totally rejected. Soloistic freedoms reappeared as a backlash response to the big-band ensembles, where long improvisations were impossible.

The emphasis on improvisation not only created new melodies for old songs but also often eliminated the original melody entirely. In the *Smithsonian Collection*'s two performances of Gershwin's "Embraceable You" (SCCJ Disc 3, Cuts 14 & 15), the melody is completely disguised. The original chords are all that remain. In addition to borrowing older songs as a basis for solos, bebop musicians composed new tunes that minimized the written melody and expanded the time for solos. They followed the standard 32-measure **AABA** form, with the 8-measure (A) section having the only written melody. This form was not new; for years it supplied a fundamental structure for songs in many different styles. Its flexibility once again surfaced, becoming a vital element in bebop composition and improvisation.

Melody chords	Same melody and chords	Improvised solo and new chords	Original melody and chords
A	A	B	A

32-Measure Song Form

LISTENING GUIDE

"KoKo" (not the same as "Ko-ko" recorded by Ellington) is structured in the traditional bebop AABA form. The tempo is very fast, with a bass note played on each beat. Playing the solo double time is quite a feat at this tempo.

"KoKo" was not an entirely original composition. As was frequently the case in bebop, Parker composed a new melody on the harmonic progression of a popular standard, in this case "Cherokee."

"KoKo"'s melody requires great technical skill and acts as a springboard to fast, fluid solos. Parker and Gillespie play the melody in flawless unison. The solos, at breakneck speed, exhibit the discipline and control required of bebop musicians. In his drum solo, Max Roach creates a steady roar with his stick work. Accents float out, adding rhythmic complexity to the very fast beat. Notice how the drumming dominates the rest of the rhythm section.

"KoKo"—1945 (Intro. to Jazz Disc 1, Cut 9)

Alto sax—Charlie Parker
Trumpet and piano—Dizzy Gillespie
Bass—Curley Russell
Drums—Max Roach

.00	Introduction begins with a double-time unison melody by the alto sax and the muted trumpet.
.06	Trumpet solo with drum accompaniment (brushes); notice the bombs.
.12	Sax solo with drums.
.18	Duet (harmonized melody), drums continue; notice the uniformity of inflections as both play the last double-time phrase.
.25	1st chorus (AA) : Alto sax solo, bass walks, drums play ride pattern, piano comps.
.50	Bridge (B) : Notice the last notes of each phrase (extensions).
1.03	Last (A) of the 1st chorus.
1.15	2nd chorus (AA).
1.40	Bridge (B) : A very complicated pattern.
1.54	Last (A) of 2nd chorus.
2.06	Drum solo: Bass drum and snare drum, accents on the snare drum; the beat becomes increasingly difficult to find.
2.29	Unison melody line returns
2.35	Muted trumpet solo with drum (cymbals) accompaniment.
2.41	Sax solo with drums.
2.47	Duet ending.
2.51	End.

Bebop is not all fast and furious. The complex melodic structures, when slowed down, reveal an underlying beauty. "Parker's Mood" combines the solidarity of the blues with the intensity of bebop. The lyric piano solo by John Lewis is a perfect complement to Parker's masterful improvisation. The solo does not compete with Parker's style but acts as a balancing interlude. Parker and Lewis show a relaxed familiarity with the blues.

"Parker's Mood"—1948 (SCCJ Disc 3, Cut 19)

Alto sax—Charlie Parker
Piano—John Lewis
Bass—Curley Russell
Drums—Max Roach

.00 Alto sax makes the opening statement.

.05 Piano continues, bass walks, drums start playing steady time, a 12-measure blues.

.16 1st chorus: Alto solo, piano comps and fills, drums and bass continue.

.29 Repeated melodic pattern.

.37 Double-time melody.

.52 2nd chorus: Relaxed lay-back style.

1.22 Extended harmonic **changes** leading into the next chorus (Parker leads the way).

1.30 3rd chorus: Piano solo, with Lewis humming; a lyric, simple melody.

2.06 4th chorus: Notice the many inflections.

2.46 Coda (same as the introduction): Alto sax followed by piano, bass and drums stop.

3.00 End.

CHARLIE "BIRD" PARKER (1920–1955)

In the 1940s, jazz made an abrupt change of direction from the classically based harmonies and melodies of big-band swing to bebop. Actually, precursors to the style had appeared in the music of Lester Young, Roy Eldridge, and a few others in the late 1930s; and even though Dizzy Gillespie and Thelonious Monk contributed as much as any to bop's creation, one name stands above the rest: Charlie "Bird" Parker.

Speculation regarding the source of his nickname has produced so many stories that truth and fantasy have become indistinguishable, but whatever prompted the appellation, to jazz lovers the word Bird means only one person

Charlie Parker

and one thing: Charlie Parker and bebop. If Louis Armstrong redirected the course of jazz at least ninety degrees in the 1920s, Parker wrenched it around just as severely in the 1940s.

Charles Christopher Parker, Jr., was born on August 29, 1920. Less than thirty-five years later, the ravages of the substances he had swallowed, inhaled, and forced into his bloodstream misled the coroner into estimating his age at death to be fifty-five.

In grade school, Charlie was a bright, diligent student; but when he reached thirteen, supported only by his mother's nighttime job, he became absorbed in jazz and the activities surrounding it. The Parker house was close to the Kansas City nightclub district, and Charlie, unsupervised during the night hours, began to frequent the clubs. Having no instrument of his own, he accepted the loan of a brass horn from the school but found he did not like it. His mother, with characteristic sacrifice, bought him an ancient alto sax for forty-five dollars. The keys leaked badly and it was hard to blow, but Charlie set about teaching himself to play. Soon he joined an amateur dance band, the Deans of Swing. At fifteen, he gave up school altogether, married nineteen-year-old Rebecca Ruffing, and let his wife and his mother support him while he roamed the nightspots listening, learning Kansas City jazz, and occasionally sitting in.

An insurance claim gave him enough money for a new sax in 1936, the same year his son Leon was born. He continued to listen and play. One of the musicians he most admired was Lester Young, the tenor saxophonist with Count Basie's band. Parker thought he was reaching the point where he could **jam** with players of that caliber. One night in the spring of 1937 Charlie got up, uninvited, to play with the famous Basie drummer Jo Jones, who was sitting in at a nightclub called the Reno Club. At first his solo progressed well, but before long he became lost in the harmonic changes of the tune. Jones stopped drumming, snatched a cymbal off his set, and threw it at Bird's feet in disgust. The experience was only a temporary setback. That summer he took a job playing in a dance band at Lake Taneycomo in the Ozark Mountains. He took along every Lester Young record he could get hold of, and during his free time, he committed Young's solos to memory. His first stop when he returned to Kansas City in the fall of 1937 was the Reno Club. Nobody threw a cymbal at him this time.

In 1938 he was hired by Tommy Douglas, a conservatory-trained leader, who helped Bird with music theory. Another sax player in the orchestra, Buster Smith, was one of the Kansas City's top jazz musicians. Charlie stayed close to him, following each Smith solo with one of his own until he could play better— even by Smith's own admission.

That summer his mother and his wife suggested Charlie move out, so he pawned his horn and left. In New York, Charlie took a job washing dishes at Jimmy's Chicken Shack in lower Harlem. As it happened, Art Tatum was playing piano there, and the pianist's lightning arpeggios and unconventional harmonic voicings undoubtedly stimulated Charlie, perhaps planting seeds for the future.

Parker's Professional Career

Charlie's first playing job in New York was at the Parisien Ballroom, a **taxi dance hall.** His fellow bandsmen were mostly old-time musicians, but the job provided unique and valuable training. Every sixty seconds a buzzer sounded backstage and the band **segued** to a new tune. Each customer had to surrender another ticket with every song or lose his dance partner. There was no written music and the band glibly transitioned from song to song, many of which Charlie had never heard before. He was forced to expand his mental library at a prodigious rate. After hours Parker often went to Clark Monroe's Uptown House, where musicians were free to play jazz as radically as they wished. In this and similar after-hours clubs, the revolution against swing was taking shape.

Bird joined Jay McShann in Kansas City, a band that was second in popularity only to Basie's. He toured the South and the Midwest until the summer of 1942. When the band traveled east to New York, Charlie decided to withdraw from the big-band scene and concentrate on small groups. This lasted until he joined the Earl Hines band in 1943. For the first time, he worked on a regular basis with Dizzy Gillespie, the trumpeter who was as much a force in the spread of bebop as Parker. Together Bird and Dizzy sharpened their skills during off-hours by practicing formal brass and woodwind instructional studies at speeds previously thought impossible. It was then that the characteristic bebop sax-trumpet unison lines developed.

In 1945 Charlie confined his activities to New York—specifically to Fifty-second Street. He organized small groups, recorded frequently, and secured Miles Davis as a sideman. Charlie's career accelerated sharply in 1945, the same year he recorded "Koko." In December he, Dizzy, vibraphonist Milt Jackson, bassist Ray Brown, drummer Stan Levey, and pianist Al Haig were booked at Billy Berg's in Hollywood, California. The West Coast showed little enthusiasm. After only two months, the group returned to the East—all except Parker, who had turned in his return ticket for drug money.

By mid-1946 Charlie's narcotic habit, which began when he was fifteen, took him over the edge. After he spoiled a recording session by his inability to play, Parker went back to the hotel and set fire to his room. After several days, a court committed him to Camarillo State Hospital for the mentally disordered. He was an inmate there from July 1946 to January 1947. Upon release he was greatly improved physically and mentally. He made several first-class recordings for Dial, among them the acclaimed "Relaxin' at Camarillo."

The years from 1947 to 1950 were probably Parker's most productive. He worked and recorded entirely with small groups made up of the elite of the be-bop movement. His health, however, was on the decline. In 1948 he was hospitalized with ulcers.

Back in New York, Charlie began a relationship with Chan Richardson, a girl he had known and occasionally dated since 1946. She would be his last "wife" (of four) and would have his only daughter and a son.

In 1949 Parker fulfilled a wish he had had for some time, to play with strings. Some of his best solos were played with string accompaniment, but the change seemed to herald the decline of Charlie's career. In 1951 he lost his New York City cabaret license. He could no longer play anywhere in the city where liquor was sold. This left him only theater concerts, recording dates, and out-of-town engagements.

His professional appearances revealed his steadily deteriorating skills. In August 1954 Charlie was booked into Birdland, the New York nightclub named for him. Bird brought his string orchestra. A few days after the opening, Charlie, irrational from liquor, fired the string players in the middle of a set. A monumental uproar ensued and Parker stalked out, went home, drank a bottle of iodine, and swallowed a bottle of aspirin. Quick action in getting him to Bellevue Hospital saved his life. But a month later he committed himself to the Psychiatric Pavillion.

This marked the end of his career and, soon, his life. On March 12, 1955, Charlie died at the home of a friend. The mystique that had begun forming before his death blossomed into cult proportions. Signs proclaiming "Bird Lives!" appeared across the country. In a sense it is still true. The genius of Parker lives in all of today's bebop-related styles.

JOHN BIRKS "DIZZY" GILLESPIE (1917–1993)

From the time in the late 1940s when bebop became widely recognized, the figure who instantly personified this musical revolution was Dizzy Gillespie. He wore horn-rimmed glasses, a beret, and "cool threads." He sported a goatee, and when he played the trumpet his cheeks bulged out. He behaved irrepressibly and made outrageous statements. But far more important, he, together with a handful of other musicians, created something brand new in jazz.

Gillespie was born in Cheraw, South Carolina, the last of nine children. It might be safe to suppose that with eight others competing for attention, Dizzy's assertiveness developed early. His father led a local band, and there were always instruments lying around. By the time he was four, Dizzy could bang out tunes on the piano, and when he was ten, he received a music scholarship to Laurinburg Institute in North Carolina, where he changed from trombone to trumpet and studied music theory.

In 1935 Gillespie moved to Philadelphia, got a job in Frank Fairfax's band as a result of sounding like his idol, Roy Eldridge, and, because of his antics, received his nickname. Two years later Gillespie went to the Teddy Hill band, where he took over Eldridge's chair and made his first record. In 1939 Dizzy joined the Cab Calloway orchestra; he stayed there until the famous incident in 1941 when Calloway fired him. It seems someone had been peppering Cab with spitballs onstage when his back was turned, and Cab accused Dizzy. Gillespie denied it and a scuffle ensued, during which Dizzy laid hold of a knife and cut his boss's posterior. Grounds for dismissal. It turns out that trumpeter Jonah Jones and bassist Milt Hinton were the culprits, and Cab and Dizzy made up. Dizzy went right to work for Ella Fitzgerald, then held positions with Charlie Barnet and Benny Carter.

Nineteen forty-two was the pivotal year in Gillespie's career. He had been playing in Les Hite's band, and the two had not gotten along. Hite disbanded rather than fire Gillespie outright and risk Dizzy's anger and possible retaliation à la Calloway. Hite then reorganized without Gillespie. This left Dizzy with time to experiment. The site of this effort was Minton's Playhouse in Harlem, where musicians from all over New York City came to jam and try new ideas. The central characters were Thelonious Monk, drummer Kenny Clarke, saxophonist Don Byas, guitarist Charlie Christian, Charlie Parker, and, of course, Dizzy. To scare off less talented musicians who came at night, Gillespie and Monk would prepare complex chord variations during the afternoon to challenge the upstarts. As these variations evolved and grew in number, the inner core of musicians began to see a new form developing. It was bebop.

From 1943 on, Gillespie played with a number of front-rank bands—Earl Hines, Coleman Hawkins, Boyd Raeburn, and Duke Ellington (for only three weeks, since the two strong personalities did not see eye to eye)—and led his own small combos from time to time. His position as musical director of the Billy Eckstine band in 1944 was significant to the advancement of bebop, since

Charlie Parker played in the sax section, other members of the band were bebop oriented, and Eckstine was enthusiastic about the new style. A big band playing bebop represented a departure from the normally accepted instrumentation of two or three horns and a rhythm section, and was rarely copied afterward except by Gillespie's own band, which he led from 1945 to 1948.

The intervening years continued to find Gillespie in the musical and, occasionally, the political limelight. In 1964 he ran for the United States presidency on a platform of total withdrawal from Viet Nam, a national lottery, and abolition of segregation. In 1977 he paid a visit to Cuba, where, to the discomfort of the State Department, he was photographed with Fidel Castro. Yet in 1978 he was invited, together with a number of other jazz greats, to the White House by President Jimmy Carter. Gillespie's musical setting was usually as leader of a small combo or as guest artist; however, in addition to his 1945 big band, he fronted big bands again in 1951–52, whence came the Modern Jazz Quartet, and in 1956–59, which took an international tour for the State Department. In 1986 he told an interviewer he would never again have a big band, but in the summer of 1987 he toured Europe, Japan, and the United States with a big band that included Dizzy's protégé, John Faddis, in the trumpet section.

Gillespie's bandstand persona tended to disguise the man. He was an astute businessman and an efficient organizer. He was kind and generous of his time and talent and never felt the need to use alcohol or drugs. He met his wife, Lorraine, in 1937 when she was a stage dancer; they were married in 1940, and they remained married. Lorraine, who is as retiring and private as Dizzy was extroverted, was his bulwark and center. They bought a house in Englewood, New Jersey, in 1965 and lived there until his death of pancreatic cancer in January 1993. If there were ever a need to refute the stereotype of the dissipated jazz musician, Gillespie would have been the example.

Dizzy, in his final years, achieved the deserved status of "legend in his own time." His puffed cheeks, which he says began developing unbidden in the late 1940s from his explosive attack of notes, and his upswept trumpet, which was derived from the horn that was accidentally bent at Lorraine's birthday party in 1954, defined his image. His legacy is of vastly greater importance. He surely must stand beside Buddy Bolden and Louis Armstrong and Duke Ellington and, certainly, Charlie Parker as one who found a new way.

SUGGESTED LISTENING

Dizzy Gillespie: *Jazz at Massey Hall* (with Charlie Parker, Bud Powell, Charles Mingus, and Max Roach). Fantasy/OJC OJCCD-044-2.

Charlie Parker: *Bird's Night—The Music of Charlie Parker.* Savoy Jazz SJL 2257. 2-LP set.

Bebop Piano: Thelonious Monk and Bud Powell

19

Thelonius Monk

Bebop developed a cult identity that popularized the wearing of berets, sunglasses, zoot suits, and string ties. Bop jokes, slang, and other trappings gave bebop national exposure and served notice that it was not just antitraditional music, it was a subculture in rebellion. Two of the fathers of bebop, Thelonious Monk and Dizzy Gillespie, were walking symbols, down to the popular goatee, of the bebop social revolution; but whereas Gillespie was friendly and humorous, Thelonious was detached and eccentric. This contrast was partly responsible for Dizzy's immediate popularity and Monk's twenty-year isolation from all but the innermost circle of musical revolutionaries. Not until the early to mid-1960s was Monk accepted as one of jazz's most influential and innovative composers.

Not all the characteristics of bebop outlined in the last chapter were reflected in Monk's playing. The factor most obviously lacking was a fast, brilliant technique. Despite his stride piano background, Monk rarely displayed a typical bebop technique. In the bebop movement, he was a leader in the realm of harmony and structure. Monk spent most of his time working with notes distantly related to the chords. As a result, his melodies and accompaniments were not always typical of bebop solos; they were, however, a reflection of the thinking that gave birth to bebop. In addition, the nonconforming, dissonant quality of his playing influenced the avant-garde movement.

Thelonious Sphere Monk was born in Rocky Mount, North Carolina, on October 10, 1917 (some sources say 1918 or 1920). His parents moved to a Manhattan neighborhood known as San Juan Hill when Thelonious was four. After his father left the family, returning to North Carolina, Thelonious grew very close to his mother. Thelonious developed an almost obsessive attachment to home. He lived in the same house, first with his mother and later with his wife, Nellie, and two children, Thelonious and Barbara, for more than forty years, until the city demolished it.

Thelonious was a withdrawn child. His name, which got teasingly changed to "Monkey," further alienated him from his peers. To escape the discomfort of social contact, he turned to music. He started picking out tunes by ear when he was six and began piano lessons when he was eleven. He quickly formed strong preferences for certain pianists, the early favorites being Fats Waller, Duke Ellington, and James P. Johnson. He directed his own studies toward the stride piano style, eventually winning several amateur-night competitions at the Apollo Theater; otherwise, his public performances were confined to rent parties in Harlem. In addition to the piano, he played the organ in church for a couple of years, but he disliked the music and eventually rejected it.

His first break from ghetto life came when he was sixteen. He quit high school and toured the country for a year with a woman evangelist and faith healer. When he returned to New York, he found some work in the Fifty-second Street clubs; there he gradually surrounded himself with the musicians who, with him, decisively turned jazz in a new direction. He played in a few bands with Gillespie and Parker; however, in the 1930s and early 1940s he worked almost exclusively in trios and quartets.

The most significant time in his early career came in 1939 at Minton's Playhouse, where, as a member of the house band, he and a handful of innovators developed a new style that was intended to reestablish black dominance in jazz. Monk named the new music "bipbop," a label that eventually became "bebop." Monk was surrounded by the enormous talents of Dizzy Gillespie, drummer Kenny Clarke, Charlie Parker, and guitarist Charlie Christian. At that time, only a few musicians were able to master the difficult bebop technique. Monk stimulated these great musicians with his clever rhythmic ideas and intriguing melodic lines. His position as house pianist put him at the forefront of the new style. His job at Minton's lasted only a short time, and for the next eight years, he found employment in low-paying, nonunion night spots. He could have found regular work playing conventional cocktail piano music, but he refused to compromise.

In 1948 Monk led the first bebop group at the Village Vanguard in Greenwich Village, but at the same time, he was drifting away from mainstream bebop to further develop his own musical personality. His increasing dissonances and angular rhythms began to alienate his fellow musicians and listeners alike and made it difficult for him to find work. His wife, Nellie, whom he had married in 1948, was forced to take a job as a clerk. He continued to compose during this period, however. In the recording of "Misterioso," his sharply defined personal sound is evident.

LISTENING GUIDE

"Misterioso"—1948 (SCCJ Disc 4, Cut 6)

Piano—Thelonious Monk
Vibraphone—Milt Jackson
Bass—John Simmons
Drums—Shadow Wilson

.00	Introduction made up of the 1st 4 measures of the tune (2 phrases).
.11	The written melody is played by the piano, vibes, and bass. The melody is heard in the bottom notes of the "walking sixths" (played louder by Monk).
.46	Vibraphone solo (blues): The piano plays a low note followed immediately by the 7th of the chord; no chords are used as accompaniment.
1.23	Piano solo: Dissonant extensions end the phrases, no accompaniment from the vibraphone.

1.42   Ascending runs ending on dissonant notes.

1.50   Again, ascending runs up to dissonant notes (although these might sound like mistakes).

1.59   2nd solo chorus by Monk: The obvious dissonant intervals are minor 2nds.

2.04   Large melodic leaps.

2.40   Vibraphone enters with the melody, piano develops accompaniment idea (low note–high note), Monk creates melodic and rhythmic tensions.

3.03   Piano joins vibes with the melody.

3.15   Ending (improvised).

3.19   End.

This blues is typical not only of Monk but also of the revolutionary spirit of bebop. The melody is instrumental—that is, it would be very difficult to sing; in fact, it is awkward even for most wind instruments. Swing musicians had a difficult time understanding this new intellectual approach to melody and had an even more difficult time playing it. Monk's solo demonstrates his harmonic thought: **Extensions** are unadorned; dissonances stand out as isolated statements. The short quips that make up his solos and accompaniments complicate the otherwise stable structure of his blues. Notice the difference between Milt Jackson's solo and Monk's. Jackson's fluid technique contrasts sharply with Monk's **disjunct** angularity. Monk's style led many listeners to conclude that he was a poor technician. That and his eccentric displays on stage led them to consider his performances to be mere shows instead of serious musical endeavors.

As Monk's style developed, he had difficulty finding steady work. His lifestyle became unpredictable and unstable. He worked in small, unknown clubs and only occasionally encountered popular bebop performers. In 1951 he was arrested with Bud Powell for possession of heroin. Although Monk was not a drug user, he insisted on keeping quiet and being convicted with Powell. When he was released after sixty days in jail, his cabaret card was cancelled and he was no longer able to play in New York nightclubs. The only work he could find was on the road and occasionally in a recording studio. Nellie continued to work as a clerk to make ends meet.

The daughter of the late British banker Nathaniel Rothschild, Baroness Pannonica ("Nica") de Koenigswarter, stepped in and bailed Monk out of trouble. The baroness, wealthy and eccentric, was a well-known benefactress of New York jazz musicians. Because of her social standing, she was able to open the right doors and have Monk's cabaret card renewed in 1957. Public taste had changed during Monk's enforced absence, and his return to the New York jazz scene was greeted with enthusiasm. He opened at the Five Spot with John Coltrane on tenor sax, Wilbur Ware on bass, and Shadow Wilson on drums. He soon received more popular acclaim than at any time in his life. His newfound celebrity did nothing to change him, however. On stage, he would often leave the piano to "dance" alone in order to communicate a rhythmic feeling to the other musicians or to ride the rhythmic wave that was being created.

His unpredictable actions were not limited to his performances. His somewhat bizarre appearance led to another run-in with the law in which he was charged with disturbing the peace; once again he lost his cabaret card, this time for two years.

Barred from performing in nightclubs, he made his first concert appearance at Town Hall in New York in 1959. His ten-piece band played arrangements by Hall Overton and elicited only a lukewarm response. A concert hall was the wrong setting for Monk. To be properly appreciated, he had to be heard playing his own compositions in informal, compatible surroundings where he could turn his creativity loose. His improvisations were more like compositions than repetitive embellishments. At times he literally stumbled onto ideas that he subsequently developed imaginatively and logically. He worked hard and sometimes long over his compositions. Many are tightly woven and complex, though they may sound deceptively unstructured. Typical of his unique compositional ability are "Round Midnight," "Evidence," "Ruby, My Dear," "Well You Needn't," and "Blue Monk."

Monk enjoyed increasing success into the 1960s, playing numerous concerts and club dates. His eccentricities were considered to be entertaining rather than bewildering. Audiences all over the world crowded into his concerts. Although the 1960s was his most successful period, his most representative recordings were made between 1947 and 1952. In 1958, 1959, and 1960, he won *Down Beat* magazine's International Critic's Poll.

Monk continued to lead a fine quartet, with Charlie Rouse on tenor sax, throughout the 1960s. In the early 1970s he toured with a group called the Giants of Jazz, which included Dizzy Gillespie and other bebop greats. Monk's health forced him to withdraw from the jazz scene for a year in 1973. He performed very successfully at the 1975 Newport Jazz Festival, with his son, Thelonious Monk, Jr., on drums. That year he was also awarded a Guggenheim fellowship. He curtailed his activities sharply in his last few years, but by the time of his death (on February 17, 1982), his place in jazz history had been firmly established. Critic Martin Williams considered Monk to be the most significant composer since Duke Ellington. Although such recognition probably pleased Monk, it did nothing to change him. He remained his own man to the end.

BUD POWELL (1924–1966)

In his prime, Bud Powell was probably the most brilliant of the boppers. His best performing years occurred before 1950, although he continued to perform into the 1960s. His career after 1945 was interrupted by extended commitments to mental hospitals. It is a pity that he is often remembered more for his periodic retreats from normality than for his music.

Powell was born in New York City to a musical family. His grandfather, father, and two brothers were musicians. He began studying classical music on the piano at age six and continued for the next seven years. His early awareness of jazz guided his growing technical abilities in both classical and jazz piano styles. At age fifteen he left high school to play professionally, and his wanderings took him to Minton's Playhouse, where he encountered Thelonious Monk. He was fascinated by the new jazz and Monk's unorthodox style. Although Powell was

Earl "Bud" Powell

Photo by Duncan Schiedt

withdrawn, Monk encouraged and helped him, and he soon exhibited the inventiveness and technique that later inspired such awe.

Powell's inner torment drove him to seek relief in alcohol, which, of course, only added to his suffering. In 1949 he spent ten months in Pilgrim State Hospital in New York. After his release, he spent his most productive years until 1951 playing with such giants as Sonny Stitt, J. J. Johnson, Max Roach, Milt Jackson, and above all, Charlie Parker. Powell had based his style on the styles of Earl Hines and Art Tatum, but it was Parker who was his inspiration.

In 1953 Powell married Alteria, a woman of great understanding and devotion to him, whom he called Buttercup. The couple had two children, Celia and John. In 1959 they moved to Paris, where they benefited from the more tolerant racial attitudes and relaxed atmosphere and where Powell could play regularly. In 1964 he returned to the United States. He appeared in a 1965 Carnegie Hall concert commemorating Charlie Parker, but his skills had deteriorated badly, and his part of the concert was a disappointment. He made only one more appearance before his death in 1966.

Serious followers of jazz piano agree that, Thelonious Monk aside, the bebop revolution had no pianistic standard-bearer until Powell came along. He was able to distill the new sounds blown through the horns of Charlie Parker and Dizzy Gillespie and convert them into a piano style that fit the moment. In addition, he created his own new sound, one that stimulated inspiration in his fellow musicians during his lifetime and that still can be felt.

LISTENING GUIDE

"Night in Tunisia"—1951 (SCCJ Disc 3, Cut 21)

Piano—Bud Powell
Bass—Curly Russell
Drums—Max Roach

.00   Introduction, drums play a Latin pattern using the crown of the cymbal. Bass enters, the piano follows with a short melodic pattern in the lower range.
.16   (A) Main motive of the song (8 measures).
.24   Brief mix of swing and Latin leads into a repeat of the first 8 measures (A).
.38   (B) Bridge section (8 measures) moves to melodic and rhythmic swing patterns.
.49   (A) Return to Latin patterns and original melody, last 8 measures of the chorus.

1.00	Interlude chorus is made up of a repeated melodic pattern that is kicked by the drums and bass. The last 4 measures are an impressive double-time solo break on piano.
1.23	Bebop solo. The Latin sections are played in swing but with the original chords.
1.45	Bridge; notice the vocalizations in the background.
1.57	(A).
2.08	2nd chorus of the solo begins with (A) but is not repeated before the bridge (B).
2.32	(A) Last 8 measures of the 2nd solo chorus.
2.43	(A) Original melody returns but is changed for the repeat of (A).
3.06	(B) Long bebop melodic line contrasts his earlier rifflike melodies.
3.18	Final (A) of 3rd solo chorus.
3.30	(A) is repeated twice as a vamp before the ending.
3.52	Open piano solo break.
4.12	End.

This trio performance is a prime example of the development of the bebop style specifically for the piano. The piano has the unique ability to join the rhythm section using rhythmic and harmonic patterns while developing powerful melodic lines at the same time. Powell displays technical precision as he effortlessly constructs complicated solo lines using accents and riffs typical of the horn lines of Parker and Gillespie.

SUGGESTED LISTENING

Monk's Music. Fantasy/OJC OJCCD-084-2.
Bud Powell: *The Complete Blue Note Recordings.* Mosaic MR 5-116.

Hard Bop (Straight Ahead and Funky)

20

Horace Silver

Following the death of Charlie Parker in 1955, several performers surfaced to continue bebop's development. Parker's influence was such that most young performers were classified as beboppers without much regard to individual differences. It is true that the main substance of their style was bebop, but each individual's creative ability gave new life to the well-defined Parker sound.[1] In addition, the cool, or West Coast, style was emerging with a character all its own. Bebop and cool (or, in many cases, cool bebop) attracted many of the performers of the 1940s. For example, the Modern Jazz Quartet, with John Lewis and Milt Jackson, became the model group in this style. At the same time, however, traditional blues elements were reentering jazz performance practice. Retrenchment in the blues was typical of the 1950s and 1960s. The blues-flavored bebop sound was popular with both performers and listeners.

HORACE SILVER

The names most often given to the reconditioned blues were *hard bop, funky,* and sometimes *soul jazz.* Pianist Horace Silver and drummer Art Blakey gave definition to these terms when they organized the Jazz Messengers in 1956. The funky style is characterized by a hard-driving rhythmic feeling that supports melodies full of cliché-like blues motives and inflections. The fine bebop solos of Hank Mobley on tenor sax and Kenny Dorham on trumpet contrasted greatly with the blues solo style of Silver. As leader and musical director, Silver organized small-group arrangements to help build intensity and swing. Listen to "Sister Sadie" on *Blowin' the Blues Away* (Blue Note 4017). Using only two horns, Silver created a big-band impression with shouts and tutti shout choruses. The structure of the piece's arrangement was so complete that Buddy Rich had to make only minor changes when he recorded it later with his big band. The funky qualities remain intact with big-band scoring just as they did with the quintet.

Art Blakey, the splashy drummer in the quintet, later left Silver to form another group, called the Jazz Messengers. The funky sound became popular in musical sound tracks, and even, with performers like Ramsey Lewis, on top-forty radio. Hard bop successfully brought back some of the basic musical pleasures associated with early jazz.

---

[1]A common term used to describe this style is *straight ahead jazz*. The term is very broad and deals mostly with small-group improvisations on standard tunes.

LISTENING GUIDE

"Moon Rays"—1958 (SCCJ Disc 4, Cut 11)

Piano—Horace Silver
Trumpet—Art Farmer
Tenor sax—Clifford Jordan
Bass—Teddy Kotick
Drums—Louis Hayes

.00   Introduction, soli horns and pedal point in the bass.
.31   Repeat. The cool sound continues.
.59   Bridge. The same texture continues but with new chords.
1.30   Return to the opening theme, completing the AABA structure.
1.58   The solos begin with the tenor sax, ride patterns in the drums, comping in the piano.
2.29   Bridge. During the solos, the cool elements of the arranged melody are replaced with a more aggressive hard-bop texture.
2.56   The solo continues (2nd chorus) with a relaxed bebop melodic line.
3.54   Trumpet solo, again a relaxed solo line, the rhythm section continues to supply walking and comping patterns.
4.22   Bridge.
4.51   Beginning of the 2nd solo chorus.
5.21   Bridge.
5.50   Piano solo, clear melodic right hand and sparse chords in accompaniment, sometimes just single notes.
6.45   2nd solo chorus. Single-note accompaniment continues.
7.18   Blues motives.
7.43   Horns enter with a new tutti theme, which moves into a soli.
8.13   Repeat.
8.39   Another new unison melody.
8.55   Shoutlike riff.
9.38   Return to the main theme with the bass playing the pedal point.
10.10   Repeat.
10.40   Ending.
10.51   End.

Notice the organizational "tightness" of the opening chorus. The bass is very important to the definition of the ensemble, changing patterns and kicks throughout. The improvisational section opens explosively with a sense of freedom and looseness. This straight ahead performance is stable and generally predictable. Notice the refined control and "coolness" of the performers during the arranged ensemble sections. This straight ahead selection also exhibits elements of two other jazz styles developing at the same time, cool and third stream (see Chapter 22).

ART BLAKEY (1919–1990)

Most of the great jazz musicians who have influenced change have done so directly, by example, by how and what they played. There have been, however, a small number of musicians who have gathered promising young talents for training and polishing before sending them out to spread the word, not necessarily as reflections of the teachers, but as innovators in their own right. For the thirty-five years following 1955, no teacher was more effective or produced a greater number of jazz luminaries than the chief of all Jazz Messengers, Art Blakey.

Art Blakey

LISTENING GUIDE

"E.T.A."—1981 (Intro. to Jazz Disc 1, Cut 10)

Drums—Art Blakey
Trumpet—Wynton Marsalis
Tenor sax—Bill Pierce
Alto sax—Bobby Watson
Piano—James Williams
Bass—Charles Fambrough

.00	The selection begins with a drum solo, steady, busy snare drum continues throughout.
.26	Horns enter in a very tight soli line.
.37	Softer contrasting phrase, the drums continue a similar ride pattern.
.48	Alto sax solo, drums stop momentarily. Long flowing double-time melody, bass walks relentlessly, piano comps sparsely.
1.10	2nd solo chorus.
1.32	3rd solo chorus. Horns play an accompanying line softly in the background.
1.54	Trumpet solo begins with short statements and soon falls into double-time melody. There continue to be brief breaks in the double time, but it always returns.
2.15	2nd solo chorus.
2.37	3rd solo chorus with soft horn accompaniment.
2.59	Tenor sax solo starts immediately with double time. Notice the ride cymbal and how it, with the walking bass, drives the rhythm forward.
3.20	Second solo chorus. Accompanying horn line returns.
3.41	Piano solo. Notice how little the drums play at first. Accented notes slowly creep into the texture. 2 solo choruses.
4.25	A fast unison line is played by the 3 wind instruments (double time).
4.47	Drum solo starts with cymbals, bass drum, and snare. It moves to the snare and returns to the cymbals.
5.32	The main theme is played as in the beginning.
5.56	Ending, long note with drum solo.
6.09	End.

This performance is full of the fire and complexity found in the extended bebop style. Although there are moments of more traditional bebop and even swing, there is no doubt that the primary focus is extended technique. The level of virtuosity of the soloists and the difficult unison lines are indicative of the extended concepts of bebop in the 1980s and 1990s.

Until he was eleven, Blakey was cared for by a Pittsburgh woman who brought the abandoned child home against her husband's wishes. Blakey never knew his mother, and his father was only a vague phantom, but his foster mother impressed upon him values of self-reliance and honesty that stayed with him the rest of his life. When he was eleven, he was taken in by a madam who put him up in a brothel where there happened to be a piano. He taught himself to play in one key, and having done that, he organized a band.

He switched to drums and began changing the role of the drummer from that of keeping time to that of sharing in the melodic development. He learned to play with such energy and force that his fellow band members were compelled to play to their limits. His reputation grew while he was still in his teens, and he went on to play with Mary Lou Williams, Fletcher Henderson, Billy Eckstine (where he played alongside Charlie Parker and Dizzy Gillespie), Thelonious Monk, and Miles Davis.

In 1955, together with pianist Horace Silver, Blakey formed the Jazz Messengers, with tenor saxophonist Hank Mobley, trumpeter Kenny Dorham, and bassist Doug Watkins. Silver left in 1956, and a new cast of players was formed. Thereafter, the cavalcade of musicians who became Messengers, graduated, and moved on is almost too lengthy to catalog: trumpeters Lee Morgan, Woody Shaw, Freddie Hubbard, Chuck Mangione, Art Farmer, Donald Byrd, Ira Sullivan, Wynton Marsalis; saxophonists Wayne Shorter, Benny Golson, Jacky McLean, Billy Pierce, Branford Marsalis; pianists Cedar Walton, Keith Jarrett, JoAnne Brackeen, James Williams, Donald Brown; and a great many more.

Trumpeter Brian Lynch, who appears on a number of Messenger recordings and who played in Japan with Blakey before his terminal illness forced the drummer to return home for the last time, says of Blakey, "Art never dictated, but somehow he made us grow individually. He never discouraged us from reaching out. In fact, he encouraged that. He'd say, 'Use your imagination. If you make a mistake, make it loud.'"

SONNY ROLLINS AND CLIFFORD BROWN

Bop continued in the late 1950s in a rather pure state with the electrifying recordings of the Max Roach–Clifford Brown Quintet. This quintet used a mature bebop format that spotlighted the fluid proficiency of Brown and the long, motivically conceived solos of Sonny Rollins. Brown died at the age of twenty-six in an auto accident in 1956 before the jazz community could really benefit from

Sonny Rollins

his extraordinary talent. Sonny Rollins went on to further develop his own unique style. Rollins constructs solos on very small ideas and methodically builds idea after idea on a single melodic motive. His style is so personalized today that he should rightfully be placed next to Lester Young, John Coltrane, and even Ornette Coleman.

Joe Henderson

When Joe Henderson, born in Lima, Ohio, in 1937, took a music aptitude test at the age of nine, he demonstrated such potential that he was advised that he could go in any musical direction he wanted. He has since stated that his decision to select the tenor saxophone was almost preordained. His affinity for and mastery of the horn were evident from the beginning. His early influences were Lester Young, Flip Phillips, Stan Getz, and Charlie Parker, so there was never any question that jazz would be his métier.

After high school he studied for a year at Kentucky State and for four years at Wayne State in Detroit, where he played gigs with Yusef Lateef, Barry Harris, and Donald Byrd. He was drafted into the Army in 1960, played in a traveling military musical show, and settled in New

Clifford Brown

York City in 1962 after his discharge. He became associated with trumpeter Kenny Dorham, who was then at the forefront of jazz innovation.

Henderson never lacked the admiration of his peers. He was in constant demand as sideman for recording sessions led by jazz giants such as trumpeters Lee Morgan, Freddie Hubbard, Wynton Marsalis, Miles Davis, and Dorham; and pianists Andrew Hill, McCoy Tyner, Herbie Hancock, and Horace Silver. He also fronted his own band on innumerable occasions, both in America and abroad.

In one of the curiosities of the entertainment industry, Henderson, who had been held in the highest esteem in Europe for decades, was "discovered" in the United States in 1992. He was selected by the critics as Jazz Artist of the Year, and his recording So Near, So Far *was Jazz Album of the Year. He suddenly found himself a celebrity, invited to the White House and lionized on every side. Although pleased by the deferred acclaim, he looked on himself as being the same musician, the same artist, he had been for more than thirty years.*

FOLLOWERS OF PARKER

The many performers who continue in the bebop tradition are often called Parkerites. The melodic patterns developed by Parker are still very much alive in the playing of Phil Woods and Charles McPherson on alto sax. Many excellent bop players are active today in every instrumental field: guitarist John Scofield, trumpeter Wallace Roney, and pianists Oscar Peterson and McCoy Tyner.

Bop can be detected in many musical styles that are developing today. There is even a popular country style in which bop and traditional country players perform in the same band. There is hardly a jazz style today that has not been affected by the bebop revolution.

SUGGESTED LISTENING

Art Blakey and Horace Silver: *A Night at Birdland.* 2 vols. Blue Note CDP7-46519, CDP7-46520

Sonny Rollins: 1951–56. With Clifford Brown, John Coltrane, Max Roach, and others. Prestige 24004. 2-LP set.

Bebop: In the Mainstream Today   21

Wynton Marsalis

All the streams of jazz proceed through the 1980s with continued modifications, as seen in the development of fusion. The refinement of Dixieland groups as witnessed in college competitions, big bands using fusion arrangements, and the joining of **acoustic** and electric instruments all show such modifications. In most cases, technical advancement has had the greatest impact on each style. Bebop has probably been affected the most by virtuosity. It has continued to develop vigorously through such greats as Herbie Hancock, Wynton Marsalis, and Tony Williams. There is no question that the technical level of these latter-day beboppers is as exciting as that which amazed listeners when bebop first appeared.

The rhythm section. The bass in a contemporary bebop group is freed from walking most of the time; it now is required to complement and augment complicated drum rhythms to create a new, more elusive sense of tempo. When patterns are played, they are not carried for such long periods of time. In fact, bass players often give the impression of comping around a time framework that must be borne equally by all players. The drumming style is very aggressive and may reflect the activity of all the other players. It sounds soloistic even when the melody or solo is carried elsewhere. The piano's role is most similar to that of the bebop pianists of the late 1940s. It must play the same difficult melodies as the horns and provide interesting comping as well.

Tightening of the ensemble. Contemporary bebop groups are composed of sections that collaborate in employing punches and kicks that are derivatives of the kind found in fusion. These are either unison rhythmic ideas with additional fills coming from the drummer, or a very complicated network of activities between the melody and rhythm sections. During the open solo interludes, the group often improvises similar kicks to accompany the curve of the soloist. Such playing demonstrates the high level of communication that exists at the heart of this style.

Arrangements and compositions. Just as in early bebop, standard songs often provide the harmonic structure for performances. "Standards" are compositions written before and during the bebop revolution of the 1940s; however, the treatment of these pieces is shaped by the new roles of the rhythm section, and the pieces are often played at breakneck speeds. New compositions are often designed specifically to display the prowess of both the ensemble and its soloists.

THE MARSALIS FAMILY

Musical talent has always tended to run in families. Consider Johann Sebastian Bach and all his musical children. In jazz there have been Johnny and Baby Dodds, Tommy and Jimmy Dorsey, the Heath brothers, and Duke and Mercer Ellington. Any number of family names come to mind. However, nowhere has the gift of talented genes been more generously conferred than in the Marsalis family.

Ellis Marsalis, for years the instructor of jazz improvisation at the New Orleans Center for Creative Arts, and his wife, Dolores, who used to sing with jazz groups, produced six sons. First Branford in 1960, then Wynton, Ellis III, Delfeayo, MBoya, and finally Jason in 1977. Unlike many highly gifted children, the two older boys did not exhibit very early evidence of their abilities. Not until they were almost teenagers did they select and set about conquering their primary instruments, Branford the saxophone and Wynton the trumpet.

Wynton's mastery of his instrument was first to be widely recognized. He was chosen to play first trumpet in the New Orleans Civic Orchestra while still in high school. At the age of seventeen he was accepted at the Berkshire Music Center and at eighteen received a scholarship to Juilliard. He did not graduate because Art Blakey heard Wynton soon after his arrival in New York and persuaded him to join the Jazz Messengers. After touring with Blakey, he went on to play with Herbie Hancock and then to form his own quintet. By the time he was twenty-two, Wynton had won the *Down Beat* best jazz trumpeter's award, had received two Grammys in the same year, one for a jazz and one for a classical recording, was the subject of feature articles in at least ten national and international publications, and could be seen on several video shows.

The attenion was deserved. Marsalis's technique is awe-inspiring. Maurice André, probably the world's foremost classical trumpeter, says Wynton could become the finest trumpeter in history. He is at ease in any setting but considers jazz the most demanding and deserving of artistic respect. He admits to being on a crusade to define and bring fitting recognition to real jazz, from which he excludes fusion, crossover, funk, and any other adulterated style.

Meanwhile, Branford was making a name for himself as a first-rank saxophonist. In fact, there are those who feel that his technique is as advanced as Wynton's and that he has a more fully developed jazz understanding. His opinions about music are as definite as Wynton's, though perhaps a bit more liberal. He recorded and toured as a member of Sting's band and has cut a number of records in his own name. He vaulted into prominence when the host of the Tonight Show, Jay Leno, selected Branford to be leader of the high-profile show band.

Others of the Marsalis brothers are musicians as well. Delfeayo has received recognition as trombonist and record producer, and Wynton thinks that Jason may soon become one of the premier drummers in jazz.

The Marsalises, in some respects, are an anachronism. Their sounds are acoustic, or as acoustic as is possible in an era when virtually every performance is electrically amplified. Listeners clearly hear the tones and timbres created by the musicians, not what an engineer concocts. Their mission is also clear: to define jazz, to play it better than it has ever been played, and to convince the country of its origin that it is an art form worthy of preservation.

Roy Hargrove

Roy Hargrove and Joshua Redman

Trumpeter Roy Hargrove, born in 1970, was discovered by Wynton Marsalis at Booker T. Washington High School in Dallas. He attended the Berklee music school on a scholarship and since has achieved wide acceptance as one of the leaders of the new generation of pretenders. He is a disciple of Marsalis and agrees with the essentiality of building on traditional styles, but he has come under some criticism for not having yet broken new ground. He has found steady work and has made a number of recordings.

Suggested Listening

The Vibe. BMG/Novus 63132.

Tenor saxophonist Joshua Redman is the son of the established and well-regarded tenor-man Dewey Redman. Joshua grew up in Berkeley, California, never intending to become a professional musician, having seen what a struggle it had been for his father. Instead, after graduating from high school in 1986 as class valedictorian, he entered Harvard on a full scholarship with plans to become a doctor, changed his major to social studies, graduated summa cum laude, and applied to and was accepted by Yale Law School. His plans were interrupted when he won the Jazz Saxophone Competition at the Thelonious Monk Institute in 1991. His accep-

Photo by Marc Hom

Joshua Redman

tance and recognition by the hierarchy of the jazz community were almost instantaneous. He signed to record for Warner Brothers; by 1993 he had completed two albums under his own name and had participated in several more as sideman, including one with his father.

Redman seems to possess the rare combination of intellect and common sense. He is not very impressed by his rapid rise and is aware that his ability to play in top form without having to practice much is an uncommon gift. He is making money, but he says that is secondary to the fulfillment of participating in the creation of music.

Suggested Listening

Wish. Warner Bros. 9 45365-2

Several unique styles have emerged on the strength of individual techniques. Two performers in particular deserve notice: guitarist Stanley Jordan and vocalist Bobby McFerrin.

STANLEY JORDAN

By tuning all his guitar strings at intervals of a fourth and playing notes by tapping the strings on the frets with the fingers of both hands, Stanley Jordan has brought a new style to jazz. The technique approaches that of the pianist who can play ten notes simultaneously. Jordan plays bass lines and comps chords with his left hand while he improvises melodies with his right. His hands move independently on the neck of the guitar, not unlike those of a pianist on a keyboard. When first introduced, the technique opened entirely new avenues to guitarists. Jordan's technique is not merely an awe-inspiring novelty, however. He uses it to enhance his innate musicality and sensitivity.

LISTENING GUIDE

"Eleanor Rigby"—1985 (From *Magic Touch*, Blue Note BT 85101)

Composers—Lennon and McCartney
Guitar—Stanley Jordan
Percussion—Sammy Figueroa

.00	Introduction, arpeggios.
.11	Repeat of first phrase, bell tree.
.21	New idea.
.45	Melodic idea from the original tune, duet.
.57	Repeat.
1.13	Rhythmic texture, bass line, comping and melody, idea from the 3rd part of the tune.
1.40	The melody begins, 1st part of the tune (8 measures).
1.54	2nd part of the tune (8 measures).
2.07	3rd part of the tune (16 measures); this idea supplied the motive for the introduction.
2.30	2nd chorus, melody is an octave higher.
2.47	Improvisation begins to dominate the original melody.
3.00	3rd part of the song is used for improvisation.
3.14	3rd chorus.
3.21	Melodic extensions are used over a **pedal point** on the lowest string.
3.39	Vamp, bass becomes predominant, balanced with comping and brief treble statements.
3.57	Treble melody returns.
3.59	Accompaniment chords ascend and descend, very short.
4.05	Rhythmic texture thins into a free-floating improvisation.

4.25	Duet texture returns.
4.40	**Counterpoint** intensifies.
5.00	Duet continues, treble line against bass line.
5.13	Melody returns (3rd part of tune).
5.36	Beginning of melody (last chorus).
5.43	Repeat; notice the temple blocks in the background.
5.50	2nd part of the melody.
6.00	This part is extended to structure an ending.
6.18	Rhythm becomes free again, with a fast running melody from the high range into the low range.
7.00	End.

STANLEY JORDAN (b. 1959)

Stanley Jordan burst on the jazz scene at the 1984 New York Kool Jazz Festival. It was learned that for the year preceding, he had been playing for handouts on

Stanley Jordan

the streets of New York, and enthusiasts concluded that he was a self-taught guitar prodigy.

In fact, he began classical piano lessons at the age of six. His parents divorced when Stanley was eleven, and his father sold the piano, forcing the boy to take up a less expensive instrument. He became absorbed in rock and roll and the blues and learned how to execute the **licks** and **harmonics** played by Jimi Hendrix, and later turned to jazz.

He studied the techniques of guitarist Wes Montgomery and pianist Art Tatum and, while in college, began experimenting with unorthodox tunings and with a two-handed touch technique that would let him play the guitar like a piano. The method would have been impossible without the electric guitar and even so required much experimentation and instrument modification.

Bobby McFerrin

In 1981 Stanley graduated from Princeton University, where he had studied music composition and theory. He went to the Midwest to further refine his system and in 1982 moved to New York City.

Since the 1984 festival, the doors of the world have opened to Jordan. Tours have taken him to Europe, Australia, and Japan. He has appeared on the Tonight Show and on the Merv Griffin Show. He has a contract with a major record company and is writing a book on guitar technique. His 1985 album, *Magic Touch,* on Blue Note, stayed at the top of the jazz charts for thirty weeks and was a best-seller in the pop field as well. This crossover success is not surprising in light of the selections: Thelonious Monk's "Round Midnight," Michael Jackson's "Lady of My Life," and The Beatles' "Eleanor Rigby." They reflect Jordan's truly eclectic taste.

BOBBY McFERRIN

Bobby McFerrin, like Stanley Jordan, is a one-person show. He slaps his chest to establish time while singing melodies far into the treble range, and effortlessly interjects low bass notes to underpin the melodies. This three-part *tour de force* provides all the musical components required of a small ensemble. The most interesting aspect of this new technique is the vocabulary of new sounds he has invented to imitate acoustic or electric instruments. One of his albums contains overdubbing in which he even mimics traditional drumset sounds vocally. His collaboration with the Manhattan Transfer vocal jazz group proved his ability to share his prodigious soloistic skill in an ensemble setting.

LISTENING GUIDE

"Another Night in Tunisia"—1986 (Intro. to Jazz Disc 1, Cut 11)

Music—Frank Paparelli and John "Dizzy" Gillespie
Arrangers—Cheryl Bentyne/Bobby McFerrin
Vocal lead, bass, and percussion—Bobby McFerrin
Vocals—The Manhattan Transfer (Cheryl Bentyne, Tim Hauser, Alan Paul, and Janis Siegel)
Soloist and lyricist—Jon Hendricks

.00   Bass and percussion introduction, all vocal.
.11   Vocal backup (soli), scat syllables.
.21   First (A) section (8 measures), lead vocal as backup continues.
.34   Ending of the 1st (A) section.

.38   Repeat of (A).
.56   (B) section, walking vocal bass with soli vocal backups.
1.09 (A) section returns, vocal shouts are more predominant.
1.25 Bridge or interlude idea, new material.
1.44 Solo break, Jon Hendricks singing a vocal solo with lyrics that are so fast they are difficult to understand.
1.49 Walking bass as Hendricks sings a solo over the 1st 2 (A) sections of the song, vocal backups continue.
2.12 Interlude built on the chords of the (B) section, use of counterpoint, no bass or percussion sounds.
2.24 Last (A) section, use of words briefly by the vocal backups, rhythm section returns.
2.35 Percussion alone, all vocal sounds.
2.57 Motives from the main melody, use of a digital delay to create echoes.
3.14 Vocals stop and only the percussion and bass vocals remain.
3.20 Return of the (A) section (lead and backups).
3.39 (A) section repeats and shouts intensify.
3.56 Fade out.

The fascinating aspect of this performance is that McFerrin produces all the percussion and bass sounds vocally, demonstrating his expanded use of the voice to imitate traditional instruments. The soloist in this recording, Jon Hendricks, and The Manhattan Transfer are familiar to vocal jazz fans. Hendricks was first to set words to famous recorded instrumental solos, such as Coleman Hawkins's "Body and Soul," for which the term *vocalese* was coined. Many of The Manhattan Transfer arrangements are his. His own improvised solos speak to the hornlike concepts with which he has been involved since vocal bebop began.

Each era tends to believe the limits of instrumental and vocal techniques have been reached; however, as the foregoing musicians demonstrate, all jazz styles are continually open to new, borrowed, and even expanded technical modifications. Exploding technical development together with the appearance of new instruments is bound to yield continued and unexpected advancements.

SUGGESTED LISTENING

Stanley Jordan: *Magic Touch*. Blue Note CDP7-46092.
Bobby McFerrin: *Spontaneous Inventions*. Blue Note CDP7-46298.

The Manhattan Transfer: *Vocalese*. Atlantic 81266-2.

Wynton Marsalis: *Wynton Marsalis*. Columbia CK-37574.

Branford Marsalis: *Bloomington*. Columbia 52461.

SUPPLEMENTAL LISTENING GUIDE FOR PART 5

"I Got Rhythm"—1945 (Don Byas; SCCJ Disc 3, Cut 9)

Tenor sax—Don Byas
Bass—Slam Stewart

.00	Short bass intro, uses slap technique (pulls strings out so they slap against the fingerboard).
.03	Tenor sax enters playing the melody, (AA), almost as written.
.16	Bridge (B).
.29	2nd chorus, tenor sax plays double-time solo against the walking bass (upper register).
.42	Bridge (change of chords).
.54	3rd chorus, texture remains the same.
1.08	Bridge (B), bass uses slap technique again.
1.20	4th chorus, tenor sax plays a descending melodic pattern.
1.32	Bridge (B).
1.39	Last (A) section.
1.46	5th chorus.
2.00	Bridge (B).
2.06	Last (A) section.
2.13	6th chorus, bass solo begins, bowed bass while singing the same notes, a trademark of Slam Stewart.
2.25	Bridge (B).
2.32	Last (A) section.
2.38	7th chorus, bass continues bowing.
2.51	Bridge (B).
2.57	Last (A) section.
3.04	8th chorus, tenor sax returns for an entire chorus.
3.22	Descending melodic pattern by the sax.
3.29	9th chorus.
3.41	Bridge, large melodic intervals in the solo.
3.54	10th chorus, solo continues and walking bass intensifies.
4.19	Melodic ideas slow down but inflections increase.

4.45 Ending.
4.56 End.

The tempo here is over 300 beats a minute, which, when factored by the rush of continuous improvised eighth notes, yields more than 10 notes a second. It is difficult to follow for those who are not experienced at hearing the AABA form; therefore, the form is pointed out where sections are easiest to perceive. The form (and chord progression) of this song has become a traditional favorite of all bebop enthusiasts. This solo, however, falls somewhere between the fluid soloing of Coleman Hawkins and the intense patterns of Charlie Parker. It contains a hint of the coming bebop practice of carrying phrases not only across bar lines but also beyond sections, thereby delaying succeeding sections by as much as a measure. Try to differentiate between the fluid melodic ideas of the swing tradition and the patterned ideas common to the current bebop tradition, both of which can be found in this selection. Slam Stewart's solo is representative of his entertaining and well-developed melodic ability, especially while using the bow.

"I Should Care"—1957 (Theolonious Monk; SCCJ Disc 4, Cut 10)

Thelonious Monk—piano

.00 Opening chords are free rhythmically and carry the melody as the top note, the bass melody fills the space between melodic (chordal) ideas.

.21 Arpeggios in the right hand.

.39 2nd 8 measures of the 32-measure song begin.

1.07 Notice the melodic extensions.

1.17 Octave trills and ascending arpeggios (chords spelled out one note at a time).

1.51 Last 8 measures of the song begin.

2.02 Single-note technique; that is, a dissonant chord is played and stopped quickly but one note is not released.

2.08 Octave trills and arpeggios reappear.

2.28 Double-time melodic idea swings in contrast to the preceding chordal ideas.

2.33 Monk plays a descending melody, one he often used when improvising.

2.50 The single-note technique reappears with an intense clarity, the chords surrounding the single notes are dissonant and very short lived.

3.03 Ending.

3.11 End.

This improvisation demonstrates Monk's preference for musical design, even if very stark, over the brilliant technique typical of most bebop soloists. Extensions are exposed without the buffer of the entire chord, revealing an intensity that characterizes his personal style. The entire cut offers only one chorus of this swing-era ballad. Note that the form of this song is somewhat unconventional: ABAC, the final four bars of the C section returning to the initial motive of the improvisation. The basic melody is clearly heard throughout. The improvisation is basically a harmonic treatment. Brief as it is, this recording tells much about the depth of Monk's musical intellect.

"Pent-Up House"—1959 (Sonny Rollins, Clifford Brown; SCCJ Disc 4, Cut 15)

Tenor sax—Sonny Rollins
Trumpet—Clifford Brown
Piano—Richie Powell
Bass—George Morrow
Drums—Max Roach

.00   Begins with the melody of a 16-measure (4/4) song, 4-measure phrases, drummer plays the rhythm of the melody on the cymbal.
.19   Repeat of the melody.
.40   Trumpet solo, **ride** pattern on the cymbal, bass walks.
.51   Short melodic phrases (trumpet).
.59   2nd chorus.
1.19 3rd chorus.
1.39 Climax, trumpet uses upper range, 4th chorus.
1.59 The pattern that begins this 5th chorus becomes the main idea of the rest of the chorus.
2.19 6th solo chorus, ends on a melodic extension.
2.44 Tenor sax solo echoes the same melodic extension.
2.59 2nd chorus.
3.20 3rd chorus, notice the fast double-time idea (in this case, 3 notes to 1 beat).
3.40 4th chorus.
4.01 New, slower motive begins the 5th chorus.
4.22 Last solo chorus for the tenor sax.
4.44 Piano solo, the drummer plays a ride pattern on the crown of the cymbal, the melodic solo is sparse and dissonant.
5.04 2nd chorus, the melodic ideas become more flowing.
5.24 Brief 2-measure solos are exchanged by trumpet, tenor sax, and drums; the fast double-time melodies appear once again.

6.03   After his last 2-measure solo the drummer plays a longer solo, which lasts for 2 choruses.

6.44   The original melody returns.

7.05   Repeat of melody, and ending.

7.27   End.

This performance is typical of the later style bebop of the 1950s, when solos were of primary concern to the musicians. The soloists in this piece begin each chorus with some simple melodic idea or pattern, which they then develop for the remainder of the chorus. The beginning of each chorus is pointed out in the Listening Guide so that you may practice counting measures and beats. In this way, you will better relate to the four-measure phrasing and the structure of the long solos. After a little practice, you will feel the phrases and choruses without all the counting.

Third Stream and Avant-garde: Miles Davis and Bill Evans

22

The history of jazz reproduces in a microcosm some of the significant events of classical music's long history. Both jazz and classical music originated in simple dance forms, and both have developed those forms into large sophisticated structures. Today's avant-garde jazz concerts are often scarcely distinguishable from those of the classical avant-garde. The two musical streams have influenced each other greatly since the sixties. Not only have jazz composers incorporated the advanced harmonies and extended forms of classical composers, but also European and American classical composers have borrowed many elements from jazz. Charles Ives adopted ragtime rhythms, and Igor Stravinsky wrote ragtime pieces, as well as the *Ebony Concerto* for jazz clarinetist Woody Herman. George Gershwin flavored classical forms with blues rhythms, melodies, and inflections, and is claimed by both the classical and the jazz communities.

Third stream music represents a merger of classical music and jazz. The term was coined to describe music that channeled jazz and classical elements into a new, third stream. As this style evolved, jazz adopted such forms as the concerto, sonata, canon, and theme and variations in place of the 12-bar blues and the 32-bar song. It applied the modern harmonies of Western European music to its own advanced improvisatory practices. Third stream music has a very wide scope and may be said to have become part of all avant-garde music. The major elements of third stream music can be summarized as follows:

It combines jazz and classical composition procedures. Much modern classical composition is melodically angular and harmonically dissonant. This "atonal" style first appeared when jazz bands turned to classically trained arrangers such as Gil Evans for their scores. **Serial** (or **12-tone**) techniques invaded jazz compositions throughout the 1950s and 1960s. Twelve-tone compositions sound dissonant because they do not obey traditional melodic or harmonic rules.

It uses orchestral instruments. White bands first used strings and classical wind instruments—such as cellos, oboes, bassoons, and French horns—to introduce new sounds into traditional jazz ensembles. Many jazz composer-arrangers were eager to incorporate traditional classical timbres.

It imitates classical music. Avant-garde jazz assimilated the tonal qualities of classical composers such as Wagner, Debussy, and Schoenberg. They even directly quoted Bach and Beethoven. Jazz composers borrowed the large extended forms of the baroque and classical periods. *Mirage*, written by Pete Rugolo for the Stan Kenton orchestra, seems more like classical music than jazz (Capitol 28002 or New World Records NW216).

LISTENING GUIDE

Today, third stream is called "free" or "avant-garde," although in the 1950s and 1960s it was associated with cool or West Coast jazz. The first example is classified as cool because it was recorded when the term was in vogue. Gil Evans used orchestral instrumentation and scoring in this cool–third stream arrangement of "Summertime." His use of flutes, bass clarinet, and French horn definitely puts the arrangement into the third stream.

"Summertime"—1958 (SCCJ Disc 4, Cut 12)

Arranger—Gil Evans
Muted trumpet—Miles Davis
Trumpets—John Coles, Bernie Glow, Ernie Royal, Louis Mucci
Trombones—Joe Bennett, Frank Rehak, Jimmy Cleveland
Bass trombone—Dick Hixon
French horns—Willie Ruff, Julius Watkins, Gunther Schuller
Tuba—Bill Barber
Alto sax—Julian "Cannonball" Adderley
Flutes—Phil Bodner, Romeo Penque
Bass clarinet—Danny Bank
Bass—Paul Chambers
Drums—"Philly Joe" Jones

.00 No formal introduction; begins with melody, harmonized riff in background, bass walks, drummer plays a soft pattern.
.27 Riff stops, unison line in background.
.32 Riff returns, the ride cymbal adds a shimmering sound to the accompaniment.
.35 Improvised solo (Miles Davis): Although the melodic ideas swing hard, the muted sounds produce an unaggressive sound.
1.02 Unison line returns, no riff.
1.11 High flutes added to the riff; notice the rich chords used to harmonize the riff.
1.37 Unison line.
1.41 Tutti band (short).
2.13 Unison line, the solo remains the dominant voice.
2.25 Tuba fills.
2.57 Ending, the tuba fills between riffs.
3.16 End.

Many jazz compositions of the 1960s and later contained one or more third stream elements. As a result, the term became so all-encompassing as to be meaningless. Even the jazz/rock writings of Chick Corea and Joe Zawinul showed the influence of classical music. Consequently, a new term emerged to accommodate all the differences. The 1960s has been called the *eclectic period* in jazz history. George Russell, Don Ellis, and Charles Mingus incorporated third stream concepts into three strikingly different arrangements.[1] Miles Davis, Charles Mingus, and the Modern Jazz Quartet clearly show how jazz became cool, orchestral, third stream, or simply eclectic.

MILES DAVIS (1926–1991)

During the first half of the 1940s, jazz took a new direction. Young men and women who had gone off to fight in World War II jitterbugging to the big-band music of Duke Ellington and Glenn Miller came back to hear Charlie Parker and Dizzy Gillespie playing bebop. The angular melodic lines, taken at break-neck speed into distant harmonic extensions, sounded harsh and unintelligible to most devotees of swing. The first bebop musicians were black, and among them in 1945 was a nineteen-year-old trumpeter freshly arrived in New York City. Miles Davis did not become a leader in bebop, but he would be in the fore-front of three very important new styles of jazz.

Miles changed the sound of jazz several times during his career of forty-six years; he either led the way himself or inspired others to strike out on a differ-ent path. A comparison of Davis's recordings over the years reveals his constant changes in direction, some of them drastic. His development, following his for-mative bebop years, may be divided into three periods: cool (1949–1964), **modal** (1959–1968), and electric (after 1968).

The Move to Cool

Cool jazz began as a reaction to the explosive frenzy of bop. Its musicians strove for a more sophisticated, mature style. Composers and soloists intellectu-alized many musical elements: Chords were intensified and delicately written, phrasing was meticulously constructed, tone quality was softened and made less aggressive. Jazz had reached a period in which musicians gave more thought than before to elements of performance and the style they produced. Cool mu-sicians wished to be considered the equals of classical musicians. To that end, they borrowed many procedures from classical music.

Performer Miles Davis and composer-arranger Gil Evans oversaw the inception of this concept in jazz. Evans blended bop elements with classical con-cepts to shape a smooth ensemble sound. Melodies became slower, and instru-ments were voiced in midrange to avoid the tension-building upper register. Most arrangements sounded highly organized, solos grew shorter, and more emphasis was put on ensemble playing.

---

[1]Compare the following albums: *Let My Children Hear Music* (Mingus; Columbia KC31039); *Electric Bath* (Ellis; Columbia CL2785); and *George Russell—Outer Thoughts* (Milestone M-47027).

LISTENING GUIDE

"Boplicity"—1949 (SCCJ Disc 4, Cut 1)

Trumpet—Miles Davis
Trombone—J. J. Johnson
French horn—Sandy Siegelstein
Tuba—Bill Barber
Alto sax—Lee Konitz
Baritone sax—Gerry Mulligan
Piano—John Lewis
Bass—Nelson Boyd
Drums—Kenny Clarke

.00　1st melodic statement: Trumpet leads ensemble, walking bass, extensions within the harmonies.
.15　Repeat of (A).
.28　Middle section (B): Alto sax leads ensemble.
.42　Repeat of (A), trumpet lead.
.57　Baritone sax solo (Gerry Mulligan): Accompaniment by piano, bass, and drums; cool, unaggressive tone.
1.24　Solo ends and lead shifts to sax section.
1.35　Very short trumpet solo.
1.43　Lead shifts briefly between alto sax and trumpet.
2.00　Trumpet solo (Miles Davis): The beginning of the solo is accompanied by lush chords from the other horns.
2.08　Bebop figure in solo.
2.25　Piano solo (John Lewis): Walking bass, very light drum activity.
2.39　Ensemble returns with first melodic statement (A).
2.52　Ending is very short, 1 measure.
2.57　End.

The instrumentation of "Boplicity" reflects the move toward third stream, as shown in the use of the French horn and the tuba. Gerry Mulligan not only played in this band but also made contributions as a composer-arranger, as did pianist John Lewis. Bebop virtuosity has definitely become a secondary consideration; instead, emphasis has been put on the subtle, the low-key, the understated, the intellectual, the unemotional—in other words, the cool.

Modal Jazz: The Revolt against Abundant Chord Changes

Miles began experimenting with modal compositions in 1959. In the following years, his interest in the form continued to grow. His association with

Wayne Shorter in 1964 contributed to his decision to concentrate on a new kind of composition. Instead of the show tunes that had been a staple of the repertoire of his early quintets, Davis introduced original tunes built on very few chords. Each chord was based on a scale similar to the familiar minor scale. Slight variations in the scale produced several different modes; for this reason, the scales are referred to as modal.

Modal scales gave soloists a new freedom. Because modal forms used fewer chords, melodies were allowed to become more linear and dissonant. However, with fewer chords, the overall structure became harmonically static. Performers were forced to create new kinds of rhythmic activity and forward motion.

In "So What" (see the Listening Guide), the rhythm section develops many ideas from only two scales. The first sixteen measures of the melody remain within one scale, the middle eight measures move to a new scale, and the last eight measures return to the first scale. Compositions prior to this new style might employ five or six different harmonies in the first four measures alone.

In developing their scale-oriented solos, performers came to rely heavily on melodic extensions. They found that they could play any note of the scale over the slow-moving harmonies, and eventually even **flat** or **sharp** it to further increase the dissonance. Extensions were one product of the intellectual approach to harmony. Although melodic extensions are dissonant to the supporting chords, they are distantly related. Many older musicians called them "wrong notes," but modern jazz performers found them not only logical but also desirable. Davis carefully chose the extensions he played and often ended phrases on these unexpected notes, unadorned by complicated melodic activity.

"So What" is also noteworthy because it debuts two great soloists who exploited this new freedom, John Coltrane and Bill Evans. Evans, confined by the composition to only one prolonged harmony, varies the extensions with such ingenuity that he gives the impression of playing many chords. The two scales upon which this piece is constructed prove to be an ample playground for his talents.

LISTENING GUIDE

"So What"—1959 (SCCJ Disc 5, Cut 3)

Trumpet—Miles Davis
Alto sax—Julian "Cannonball" Adderley
Tenor sax—John Coltrane
Piano—Bill Evans
Drums—James Cobb
Bass—Paul Chambers

.00   Introduction: Call-response between bass and piano, free rhythmic flow.

.32　Melody stated by the bass (A), the piano answers each phrase with two chords; the trumpet, alto sax, and tenor sax join the piano. The drummer uses a swing pattern.

1.00　The harmony moves into another mode (B).

1.14　Return to original modal scale (A).

1.28　End of 1st chorus, beginning of trumpet solo, bass and trumpet predominant. Bass walks, drummer kicks lightly, ringing ride cymbal.

2.05　Trumpet ends phrases on extensions, piano is very sparse.

2.25　Trumpet continues with a slow-flowing melody—which is not typical of bebop style, but very typical of Davis.

2.53　(B) section, new scale.

3.20　Tenor sax solo: Extensive use of melodic extensions and patterns.

3.48　(B) section.

4.00　Bursts of bebop melodies, rhythm section continues the same texture.

4.41　(B) section.

4.50　More bebop patterns, use of intense upper range.

5.09　Alto sax solo: Much stronger bebop references, clear melodic construction.

5.33　Bridge: New scale.

5.49　Short, blueslike quotation, continues with more traditional use of extensions.

5.50　Last (A) section of chorus.

5.55　Rhythmic interplay with drummer.

6.35　Bebop melody with harsh extensions.

6.56　Piano solo: Use of thick-voiced, dissonant chords, almost no single-note melodies. Horns use 2-chord motive.

7.24　Bridge: New scale.

7.48　Horns stop 2-chord motive, piano continues motive.

7.50　Bass has very short, animated walking solo, (A).

8.04　Original melody is repeated by bass, piano and horns answer with the 2-chord motive, 2nd (A).

8.40　After (A) section chorus ends and fade-out begins.

8.52　End.

The form for one chorus is:

    (A)　eight measures
    (A)　eight measures
    (B)　eight measures—new scale (Bridge)
    (A)　eight measures—original scale

Bill Evans (1929–1980)

Evans was born in Plainfield, New Jersey. He studied flute, violin, and piano as a boy, graduated from Southeast Louisiana College, and spent four years in the Army. When he was discharged in 1954, he went to New York and began his professional career with George Russell. He burst into prominence in 1958 when he teamed with Miles Davis in the sextet that recorded the landmark album Kind of Blue. *When he left Davis, Evans organized his own trio with bassist Scott La Faro and drummer Paul Motian. The three became so integrated musically that the trio was considered a single instrument rather than piano with rhythm accompaniment. Evans's music was reflective and impressionistic; his technique was characterized by delicacy of touch and harmonic subtlety. His influence on pianists of his era, and thereafter, was profound.*

When Scott La Faro was killed in an auto accident in 1961, Evans was so depressed that he went into seclusion for almost a year. When he emerged he formed a new trio with bassist Eddie Gomez and drummer Marty Morell. They remained together for nine years. In the mid-1970s Evans defeated a drug habit, which had plagued him for two decades, married his second wife, by whom he had a son, adopted a daughter, and pursued his career with new enthusiasm. His music became less introspective and melancholy, and he appeared to be on the verge of even better things; however, his health began to deteriorate badly in the late 1970s. He refused to heed the warning signs until it was too late. He died of a massive bleeding ulcer in New York City in September 1980.

LISTENING GUIDE

"Blue in Green"—1959 (Bill Evans Trio; SCCJ Disc 5, Cut 4)

Piano—Bill Evans
Bass—Scott La Faro
Drums—Paul Motian

.00	The tempo is slow as all three musicians begin together. Notice the rich chords in the piano. Some of the notes are played very softly, giving flavor to the other notes played more forcefully at the same time (called levels of touch).
.50	Bass and drums continue a very thin texture, adding just enough to support the simple melodic ideas in the piano.
1.20	Notice the equal partnership of the three players. The bass plays melodic figures rather than the more typical walking patterns of bebop. The activity of the drums and bass increases.
1.49	A series of thickly voiced chords.
2.44	Chord solo section. The chords form a quasi stop-time effect.

3.03 Single-note melody returns, but with full chord accompaniment.

3.20 Contrasting thinner texture.

4.05 Short bass-piano dialogue.

4.20 Very thin texture. Tempo relaxes. Drums stop playing patterns. Free rhythmic flow.

5.13 Ending.

Bill Evans arranged this piece in such a way as to nearly defy the traditional feeling of a jazz chorus. One chorus has only ten measures, not the more common twelve or sixteen. The harmonic progression gives the music a sense of perpetual motion. The phrasing is also fluid because of the ten-measure structure.

Photo © Joe Alper

Bill Evans and Gary Peacock

Electric Jazz

Miles Davis's third period involved a radical change in the instrumentation of his band. Instead of the standard quintet, he introduced electric guitar (John McLaughlin), electric keyboards (Joe Zawinul, Chick Corea, and Larry Young), and electric bass. The electrically amplified and altered trumpet was another element. In addition to the electrification of the band, the musicians had new roles to play in the ensemble. The bass played continuous patterns on which the other musicians built various textures.

The intensity of the music fluctuated in direct relation to the activity of the musicians. As they became more active musically, the texture thickened, producing a more agitated atmosphere. Traditional concepts of melody, harmony, and phrasing had been replaced by repetition and hypnotic rhythms. The texture created by the composite group was the important aspect of this music.

The substance of this new style was a pyramiding of rhythmic motives that was similar to the chanting rites of preliterate societies. The motives were usually short ideas, sometimes only two or three notes, that were repeated in a hypnotic manner to form a foundation of sound for the soloists. As one musician initiated a motive, the others responded with complementary ideas and strove to produce a full and complex texture. The resulting patterns took several forms; at times, every performer seemed to be equally important; at other times, all activity seemed to rotate around the melodic center of Miles Davis's trumpet.

Davis's electric rhythm section unavoidably identified his music with rock and roll. Davis did not dispute the contention. He even came to believe that true black jazz was rock oriented. He said that traditional jazz, even the word *jazz,* was a product of white America, whereas jazz/rock was the true expression of black music. Ironically, he was attacking the very styles that he had helped initiate.

LISTENING GUIDE

Rock style is evident in "Miles Runs the Voodoo Down" from *Bitches Brew.* This arrangement includes two electric pianos, one of which employs distorted sound effects and **tone clusters** (groupings of unrelated notes). The unchanging harmony produces the impression of a continuous vamp (a repeated and seemingly directionless idea).

"Miles Runs the Voodoo Down"—(from *Bitches Brew,* Intro. to Jazz Disc 1, Cut 12)

Trumpet—Miles Davis
Soprano sax—Wayne Shorter

Drums—Lenny White
Bass clarinet—Bennie Maupin
Electric pianos—Chick Corea, Larry Young
Percussion—Jim Riley
Drums—Jack De Johnette, Charles Alias
Fender bass—Harvey Brook
Bass—David Holland
Electric guitar—John McLaughlin

.00   Bass and drums begin with melodic and rhythmic patterns, soft piano.
.16   Guitar enters; notice the bass clarinet.
.35   Trumpet enters in the low register and slowly moves up in pitch.
1.45   Trumpet plays over a large range (high to low register); the bass finally creates the pattern that remains for the entire selection and establishes the tonal center.
2.00   Textural sound effects by the trumpet.
2.15   Intensification of rock patterns.
2.30   Melodic pattern built on wide intervals.
2.58   Long notes with changes in tone quality.
3.28   Use of bebop melodic ideas.
4.07   Trumpet stops.
4.10   Piano and guitar dialogue creates a texture from various electronic effects (distortion).
5.30   Guitar assumes a solo role, all others maintain vamping patterns.
5.45   Piano becomes more soloistic, plays large intervals, and uses distortion.
6.10   Soprano sax solo (Wayne Shorter); bass clarinet (Bennie Maupin) accompanies softly.
7.15   Thick collective improvisation.
8.00   Piano solos much more dominantly, uses distortion and angular melodic lines; the solo is more rhythmic than melodic.
9.05   Intensity increases throughout the band, piano creates a frantic texture, drummer kicks explosively.
10.00 Distortion increases.
10.20 Texture begins to thin.
10.40 Trumpet reenters.
10.52 Trumpet uses extensions almost exclusively, pitches seem to slide into each other.
11.35 Beginning of a musical climax.
11.55 Peak of climax, high range of the trumpet.
12.28 Low range of the trumpet.

12.52	Trumpet drops melodic role and becomes a rhythmic element in the texture.
13.22	Trumpet reassumes the melodic role.
13.32	Trumpet stops.
13.35	Music fades out.

Davis electronically amplified his trumpet to produce **echo-plex, reverb, phase shifting** effects. An electronic amplifier interrupts the sound signal and treats it before it goes to the speaker. The resulting sounds differ greatly from the pure vibratoless trumpet tone that had become Davis's trademark. Despite the use of electronic devices, however, Miles still sounds like "Miles"—solitary, sad, and plaintive. This recording illustrates the vast difference between cool and modal jazz and the new world of electric sound.

Davis's Early Years

Miles Davis was born on May 25, 1926, in Alton Illinois. A couple of years later, he and his family moved to East St. Louis, Illinois, where he grew up. His father was a dental surgeon and saw to it that the family was never in financial want. His mother was determined that the children receive cultural enrichment, which included music lessons. On Miles's thirteenth birthday, his father went against his mother's wishes and gave Miles a trumpet instead of a violin. It was a prophetic choice.

Of his various music teachers the most influential was a local trumpeter, Elwood Buchanon, who disdained any kind of wavering vibrato sound. The motionless tone that was Davis's trademark can be traced to this early training. Much has been written about Miles's early lack of technique and finesse, but by the time he was sixteen, he was playing regularly with a local band, Randolph's Blue Devils. In 1942 Tiny Bradshaw brought his band to town and asked Miles to join them at sixty dollars a week, but Miles's mother vetoed that proposal and insisted that he complete high school. In the summer of 1944, when Billy Eckstine's orchestra arrived in need of a trumpeter, Miles filled in for three weeks. He played with both Charlie Parker and Dizzy Gillespie, who were with Eckstine then, though at the time he could not match the ability of those giants.

When he graduated from high school, Davis talked his parents into sending him to New York, where Parker and Gillespie were working. Miles had married at age sixteen; when he left East St. Louis, he also left his wife, who was awaiting the arrival of their first child. Miles had been accepted by the prestigious Juilliard School of Music in Manhattan, but as soon as he arrived in New York, he set out in search of Charlie Parker. Although Miles went to Juilliard for one semester, most of his real schooling occurred during his frequent trips to Fifty-second Street, where he received encouragement from musicians such as

Thelonious Monk, Tadd Dameron, and Dizzy Gillespie. He went to school only to use the practice rooms, where he could try out the chord progressions and tunes he had heard the night before.

Parker had much to do with the musical force-feeding that propelled Miles into early recognition. Bird often insisted that Davis join him on the bandstand, even though Miles felt himself to be inadequate. He and Parker were rooming together, with Davis paying the rent; Miles must have considered it little enough to pay in exchange for being associated with a musician of Parker's stature.

Between 1945 and 1949, Miles worked in the bands of Charlie Parker, Billy Eckstine, and Benny Carter, not only in New York, but also on tours to the West Coast. In 1948 he fronted his own bands; after returning from the Paris jazz festival in mid-1949 he, together with arranger Gil Evans, launched the landmark series of recordings later known as *The Complete Birth of the Cool.*

In 1949, while in Paris, Miles succumbed to the lure of heroin. In 1954, having almost reached the point of no return, he decided he had had enough, and in a twelve-day period, he broke the habit on his own. However, his victory had not occurred soon enough to salvage his marriage, which by this time had produced two more children.

In 1954 his creative powers began to reassert themselves. A triumphant appearance at the 1955 Newport Jazz Festival put his career once more on the rise.

Miles Davis

He claimed that his playing at Newport was no different from what it had been for years, but his ability to select, hold, and direct virtuoso sidemen had vastly increased. A complete list of the various band members who played with Miles in his cool and modal periods would constitute a sizable percentage of the Who's Who of jazz. Probably the most influential of these was John Coltrane, who joined Davis in 1955.

During the cool and modal years, Miles performed in many settings. He did show-tune albums with large orchestras, he toured with small groups playing standards and original bebop numbers, he traveled to Europe, and he experimented with combinations of sounds. Although he inaugurated several different styles during his career, it is impossible to assign a specific date for any one of them. As is usually the case, Davis's stylistic shifts took place over a period of time.

By 1968 Miles was beginning to feel pressure from two directions. After John Coltrane's death in 1967, Davis believed that he was carrying the entire burden of innovation in jazz. In addition, his most recent record releases had hardly sold 25,000 copies each. If it had not been for the mutually profitable relationship Miles had started in 1956 with Columbia Records—at one point, Columbia paid a $39,000 tax bill Miles had incurred—he would have been financially strapped. In any event, Miles decided it was time to start using amplified sound and incorporate the heavy beat associated with rock music.

Whatever the reason for the radical stylistic change, Miles cast off all ties with the past. He told Leonard Feather that he even stopped listening to his old records.[2] Some suspected that Miles's change of direction was commercially motivated; however, if he did make musical compromises, he could take comfort from his expanded income: *Bitches Brew*, recorded in 1969, sold 400,000 copies.

Poor health and an overriding desire for privacy influenced Miles to withdraw from public life for several years. Columbia released a two-record album of Davis's music in late 1979, *Circle in the Round*. It contained no new material, however, but was composed of ten previously unreleased recordings made between 1955 and 1970. Although he said in 1976 that he had played his last concert, he returned in the summer of 1981 to play at the Kool Jazz Festival (formerly the Newport Jazz Festival). The program received generally favorable, if not wildly enthusiastic, reviews, but Miles was encouraged to assemble a series of successful groups over the next ten years. Composed largely of rock-oriented white musicians, these bands toured extensively and recorded several albums: *The Man with the Horn, We Want Miles, Star People, Decoy, "TUTU,"* and *You're Under Arrest*.

Miles said his health had been restored, after a stroke, by acupuncture and the care of his wife at that time, actress Cicely Tyson. He remained vigorous throughout and beyond the 1980s. At the request of Quincy Jones, he appeared for a reprise of Gil Evans music in July at the 1991 Montreux Jazz Festival.

[2]Copyright © 1972 by Leonard Feather from the book *From Satchmo to Miles*, reprinted with permission of Stein and Day Pubishers, and Leonard Feather, p. 227.

However, in August 1991, five days after playing a concert at the Hollywood Bowl, Miles was hospitalized in Santa Monica, California, with pneumonia and died of a stroke and respiratory failure on September 28.

There has probably been no other musical innovator who has founded and promoted more movements only to abandon them, recruited more enthusiastic disciples only to desert them, gathered more ardent converts only to leave them enraged, than Miles Davis. He was more than a musician, he was a social phenomenon. He was an influence in jazz beyond measure.

SUGGESTED LISTENING

Bitches Brew. 1970. Columbia Jazz Masterpieces G2K-40577.
Decoy. 1984. Columbia CK-38991.
Kind of Blue. 1959. Columbia Jazz Masterpieces CK-40579.

Charles Mingus and the Modern Jazz Quartet

23

Charles Mingus

CHARLES MINGUS (1922–1979)

Charles Mingus, the free-spirited composer and bass player, is difficult to categorize musically. His taste was shaped by such strong personalities as Duke Ellington, Charlie Parker, and Art Tatum. In addition, he studied and absorbed the works of classical composers such as Richard Strauss, Debussy, and Ravel. This extensive background spawned compositions imbued with jazz and classical elements. The Mingus style is best characterized as third stream or avantgarde. He never followed a predictable path or conformed to fashion. His unique approach to music placed him outside traditional jazz and classical styles, but he did retain a fundamental gospel and blues approach in his diverse musical performances. He expressed strong feelings in his music, which, depending on his frame of mind, could sound bitter, happy, sad, or angry. Whatever the mood, the music exhibited tremendous energy and was propelled by his powerful, technically brilliant bass playing.

Mingus expected his sidemen to adhere to the same high standards he did and often interrupted a performance to correct someone in the band. When sufficiently exasperated, he became violent. Once, in a fit of temper, he knocked out trombonist Jimmy Knepper with a punch in the stomach. His stopping in mid-performance to fire or hire musicians became part of jazz lore. It was also not uncommon for Mingus to lecture the audience on proper conduct and musical taste.

LISTENING GUIDE

"Haitian Fight Song"—1957 (Charles Mingus Quintet; SCCJ Disc 4, Cut 13)

Trombone—Jimmy Knepper
Alto sax—Curtis Porter
Piano—Wade Legge
Bass and arranger—Charles Mingus
Drums—Danny Richmond

.00   Introduction is a free solo on bass.
.52   A strong rhythmic pattern is established.
1.10   The drums start a ride pattern while the trombone and alto sax start playing independent lines in the background.
1.42   The intensity and volume grow steadily.
2.13   Trombone solos alone with the rhythm section. The sax plays softly in the background.
2.45   A sudden doubling of tempo.

3.04	A slower stop-time figure replaces the frantic double-time tempo.
3.20	Big rhythmic lead-in to the original tempo, the trombone continues to solo.
3.42	Piano solo, bass walks, ride pattern continues in the drums.
4.21	Stop-time pattern returns, piano plays bebop figures.
4.40	Time returns.
5.19	Alto sax solo, strong bebop figures are used above the rhythm section.
5.58	Double-time.
6.16	Stop-time figure returns.
6.36	Original tempo and patterns are reestablished.
6.57	Bass solo, drums continue time patterns, piano plays softly.
7.57	The comping pattern of the piano will quote "So What."
8.21	All accompaniment stops. The bass continues a rhythmic melody.
9.30	The solo becomes freer rhythmically.
9.55	Rhythmic pattern returns, soft.
10.26	The rest of the ensemble enters softly and builds in intensity as before.
11.29	Musical flow slows.
11.55	End.

This small ensemble is typical of the sound associated with Mingus. The musical texture is much freer and depends greatly on the imagination and skill of all the players. The piece does, however, have a strict formal structure. This performance spotlights the solo abilities of Mingus. His bass playing helped define the instrument soloistically, pulling it from its accompaniment function.

His Youth

Charles Mingus was born on April 22, 1922, in Nogales, Arizona. His mother died shortly after he was born, and before he was one year old, his father, an ex-Army sergeant, moved him and his two older sisters from Nogales to the Watts area of Los Angeles.

When he was five or six, Charles received a trombone from his father. Mingus wanted to join the school band but did not know how to read music, so he asked his sisters, who played piano and violin, to teach him. Not realizing that trombone music is written in the bass clef, they taught him treble clef. Although he failed a school audition because of that, he continued to practice on the instrument until his father tired of hearing the sound and traded it for a cello.

Charles and his sisters formed a trio about this time to play at the Methodist church their father attended; what Mingus really enjoyed, however, was the gospel-blues music sung and played at the Holiness Church his stepmother attended. This early exposure to gospel music was to influence everything Charles played and wrote in later years.

When Charles graduated from high school, he wanted to join a jazz band made up of musicians from his and another high school. The band had no need for a cello but it did for a string bass, so Charles, Sr., traded in the cello for a bass, and thereby put in Charles's hands the instrument that would make him famous. Charles received first-rate instruction from Red Callender, the venerable bass and tuba jazz artist, and later from H. Rheinschagen, who had played in the New York Philharmonic. He practiced furiously and invented new roles for the instrument. Callender had shown him fingerings that released him from mere two-beat timekeeping and allowed him to play melodies. Mingus studied the technique of Andrés Segovia, the master of classical Spanish guitar, and he listened intently to Jimmy Blanton, the bass frontiersman in Duke Ellington's orchestra.

It was Ellington who turned Mingus firmly onto the path of jazz. Charles listened to every Ellington record he could get hold of. "When I first heard Duke Ellington in person I almost jumped out of the balcony. One piece excited me so much that I screamed," he told writer Nat Hentoff.[1] Charles's high school jazz band profited from his dedication. He developed an unusual driving style that slightly anticipated the beat and propelled the band mercilessly. He became a standout in a band already loaded with such future stars as Britt Woodman, Dexter Gordon, Buddy Collette, Chico Hamilton, and Ernie Royal. His reputation grew proportionately. When Art Tatum came to Los Angeles and asked for bass accompaniment, Mingus, then only eighteen, was selected.

His private life also had its share of excitement. He took his girlfriend, Lee Marie Spendell, to Mexico and married her. On their return, her father had the marriage annulled, sent the girl away, and put a bullet hole in Charlie's shoulder.

His Professional Career

The early 1940s brought Mingus in contact with Louis Armstrong and later (from 1946 to 1948) with Kid Ory, Barney Bigard, Alvino Rey, and Lionel Hampton. In 1947 he recorded his first successful composition, "Mingus Fingers." It was also in 1947 that he met trumpeter Fats Navarro. Mingus became very close to Fats and adopted much of his philosophy. Navarro's death from tuberculosis and drug addiction in 1950 confirmed Charles's belief that social pressures took an appalling toll on black artists. In the late 1940s he also worked with out-

---

[1] Nat Hentoff, *The Jazz Life* (1962), p. 164. Reported by permission of Nat Hentoff.

standing bebop personalities such as Dizzy Gillespie, Bud Powell, Max Roach, and Charlie Parker. He later joined the Lionel Hampton band and toured the United States from coast to coast.

Mingus gave up music temporarily in 1950 and worked for the postal service, but in 1951 Charlie Parker persuaded him to take it up again. In 1952 Mingus and Max Roach established a recording company, Debut, in hopes of recording "workshop concerts," but the endeavor failed. Mingus felt the creative process included the developmental stages prior to performance. The workshop was designed to be a place where musical ideas could be developed and nurtured. He wanted the audience to be a part of this. The concept of a workshop performing in front of an audience was too unorthodox to be commercially viable. Despite this failure, Mingus never hesitated to rehearse a tune on the bandstand. Being concerned with the accuracy and spirit with which his music was played, he would stop and restart a tune to establish a new feeling or discuss changes. Many of his compositions were not entirely conceived until the band had "worked out" the ideas. Mingus refused to sacrifice his musical goals for the sake of appearances. He intended to lead his audiences on serious musical journeys; if that necessitated stopping and talking about the music, then so be it.

By 1956 Mingus expanded the scope of his compositions. He devised new instrumental combinations to play an increasingly dissonant music. To jazz conservatives his strange textures appeared to be composed of unrelated elements. His inventive brilliance became more and more evident in compositions that ran the gamut from simple to complex. By 1960 his musical stature had increased to the point that when enraged at the growing commerciality of the producers of the Newport Jazz Festival, he was able to organize a rival festival in another part of town that outdrew the original one. He also vehemently condemned racial discrimination and other social injustices. His strong public statements made club owners wary of booking him, despite his growing popularity. They preferred to hire lesser talent rather than risk having Mingus insult the audience.

He performed actively with the Jazz Workshop in the 1960s, but went into semiretirement from 1966 to 1970. He suffered from deep depressions during that time, spending days alone in his room, the windows boarded shut. He would stare at himself in the mirror, willing himself to die. Toward the end of that period, he committed himself briefly to the mental ward of New York's Bellevue Hospital.

Mingus's public and private lives were a strange mixture of secrecy and openness. On the stand he could express his deepest feelings both verbally and musically, but he kept silent about his three unsuccessful marriages and the lives of his six children.

His curious autobiography, *Beneath the Underdog*, published in 1971, meticulously recounted many intimate experiences, although for the most part it is a rambling conglomeration of fact and fantasy dealing mostly with sexual exploits.

His return to public performance in 1970 was moderately successful. Attempts to revitalize his music in the early 1970s produced the album *Three or Four Shades of Blues,* which featured contemporary performers such as Larry Coryell and George Coleman. Although it was his most successful album and promoted a strong revival of his music, it was personally disappointing to him. He made a brief European tour in 1972 and continued to perform until 1977, when he contracted amyotrophic lateral sclerosis, a motor-neuron disease that severely slowed him down. He continued to work on a limited schedule up to his death on January 5, 1979, in Cuernavaca, Mexico. A final collaboration with pop singer–songwriter Joni Mitchell produced a moving epitaph; however, because he was too ill to play, the album lacks the enormously powerful Mingus foundation.

Charles Mingus's life provides a revealing glimpse of the conflicting forces at work in the lives of artists in general and black jazz artists in particular. His apparent aggressiveness concealed a great deal of tenderness and vulnerability. It must have been difficult for such a man, dedicated to the beauty of music, to comment on an ugly world through a medium that should project hope and happiness.

SUGGESTED LISTENING

Joni Mitchell/Mingus. Electra 505-2.
Mirage, Avant-Garde and Third Stream. New World Records NW 216.

THE MODERN JAZZ QUARTET

The Modern Jazz Quartet (MJQ) has been classified as third stream owing to the classical concepts with which it structured its music. At the same time, the quartet was one of the best examples of musical moderation. The MJQ's sophisticated style influenced the development of many small jazz groups throughout the 1950s and 1960s. Composed of piano, vibraphone, drums, and bass, it was essentially an augmented rhythm section.

The MJQ seemed to epitomize cool jazz because of its relaxed and intellectual approach. In spite of its classification, however, the MJQ always swung with a strong foundation in the blues. Even its most intellectual compositions contained basic blues and bebop overtones.

The Modern Jazz Quartet never used amplified instruments such as electric piano or bass. The group's members felt that amplification would overpower the softer qualities of the acoustic instruments. The **dynamic** levels of the MJQ therefore ranged from very soft to almost loud. The MJQ believed that amplification would require too great a sacrifice in subtlety and "coolness." In addition, amplification would change the tone qualities of the bass and the piano that were essential to the identity of the quartet.

LISTENING GUIDE

"Django," written by John Lewis, has three distinct jazz and classical components. The first is the slow melody that begins and ends the work. It is a threnody for the guitarist Django Reinhardt, who died in 1953. The second is the rhythmic feeling, an easy, uncluttered swing. The third is the recurring pedal point, in which the bass player repeats the same note on each beat for eight measures. Pedal points are usually played in the bass and are independent of, though not necessarily dissonant to, the harmony and melody. They are of classical derivation, having first been used extensively in baroque organ music.

As usual when listening to the Modern Jazz Quartet, it is often difficult to determine which ideas have been freshly invented and which premeditated. The different ways in which the musicians treat each section show a mature and subtle ability to improvise. Both Jackson and Lewis are brilliant soloists, and their contrasting styles complement each other. Jackson's technique is more suited to bebop, whereas Lewis's is more restrained and often builds on clear melodic ideas. The clarity of Lewis's playing enhances the many textures in this recording.

"Django"—1960 (SCCJ Disc 4, Cut 14)

Vibraphone—Milt Jackson
Piano—John Lewis
Bass—Percy Heath
Drums—Connie Kay

.00	Slow beginning; the melody on the vibes is supported by chords from the piano and bass.
.14	2nd melodic idea.
.24	3rd melodic idea.
.36	Medium swing tempo is established, brushes on snare, solo by Jackson, bass plays a pattern of 2 notes to the measure.
.52	Pedal point for 8 measures, the bass repeats the same note with different chords above.
1.03	Harmonies move, bass plays a 2-beat swing pattern.
1.09	Notice the rhythmic pattern created by the bass and piano; this pattern will return several times.
1.21	Walking-bass pattern with a bebop solo by Jackson.
1.36	Return to the pedal point idea.
1.47	Harmonies move again with a solid swing feeling.
1.53	The bass and piano pattern returns.
2.20	Return to the pedal point idea.

2.31 Vibes solo continues with another swing feeling.

2.37 Bass pattern returns (with the accompanying piano chords).

2.48 Interlude: The vibes solo ends and the piano solo begins.

2.53 Piano solo: Notice the clean, delicate touch of the right hand and the sparse left-hand chords; the bass walks.

3.10 Pedal point.

3.21 Swing feeling returns.

3.27 Bass pattern returns (complementary piano pattern is not present).

3.38 Walking bass.

3.56 Pedal point.

4.06 Swing feeling.

4.12 Bass pattern returns and gradually slows down.

4.29 Return to the slow texture of the introduction.

4.50 Last idea (same as the 3rd idea of the introduction).

5.04 Final improvisatory statements by both vibes and piano.

5.21 End.

Although not immediately apparent, the contributions of the drums and the string bass to the MJQ sound are as important as those of the piano and the vibraphone. In addition to his unerring harmonic support, Heath on the string bass provides a solid rhythmic pulse. Connie Kay's drumming not only highlights and embellishes the rhythm and meter, but also adds melody-like ideas. He also colors the sound by using finger cymbals, bells, triangles, and wood blocks.

The Group's Beginning

The Modern Jazz Quartet came into existence formally on December 22, 1952, when it made a recording for Prestige Records; however, the group had been playing together for over a year as the Milt Jackson Quartet. The members were all musicians from Dizzy Gillespie's big band and had known each other for a long time. The group's original drummer, Kenny Clarke, met John Lewis in the Army during World War II. Bassist Percy Heath played in many bands around New York and became acquainted with vibraphonist Milt Jackson when they joined Gillespie in 1950. Except for the replacement of Clarke by Connie Kay in 1955, and a ten-year period beginning in 1974 when they pursued separate paths, the quartet has been a model of stability and durability.

The MJQ performed on a random schedule until 1954. In fact, John Lewis left to accompany Ella Fitzgerald on a tour to Australia in 1954; after that, however, the MJQ was in such demand that the members were able to book themselves almost exclusively on concert tours all over the world. Many of Lewis's compositions filled their repertoire, and some numbers, such as "Django," were kept actively in their book for years. However, they continued to play a number only as long as each performance produced something new. The differences in the various recordings of "Django" made over the years make an interesting study.

In June 1974 the MJQ gave what was to have been their final concert. The parting of the ways was not wholly amicable. It seems Jackson believed that he could make more money as a single. The others would have preferred to remain together, but rather than try to find a replacement for "Bags," they decided to go separate routes. They all immediately found places either as leaders or as members in bands, but the satisfaction was not there. In 1980 they began re-forming periodically for concerts, and in 1984 they decided that permanent re-constitution was the only answer. Their reappearance was enthusiastically hailed, since they have been a unique force in jazz.

John Lewis

John Aaron Lewis was born in La Grange, Illinois, on May 3, 1920. His mother was a singer, and his optometrist father played the piano and the violin. When John was seven, he began lessons on those two instruments but eventually focused on the piano. At the University of New Mexico, he majored in music. When he was drafted into the Army in 1942, he worked as a musician in Special Services for three years. After the war, Kenny Clarke took Lewis to New York to meet Dizzy Gillespie. Lewis joined the band as pianist and arranger. He also resumed his studies at the Manhattan School of Music, from which he received two degrees. He especially admired J. S. Bach and other European baroque and renaissance composers. His own many compositions, including the "Toccata for Trumpet and Orchestra," reflect his classical leaning. (This third stream work was performed by the Gillespie band at Carnegie Hall in 1947.)

In 1948, after accompanying the Gillespie band to Europe, Lewis remained in Paris for two months playing with Tony Proteau. When he returned to New York, he played with the Illinois Jacquet Band for eight months, then played and recorded with Lester Young and Charlie Parker. In 1949 he arranged and soloed in such numbers as "Budo," "Move," and "Rouge" in the famous Miles Davis nine-piece band that turned the corner into the cool period.

Lewis then rejoined Gillespie. The MJQ began to emerge, rather by chance. During band performances, Gillespie would interject change-of-pace interludes featuring vibraphonist Milt Jackson with the rhythm section. At these performances, the group developed its own identity and started to perform separately.

Milt Jackson

Milton "Bags" Jackson was born in Detroit on January 1, 1923, and studied music at Michigan State University. He was discovered by Gillespie in 1945 and came to New York City. He played with artists at the forefront of jazz innovation—Howard McGhee, Tadd Dameron, and Thelonious Monk. He was a member of the Woody Herman Big Band in 1949 before rejoining Gillespie in 1950. His vibraphone playing is distinctive. His phrasing and inflection are tinged with the blues and even gospel music. He slowed the vibraphone's mechanical vibrato to give the instrument a mellow, contemplative tone. If Lewis was the directing force of the Modern Jazz Quartet, Jackson was its most distinctive voice.

Connie Kay

Connie Kay, born April 4, 1927, in Tuckahoe, New York, began studying the piano at age six with his mother. At age ten he took up drums and eventually took lessons when he was fifteen. He quickly acquired professional experience as a jazz drummer. By the mid-1940s he played with Miles Davis and later with Lester Young. In the 1950s, before replacing Kenny Clarke in the MJQ, he performed with many of the bebop greats. After he joined the MJQ in 1955, his playing soon acquired national recognition. His subtle and responsive style added greatly to the definition of this quartet. Kay died in New York on November 30, 1994.

Percy Heath

Percy Heath was born in Wilmington, North Carolina, on April 30, 1923. He played the violin in school and in 1943 joined the Army, where he became a fighter pilot. Following his discharge, he studied bass at the Granoff School of Music in Philadelphia. In a few months he began playing professionally. Howard McGhee took him to New York in 1947 and to Paris in 1948. After leaving the McGhee sextet, he played with leading bebop players in New York before joining John Lewis in the MJQ.

SUGGESTED LISTENING

The Art of the Modern Jazz Quartet. 1957–66. Atlantic CS 2-301. (CS)
Echoes. 1984. Pablo Digital PACD 2312-142-2.
MJQ40. Atlantic 82330 (4-CD box)

Big Bands Continue

24

Don Ellis

By the late 1950s and 1960s many subsidiary jazz styles had sprung up, several of which defied classification. Cool jazz had given rise to a renewed interest in third stream, hard bop had developed a revitalized gospel sound, and bop had opened doors to **free jazz.** All in all, the spectrum of jazz had lengthened to include diverse but related jazz styles.

Eclectic is perhaps the term best suited to encompass such a cross-section of music. Most of the developments represented mergers of several styles. In addition, no single style predominated in such a way as to determine the overall direction of jazz. Many musicians probed in different directions, either in the hope of finding the most satisfactory course or because their interests had become more catholic. The music of Don Ellis shows how autonomous one performer could be.

DON ELLIS (1934–1973)

Ellis's musical background was shaped by such innovators as George Russell and Eric Dolphy. In small groups in the early 1960s, he played trumpet solos that showed a sensitivity to developing melodic ideas of the avant-garde. In 1965 Ellis began to introduce exciting new sounds with his own big band.

His innovations were wide ranging. He was inspired by the music of India, and its rhythms and melodies invaded most of his compositions. He was the first bandleader to write extensively in odd time signatures, such as 5/4, 7/4, and 3½/4. The music seemed to be something other than swing, Latin, or rock, but it had a certain appeal to almost every musical audience.

In addition to writing in these unfamiliar meters, he initiated the use of electronic instruments in the big band. From electric string quartets and amplified vocal quartets to synthesizers and echo-plex units, he never hesitated to experiment with the fast-growing world of electronics. The album *Electric Bath* (Columbia CL2785) contains many of the exotic sounds and complex meters Ellis introduced.

Besides borrowing rhythms from India, he used melodic ideas built on scales having twice as many tones as traditional Western European scales. He even devised an extra valve for his trumpet to play these in-between notes, called **quarter tones.** Quarter tones became characteristic of Ellis's solos and had the same effect as the blue notes of early blues songs.

MODERN BIG BANDS

Other big bands of the 1960s and 1970s developed along the lines of preceding jazz styles. Besides the Ellington band, those of Count Basie, Woody Herman, and Stan Kenton were among the few that survived the decline of the swing era. All these bands adopted strong jazz definitions and featured some of the best soloists available. The band most notable for its soloists was Count Basie's. Besides having outstanding rhythm sections, Basie always had exceptional trumpet soloists. Oran "Hot Lips" Page was followed by Buck Clayton, Harry Edison, and Thad Jones. His saxophone section also boasted such legendary soloists as Hershel Evans and the immortal Lester Young. In addition to great soloists, Basie hired excellent section leaders. Marshall Royal on lead alto and Snooky Young on lead trumpet became pacemakers for all hard-swinging bands.

Thad Jones, an alumnus of the Basie band, and Mel Lewis formed the hottest big band of the 1970s. Jones's writing and arranging had been instrumental in defining the Basie sound after 1954. When he formed his own band, he turned to the active rock rhythms of popular music. His band became the leader in ensemble precision.

After 1950 most big swing bands were white. The two major exceptions were Count Basie's and Duke Ellington's, but by and large the bands that retained the fifteen-person-or-more format (trumpet, trombone, sax, and rhythm sections) were white. These orchestras fell into two categories: traditional, uncompromising 1940s swing bands, and progressive bands. The former appealed to an aging audience that remembered Glenn Miller, Tommy Dorsey, and Artie Shaw in their heyday and wanted to hear nothing but the familiar arrangements unchanged, with solos transcribed verbatim. Some even kept the identities of long-departed leaders, such as "The Glenn Miller Band led by Tex Beneke." The latter fell into two categories also: big school stage bands, such as the awesome North Texas State University Lab Bands, and professional bands. The two professional organizations that led the progressive movement most vigorously were Woody Herman's and Stan Kenton's.

WOODROW CHARLES HERMAN (1913–1987)

Woody Herman was one of the last swing-era big-band leaders to keep a jazz orchestra rolling through the years of changing styles and tastes. In actuality, the band did not retain a constant character in the way Ellington's did. Herman was sensitive to musical progress and continually refreshed the band's score book with numbers that reflected current styles by a steady infusion of young, school-trained musicians who brought writing and arranging skills to the organization.

Woody was not a composer or an arranger. He has never been considered a clarinetist the equal of Benny Goodman or Artie Shaw, although in his prime he played more than passably good jazz on clarinet and alto and soprano saxes. His singing, while entertaining and musical, would not rank him with Mel Tormé. But Woody had qualities that brought him prolonged success in a business that burns out all but the most gifted and hardy in a matter of a few years, if not months. Herman's career spanned more than five decades.

His first band, formed in 1936, was a cooperative, Dixieland-flavored orchestra called "The Band that Plays the Blues." It featured novelty numbers but

Woody Herman

also a large proportion of solid jazz, which included his 1939 top-of-the-charts "Woodchopper's Ball." The band's popularity ranked just below the Ellington-Goodman-Miller level and remained so until the draft for the Second World War decimated its personnel.

In later years Herman's band was populated by a series of relatively anonymous instrumentalists, but that was not always the case. In 1944 he organized a new band that became known as Herman's Herd. This was a big, powerful, boisterous band that reflected Woody's reverence for Duke Ellington. The musicians in this band and in the Second Herd, which shortly followed, were the elite of the postwar bands: the famous Four Brothers sax section of Stan Getz, Zoot Sims, Al Cohn, and Serge Chaloff; saxophonists Herbie Steward, Flip Phillips, John LaPorta, Sal Nistico, and Gene Ammons; trumpeters Sonny Berman, Red Rodney, Shorty Rogers, and Pete and Conte Candoli; trombonist Bill Harris; pianists Ralph Burns (who also arranged) and Jimmy Rowles; vibists Red Norvo, Margie Hyams, and Milt Jackson; bassists Chubby Jackson and Oscar Pettiford; drummers Davey Tough and Dom Lamond; arranger Neal Hefti. These bands won critics' and popularity awards from *Down Beat, Metronome,* and *Billboard* in 1945 and 1946. Their performances of "Apple

Honey," "Northwest Passage," and "Bijou" are still admired as prime examples of high-energy jazz. Nineteen forty-six also saw Herman's band premier *Ebony Concerto,* a number written for them by Igor Stravinsky.

Woody disbanded the Second Herd in 1949 but came back in 1950 with the Third Herd, which took the *Metronome* award in 1953. In the next thirty-plus years, there were numerous other Herds, all exemplary.

Otto and Myrtle Herman's boy, Woodrow Charles, was precocious. Billed as The Boy Wonder, he was tap-dancing in a Milwaukee vaudeville house at the age of eight. In a matter of months he was able to buy a saxophone and a clarinet with his earnings. He played locally in dance bands until he was seventeen. Then he left for Chicago to join Tom Gerun's band at the Granada Cafe, a front for one of Al Capone's operations. One night, two of Capone's thugs shot Woody in the leg for a fancied affront, but evincing more persistence than prudence, Woody remained with the band for three years. Following his stint with Gerun, Woody played for Harry Sosnick, Gus Arnheim, and Isham Jones, from whom he recruited the nucleus of his first band when Jones folded in 1936. That was the year he married Charlotte, to whom he remained a devoted husband until her death in 1982. The couple had one child, Ingrid.

Woody's career was an almost uninterrupted success. He and the band appeared in six feature-length movies; he was invited to play at the Stravinsky Centennial at La Scala in Italy in 1982; and manuscripts of his music are contained in the University of Houston's Woody Herman Music Library. His life was not without misfortune, however. In September 1987 it was learned that in the mid-1960s a crooked manager had left Woody's payments to the Internal Revenue Service in arrears. By 1987 penalties and interest had grown to $1.6 million. In addition, Woody was bedridden with severe congestive heart disease. The IRS had confiscated all his recording royalties and auctioned his home of forty-one years for a fraction of its value. The new owner was threatening to throw Woody out.

The jazz and entertainment community rose in a body. Collections were taken, benefit concerts were arranged, and stars of every magnitude came forward. Woody's rent and medical bills were covered, and more important, he realized how much he was loved and esteemed. It was none too soon. He was hospitalized in Los Angeles on October 1 and died October 29, 1987.

STAN KENTON (1912–1979)

In the summer of 1941, the Rendezvous Ballroom in Balboa, California, introduced a new band that in sheer volume and energy surpassed anything many listeners had heard before. It was the brainchild of Stanley Newcombe Kenton and was an almost instantaneous hit, at first locally and then, after moving to the Hollywood Paladium where it was broadcast coast to coast, nationally.

Stan Kenton Band, 1945. *Left to right: Bob Ahern, guitar; Ralph Collier, drums; Vido Musso, tenor sax; John Anderson, trumpet; Stan Kenton, leader, piano; Boots Mussulli, alto sax; Milt Kabak, trombone; Buddy Childers, trumpet; Ray Wetzel, trumpet, vocals; Freddie Zito, trombone; Al Anthony, alto sax; Bob Lymperis, trumpet; Jimmy Simms, trombone; June Christy, vocalist; Russ Burgher, trumpet; Bart Varsalona, trombone; Bob Gioga, baritone sax.*

Kenton was a West Coast phenomenon. His had not been a traditional jazz education. He was a piano player whose training had been confined to furnishing background music in cocktail lounges and playing in the society dance bands of Gus Arnheim and Everett Hoagland. But he harbored the burning concept of a big, driving band that would redefine jazz, and he nurtured and promoted that concept for the rest of his life.

Kenton's first band, often labeled Artistry in Rhythm, retained its identity for about six years. This orchestra boasted jazz soloists of the caliber of tenor saxophonists Vido Musso and Stan Getz, trombonist Kai Winding, trumpeter-arranger Ray Wetzel, bassist Eddie Safranski, drummer Shelly Manne, and two top-notch jazz vocalists, first Anita O'Day and later June Christy.

In 1947 Kenton disbanded and reorganized his twenty-piece Progressive Jazz concert/dance orchestra. Keystone of the new band was composer-arranger Pete Rugolo, whose Afro-Cuban–flavored compositions often featured Brazilian jazz guitarist Laurindo Almeida. The band played some rather heavy material, *Prologue Suite in Four Movements*, for example. Notwithstanding, the *Down Beat* polls voted it the best big band in 1947 and 1948. The band toured virtually nonstop for two years. By the end of 1948, exhaustion and internal dissension were tearing it apart. In December Stan notified his sidemen that he was disbanding again.

Less than a year later, Kenton organized a forty-piece concert orchestra that included sixteen strings, tuba, oboe, English horns, French horns, and a bassoon. He called it Innovations in Modern Music. Despite its classical composition, the band carried a contingent of some of the most exciting jazz soloists in the country: flutist Bud Shank, alto saxophonist Art Pepper, trumpeters Shorty Rogers, Chico Alvarez, Buddy Childers, and the stratospheric Maynard Ferguson. In addition, no fewer than eight composer-arrangers, including Neal Hefti, wrote for it. The payroll was staggering. The orchestra took to the trail in 1950 and survived until 1952. It received great reviews but lost Kenton most of the money he had made from his previous bands. To top things off, his wife, Violet, divorced him, taking their daughter.

Kenton formed the nineteen-piece New Concepts in Artistry in Rhythm in 1952 without Shelly Manne, Maynard Ferguson, and a number of other previous regulars, but with standout saxophonists Lee Konitz and Richie Kamuca, trombonist Frank Rosolino, and trumpeters Conte Candoli and Ernie Royal. In addition, Kenton enhanced the bandbook with compositions and arrangements from Gerry Mulligan and Bill Holman. For the next four years, the band toured tirelessly, sometimes billed as The Festival of Modern American Music. It covered the United States and Europe and presented guest artists such as Charlie Parker, Dizzy Gillespie, and Billie Holiday.

In 1955 Stan married singer Ann Richards, hoping to establish a home for his daughter. The marriage lasted six years and produced two children. Kenton bought the Rendezvous Ballroom in 1957, thinking he could operate at a fixed base, thereby holding his sidemen and stabilizing his home life, but the venture failed in three months and he went back on the road. In 1959 Stan began perhaps his most significant contribution to the continued health of jazz. He started his Orchestra in Residence program at universities in Indiana and Michigan. The band would remain at schools for a week or two playing concerts, conducting clinics, and encouraging young musicians to pursue jazz as a career. This movement started by Kenton has grown nationwide, and jazz is now offered as a major subject in most big schools.

Nineteen sixty-one saw the birth of Stan's New Era in Modern American Music band, which earned the subtitle of Mellophonium Band after the name of the little-known instrument he added to the brass section. That section consisted of five trumpets, four trombones, and four mellophones, giving the orchestra a distinctly brass-heavy sound. But the public accepted it, and Stan kept it touring profitably for three years. However, in November 1963 they were booked for a concert tour in England and were virtually ignored. Kenton, imagining this the final depressing blow, came home, disbanded, and secluded himself in his Beverly Hills house for most of 1964.

In 1965 Kenton was persuaded to reorganize a band to present a series of concerts at the new Los Angeles Music Center. He called it the Neophonic

Orchestra. The concerts offered guest stars—Miles Davis, Gerry Mulligan, Dizzy Gillespie, George Shearing, The Modern Jazz Quartet—but Kenton's insistence on avant-garde material kept attendance low. It was astonishing that the band survived until mid-1967, when bankruptcy devoured it. By this time, Stan had a new wife.

In 1968 he formed another band, which by the early 1970s came to be called the Fusion Band, although it was not fusion as the term is understood today. Stan's dominance of the big-band scene waned, but he remained in front of a bandstand despite periodic attacks of illness and depression. Personnel flowed through the band, altering its flavor as time passed, but Stan never surrendered completely to current tastes.

Year after year Kenton continued to subject his mind and body to the pressures of life on the road. He was sustained by his music, but in 1979 his system finally rebelled. He suffered a fatal stroke in August of that year and was buried in Hollywood. He left a vast legacy of recorded and written music, and perhaps of more importance, his contribution to jazz in school.

LISTENING GUIDE

"Artistry in Rhythm"—1943 (Intro. to Jazz Disc 1, Cut 14)

Composed and arranged by Stan Kenton
Piano—Stan Kenton
Trumpets—John Carroll, Dick Morse, Buddy Childers, Ray Borden, Karl George
Trombones—Harry Forbes, George Faye, Bart Varsalona
Saxophones—Eddie Meyers, Art Pepper, Red Dorris, Morey Beeson, Bob Gioga
Bass—Clyde Singleton
Guitar—Bob Ahern
Drums—Joe Vernon

.00 Introduction, fanfare opening, trombone lead, saxes and trumpets have active accompaniment.

.17 Drum roll begins an extended idea that moves into a rhythmic pattern.

.27 The theme is stated by the saxes in an up-tempo rhythmic texture.

.42 The repeat of the theme is accompanied by active melodic ideas from the brass section.

.57 Interlude, the tempo slows and becomes very expressive.

1.07 Piano solo, no horn or rhythm section activity.

1.46 Rhythmic motive in the piano is picked up by the bass.

1.52   Muted brass enter, bass continues motive.
2.06   Alto sax takes the melodic lead with a full brass background.
2.18   Sax soli is accompanied by a hard-driving swing.
2.37   Trombone lead is accompanied by a stop-time figure with a separate trumpet melody.
2.57   Tutti shout.
3.07   Ending.
3.12   End.

This arrangement is typical of the full ensemble writing of Stan Kenton. His large sound was unique among big bands. The thick writing using counterpoint was one reason for the full sound associated with Kenton. The changes in tempo and texture make this music more suitable for concerts than for dancing. In the 1940s this band gave birth to a new, highly developed sound unique to both the black and the white jazz traditions.

MAYNARD FERGUSON (b. 1928)

The ability to play in the extreme upper register of their horns has been a goal of most trumpeters, but of all those who have achieved the technique, only a handful are remembered primarily for the high note. Louis Armstrong was considered remarkable in the 1920s when he could play F's above high C for sustained periods. Of course, Armstrong's many other contributions to the music eventually overshadowed mere technical prowess. In the mid-1930s Snooky Young, Jimmie Lunceford's great trumpeter, played even higher than Armstrong, and then Cat Anderson, in Duke Ellington's orchestra, learned to blow notes in the piccolo range.

Among contemporary trumpeters, the player noted largely for his screaming upper register is Maynard Ferguson. It is true that a number of other musicians can play high notes—John Faddis, who has filed a notch in a front tooth and positions his horn off center to achieve the high-frequency lip vibrations needed; Faddis's mentor, Dizzy Gillespie; Dizzy's Cuban discovery, Arturo Sandoval; and many more—but Ferguson plays across the entire range with a pure, full-throated, controlled tone all the way up to and above double high B-flat (an octave above B-flat over the treble clef). Furthermore, Ferguson can play at the extreme lower reaches of the horn, into the bass clef, with power and centered pitch. Although his technical ability is cause for awe, it is his judicious use of his high register that is admirable. All Ferguson's notes have meaning in the compositional context.

Ferguson was born and raised in Montreal, Canada, the son of a school principal and a musical mother. At four he started his studies on the piano and the violin, but when he heard a cornet played at church, he realized that was the sound he wanted to produce. At sixteen he played in his brother's band, the Montreal High School Victory Serenaders, whose pianist, incidentally, was Oscar Peterson. He went on to lead a band that played preconcert warmups for the touring bands of Count Basie, Duke Ellington, Woody Herman, Stan Kenton, and the Dorsey brothers, among others. A number of these leaders invited Ferguson to join their bands, but at the time, he had other commitments. In 1949 he came to the United States to join Kenton, who had given Ferguson a standing offer. As it happened, this was during one of Kenton's nonplaying periods, so Ferguson spent the next two years with Boyd Raeburn, Jimmy Dorsey, and Charlie Barnet. When he finally joined Kenton, his international reputation blossomed. His commanding tone could be heard a full octave above Kenton's huge brass section. Audiences were astounded.

After three years with Kenton, he spent the next three doing studio work and then formed his own band. He has had one ever since, although it has changed appreciably in size and musical direction at different times, going from rock to bop to traditional swing to funk to pop commercial and back. His pop recordings of *MacArthur Park* and *Gotta Fly Now* reached the top of the commercial charts to the benefit of his bank account if not his artistic satisfaction.

Between 1967 and 1973 Ferguson lived in Spain and England and in India, where he studied and absorbed the Eastern concepts of spirituality. He returned to south India every summer for a number of years thereafter to teach at Satya Sai Baba Institute of Higher Learning in Bangalore. He credits much of his continued enthusiasm and energy to what he learned there, and he still meditates before each concert. Whatever the source, onstage, fronting the teenagers and twenty-year-olds in his bands, in his sixties he is still the dynamo that moves the music. His tone, range, and technique are as formidable as they were forty years ago.

BOB MINTZER (b. 1953)

The Bob Mintzer big band is best known through its recordings, and although he employs the same superior musicians on most sessions, the band has been largely a showcase for Mintzer's compositional and arranging skills. Mintzer follows a trend that has appeared in recent years. He and other topflight composer-arrangers (Sammy Nestico, Lennie Niehaus, and Frank Mantooth, to name a few) are writing scores for bands at all levels of competence, from beginning student bands to professionals, and are offering them through mail-order catalogs. Thus, first-class scores have become widely available.

Besides his writing, which he started in the mid-1970s while playing in the Buddy Rich band, Mintzer plays saxophone so well that he is in constant demand as soloist, clinician, and studio sideman. In fact, Yellowjackets, the Grammy Award–winning group, were so impressed with his talent that they asked Mintzer to join after their saxophonist of six years, Marc Russo, left in 1990. It is likely that Mintzer will continue to record with a big band from time to time, but in the early 1990s his primary commitment is to Yellowjackets.

LISTENING GUIDE

"The Ring"—1985 (Intro. to Jazz Disc 1, Cut 15)

Trumpets—Marvin Stamm, Randy Brecker, Laurie Frink, Bob Millikan
Trombones—David Bargeron, Bob Smith, Keith O'Quinn, Dave Taylor
Saxophones—Bob Mintzer, Lawrence Feldman, Peter Yellin, Michael Brecker,
    Bob Malach, Roger Rosenberg
Piano—Don Grolnick
Bass—Lincoln Goines
Drums—Peter Erskine
Percussion—Frankie Malabe

.00	(A) Brass tutti begins the selection, the drum plays fill solos between the statements.
.14	(A) Saxes enter in a tight call-response with the brass, the drums continue to fill with short soloistic ideas.
.29	(B) Low brass begin each phrase, and the high brass and saxes complete them. This new rhythmic feeling will return each time the (B) section is played.
.44	(A) Return to the original brass and sax call-response.
.56	Trumpet solo, the rhythm section becomes freer and responds to soloist, the bass walks.
1.25	New rhythmic feeling, less intense (B).
1.40	Return to the hard-driving rhythm accompaniment.
1.54	2nd solo chorus. Tutti accompaniment ideas from the other horn players.
2.21	New rhythmic feeling (B), soloist continues accompanied by the entire band.
2.51	Tenor sax begins solo with the same inflection used by the trumpet to end his solo.
3.16	Contrasting rhythmic feeling returns (B).
3.30	Driving swing returns, last (A) of 1st solo chorus.
3.44	Band enters with accompanying ideas.

4.11 Rhythmic change (B).
4.25 Band shout.
4.39 Tutti, drum fills, notice how the drummer kicks the ensemble figures.
5.02 Drum solo.
5.08 Return to original sax and brass interplay.
5.33 End.

This selection is typical of the hard-driving sound of the modern big bands. The arrangement uses a traditional jazz structure, AABA. Compare the aggressive, swinging solo of Randy Brecker on trumpet with the conceptual solo of his brother, Michael Brecker, on tenor sax. This composition by Bob Mintzer displays some amazing tutti ensemble sections. The ensemble is crisp and tight; the performance demonstrates a command and control of a wide dynamic range.

Photo by Dave King

Bob Mintzer

Harry Connick, Jr. (b. 1967)

When he was one, he could keep perfect musical time with a spoon on his high chair. When he was three, he could play tunes on the piano. When he was five, he played the "Star-Spangled Banner" on the piano in the ceremony at which his father was sworn in as New Orleans District Attorney. When he was nine, he joined the musicians union. At thirteen, he started playing regularly in New Orleans nightclubs. At eighteen, he moved to New York, and at twenty, he cut an album under his own name for a major record company.

Harry Connick, Jr., no doubt was a prodigy, and his musical schooling has been extensive. He grew up in New Orleans with the Marsalis family, studied under Ellis Marsalis and James Booker, whom he considered a genius, and absorbed every style of music from classical to Michael Jackson to Thelonious Monk. As his taste matured, his appreciation for the jazz masters Armstrong, Ellington, Waller, Johnson, Hines, and Tatum grew, and he, like Wynton Marsalis, became convinced that for the sake of perpetuating traditional jazz, he would have to present it in a way that audiences could not ignore.

In some ways Connick is a throwback to earlier entertainers. He believes the public wants to see as well as hear excitement. Onstage he wears clothes that reflect both the 1940s and the present; he has slicked back hair; he croons for sensual impact, does a little dancing, and engages in light-hearted patter. At the piano he reveals an impressive bebop technique, and his singing style recalls romantic ballads of the swing era.

Before the age of twenty-five, Connick achieved success. He writes music, and he has scored movies, acted in movies, and appeared on the covers of People *and* GQ *and* Down Beat. *He has put together a high-energy stage band of young musicians that can compete with the best. He evokes matinee idol response when he performs. His music comes across as a contemporary history of musical styles. To date, he has not challenged or questioned the direction of jazz, but he has rekindled many of the exciting qualities of its tradition.*

Other new bands were formed that capitalized upon the hard-driving swing established by the Basie and Herman bands. The most popular were the Buddy Rich, the Thad Jones–Mel Lewis, and later the Toshiko Akiyoshi–Lew Tabackin bands. The powerful drummer Buddy Rich depended on the traditional arrangements available to most bands. Toshiko, on the other hand, wrote compositions that delicately mixed musical elements from the Orient with a driving, modern big-band sound.

Like big bands, small groups capitalized upon the many avenues available to them in the 1960s. It is easy to overlook musicians of the 1960s because of the popular developments of jazz/rock in the 1970s. However, the 1960s produced some of jazz history's greatest recordings. The group led by pianist-composer George Russell recorded many superior arrangements and compositions. His intellectually stimulating rendition of "You Are My Sunshine" (*Outer Thoughts*, Milestone M-47027) demonstrates that jazz of the past and the future can be combined.

SUGGESTED LISTENING

Count Basie: *Best of Basie*. Pablo 2405-408-2.

Maynard Ferguson: *Storm*. Palo Alto Records PA 8052-N.

Woody Herman: *Giant Steps*. Fantasy OJC 344.

Stan Kenton: *New Concepts of Artistry in Rhythm*. Capitol Jazz CDP7-92865.

SUPPLEMENTAL LISTENING GUIDE FOR PART 6

"Subconscious Lee"—1949 (Lennie Tristano Quintet; SCCJ Disc 4, Cut 2)

Alto sax—Lee Konitz
Piano—Lennie Tristano
Guitar—Billy Bauer
Bass—Arnold Fishkin
Drums—Shelly Manne

.00   The melody is played in unison by the alto sax and the guitar; notice the melodic accents within the fast flow of notes. The piano comps, the bass walks, and the drummer uses brushes on the snare drum.

.31   Piano solo begins with very angular melodic ideas and harmonic extensions.

.47   Double-time melodic ideas, twice as fast as the normal double time.

1.03   Guitar solo continues with melodic patterns similar to those heard in the piano solo. Notice the interesting rhythmic ideas that pull and push against the drums and bass.

1.33   Alto sax solo follows, double-time flowing melody; notice the melodic patterns used to build the longer phrases.

2.05   Piano solo begins a series of 8-measure solos. The guitar is second, and the sax follows.

2.27   Piano plays the last 8-measure solo.

2.34   Guitar and alto sax restate the opening unison melody.

2.43   Sudden stop on the last chord.

This performance is typical of the understated melodic and rhythmic activity of cool jazz. Although the tempo and the melody are fast, the aggressive elements of bebop are softened considerably. The drummer still bombs, but with brushes to lessen the explosive effects. The focus is on the long, flowing melodic ideas. The composition is based on the chord flow of Cole Porter's "What Is This Thing Called Love?"

"Fables of Faubus"—1959 (Charles Mingus; Intro. to Jazz Disc 1, Cut 13)

Bass—Charles Mingus
Piano—Horace Parlan
Alto sax—John Handy
Tenor sax—Booker Ervin
Tenor sax—Shafi Hadi
Trombone—Jimmy Knepper
Drums—Danie Richmond

.00	Introduction, unison line, rhythm instruments reinforce the melody and do not play time yet.
.16	Saxes continue and the brass enter with a new melodic idea.
.32	New unison melody. The drums and bass play time patterns for the first time.
.55	Return to the sax and brass idea.
1.11	Swing patterns return in the rhythm section.
1.30	Tenor sax solo; notice the accompaniment figures and how free and expressive they are.
1.45	Double-time rhythm section activity with a double-time alto solo while the alto solo remains in the same time. Double-time ends quickly.
1.54	Return to the sax and brass texture. The swing section follows as it did before the first solo. This arranged section will appear before each solo.
2.37	Tenor solo; notice how the rhythm section starts and ends with a limping-like rhythmic feeling.
3.49	Piano solo; notice the brief moments of double-time in the rhythm section that float in and out during the solo.
4.20	The limping feeling reappears. Straight time returns soon.
4.53	Tenor solo, the rhythm section leaves straight time again. The rhythm section continues to move in and out of straight swing patterns.
6.03	Bass solo, the rhythm section continues to move between swing and angular patterns.
7.05	Melody returns, with the free background figures. The double-time rhythm also returns.
7.35	Sax and brass dialogue returns.
8.14	End.

Mingus was an inveterate talker. He had a multitude of reasons for composing every work, and he never hesitated to tell them to anyone within earshot, although his long explanations often seemed to go in circles. His most effective statements consisted of short quips or song titles such as "All the Things You Could Be by Now if Sigmund Freud's Wife Was Your Mother." His "Original Faubus Fables" was a satirical work with biting lyrics about the segregationist governor of Arkansas. This unique musical approach to social and political problems understandably found little support in the marketplace.

Free Jazz: Ornette Coleman

25

Ornette Coleman was among the first to experiment with free jazz, a term that covers a large number of styles and sounds. There are, however, four common musical procedures in free jazz: (1) Tone color becomes a structural element; (2) a new emphasis is placed on collective improvisation; (3) new roles are assigned to soloists and to those playing accompaniments; (4) all traditional musical rules are open to question.

Tone color. For a long time, Coleman played a white plastic saxophone instead of the traditional metal instrument because he found its nasal, shallow sound better suited his style. Coleman's excessive inflections, along with the manner in which he blew through the horn, led some critics to dismiss him as a poor technician. This criticism, however, fails to recognize the validity of a personalized technique. Coleman's inflections were deliberate exaggerations of common jazz inflections. He projected an individualized sound similar to that of early blues singers, which explains why he was accepted by the rhythm and blues (R&B) bands in which he first played.

Coleman found little approval later, when he became interested in bebop and attempted to interject his style into bebop bands. The boppers especially derided his "out of tune" approach to melody, which he developed by sliding into or away from a specified melody note.

Collective improvisation. Free jazz restored a concept that jazz had minimized since the passing of Dixieland: collective improvisation. Once again, all the musicians were called upon to actively solo together. Harmonies as well as melodies were improvised; therefore, melodies were not governed by inflexible chord progressions.

To allow a free flow of harmony, Coleman seldom used any comping instruments such as piano or guitar; he felt it to be too restricting to have one player dictate the harmonies. Without a pianist, he (or any other soloist) could lead the bassist in any harmonic direction he wished. Joachim Berendt, an authority on modern jazz, describes Ornette's free-flowing concept of improvisation in this way:

> . . . released from the unifying framework of a predetermined harmonic sequence, his solos unfold with an inner logic which never loses its ability to surprise. One thought springs from another, is re-expressed, transformed and leads to yet another. But the details of this process often approach the simplicity of a folk song and only knit when brought together in a complex structure.[1]

Ensemble. Collective improvisation brought about the third aspect of free jazz: the abolition of the traditional roles of soloist and accompanist. All the performers were free to play at any time they desired. They could add sounds or rhythms to help spark the texture or add melodic ideas to complement what was

---

[1] Joachim Berendt, ed., *The Story of Jazz* (London: Hutchinson Publishing Group, Ltd., 1978), p. 121.

being developed. The performers had to decide when and what to play. Don Cherry, in discussing Ornette Coleman's music, said:

> It had the jazz sounds and the jazz quality, but in terms of the kind of love and communication that they could achieve it had the quality of some African rhythms I've heard in which the communication is more important than the music, if you could separate the two.[2]

New musical priorities. The questioning of traditional rules of music created a revised ordering of musical priorities. The free jazz musician does not abandon tradition, he leans on it, especially on the blues. The performer must trust personal expression, although it often contradicts traditional melodic and harmonic relationships.

LISTENING GUIDE

"Lonely Woman" (1959) is an exceptional example of the free-floating harmonic structure associated with Coleman and his bassist, Charlie Haden. The inflections used by Coleman in this melody are strongly reminiscent of rural blues performances. Compare this traditionally based composition with the next example, "Free Jazz."

"Lonely Woman"—1959 (SCCJ Disc 5, Cut 7)

Alto sax—Ornette Coleman
Trumpet—Don Cherry
Bass—Charlie Haden
Drums—Billy Higgins

.00   Introduction: Loose rhythmic activity by bass and drums; bass plays double stops (two notes at once) in the upper register; drums play a fast pattern on the ride cymbal with punches on the snare drum (this will continue throughout the piece).
.18   (A) section: Trumpet and sax play melody, bass and drums continue.
.30   Very brief sax statement; this motive will return.
.33   Both trumpet and sax continue in harmony.
.43   Repeat of (A) section.

[2]A. B. Spellman, *Four Lives in the Bebop Business* (New York: Pantheon Books, a Division of Random House, Inc., 1966), p. 113.

.54   Sax alone again.

.59   Both in harmony.

1.07   (B) section: Trumpet plays ascending scale, bass and drums help accent new melody, sax ends section.

1.21   (A) section: This passage is exactly like the 1st two statements of the previous (A) section.

1.46   Alto sax solo, bass in upper register; notice the changing tonal quality of the alto sax.

2.08   Blueslike melody, rhythm section supports blues feeling.

2.21   (B) section: Marked by ascending scale in trumpet entry.

2.54   (A) section: Return to original melody.

3.17   Repeat of (A) section: Trumpet personalizes his part as if it were a solo.

3.40   (B) section: Scale on trumpet is followed by melodic falls.

3.53   Last (A) section.

4.17   Ending: Introduces new melodic idea based on original melody; trumpet plays soft low notes.

4.56   End.

"Lonely Woman" followed the traditional AABA structure found so often in bebop. The rhythm section develops a free-floating unaggressive texture that creates a mood appropriate to the title of the composition.

The excerpt from "Free Jazz" (1960) is much denser, and its complexity seems baffling at first. That is because "Free Jazz" attains the harmonic and melodic freedom suggested by "Lonely Woman." There are few traditional melodies or harmonies. If plotted on a graph, the changing energy levels and the activity of the performers might look like the following:

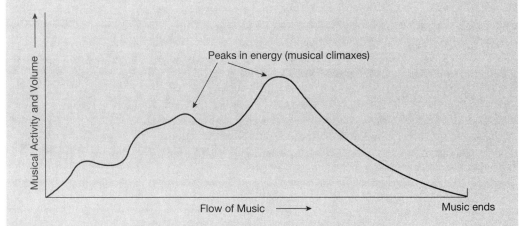

Excerpt from "Free Jazz"—1960 (SCCJ Disc 5, Cut 9)

Alto sax—Ornette Coleman
Trumpets—Donald Cherry, Freddie Hubbard
Bass clarinet—Eric Dolphy
Basses—Scott La Faro, Charlie Haden
Drums—Billy Higgins, Ed Blackwell

.00	Introduction: Everyone plays slowly, long notes.
.11	Organized Section: Bebop melody provides idea for the following improvisation.
.22	Alto sax solo: Bass walks, drummers play patterns that produce a strong feeling of swing.
1.10	Horns enter with accompaniment ideas (backup figures).
1.20	One bass player plays high, fast scales, while the other plays a more traditional bass line.
1.28	1st climactic point: Backup figures are free improvisations supporting the long sax solo.
1.40	New backup ideas: Bass clarinet plays long notes.
2.45	New backup ideas: Coleman continues the hard, rhythmic swing feeling.
3.00	Notice the bass.
3.24	Bebop pattern.
3.40	Horns enter again with related but independent ideas.
3.48	New backup ideas.
4.12	Fast solo work by Coleman, new climax.
4.25	The bowed string bass plays a separate idea.
4.42	All the horns play, increasing the density and energy.
5.00	Climax.
5.32	"Jingle Bells" quote, perhaps by accident.
5.38	Sharing of melodic ideas started by Coleman.
6.50	Very free section in which all the horns become near-equal soloists, each playing an independent idea.
7.22	Coleman takes solo ride again.
7.55	All play fast notes, increasing energy.
8.45	Horns pass around motive from the 1st part of this section.
9.15	Building to another climax.
9.51	Return to the bebop melody first heard at the beginning of this excerpt; horns play in unison.
10.01	Fade out.
10.07	End.

The bebop melody (ten seconds) at the beginning of this long improvisation returns at the end, a procedure similar to the standard bebop **head** arrangements. The horns accompanying Coleman's long solo respond freely to his ideas. Notice how Coleman maintains the swinging rhythmic feeling of long-short, long-short. This swinging feeling would be absent in freer styles of jazz.

ORNETTE COLEMAN (b. 1930)

Ornette Coleman was born in Fort Worth, Texas in 1930. His mother was a seamstress; his father died when he was seven. The atmosphere at home was caring, but Coleman says they were "po'," which he describes as a degree of poverty below poor. Ornette worked after school to help the family out. When he was fourteen his mother surprised him with the gift of an alto saxophone so that he could join his friends in the church band. Lessons were out of the question, so he began to learn the horn on his own. Some critics have speculated that his self-taught, incorrect fingering and misinterpretations of written notes have been the cause of his tonal peculiarities. However, this theory does not hold up. Coleman's cousin taught saxophone, and Coleman received adequate instruction in the high school band.

By the time he was sixteen Ornette was playing tenor sax in the high school band during the day and in R&B nightclubs in Fort Worth at night. He listened to the recordings of Louis Jordan and other R&B bands and could play their solos by ear. He also listened to and copied the bebop style of Charlie Parker. One night while working at a white club, he played a solo that was neither bebop nor R&B. He remembers it as being the awakening of his new concept. It was not well received, but he considers it a turning point.

In 1949 Coleman joined a traveling minstrel show called "Silas Green from New Orleans." The troupe toured through Oklahoma, Arkansas, Louisiana, and Mississippi. When they got to Natchez, Ornette tried to get the other tenor sax player to practice some bebop. Silas Green disliked bebop and fired Ornette on the spot. After a short stint with Clarence Samuel's Travelling Rhythm and Blues Band, Ornette joined Pee Wee Crayton's band, which was on its way to Los Angeles. By this time Coleman's style had evolved so drastically that Crayton could not tolerate it. When the band reached Los Angeles, Crayton paid him off and left him there.

With the exception of a two-year return to Fort Worth, Coleman remained in Los Angeles for the next nine years. It was a difficult time. No band would give him a job playing. In fact, whenever he tried to sit in, the other musicians would leave the stand. He worked as a baby-sitter, a porter, an elevator operator, and a stock clerk. He was not completely rejected, however, for he met and married Jayne Cortez and had a son, Ornette Denardo, who, though welcomed, further burdened Ornette's meager finances.

Ornette Coleman

Through Jayne, Coleman met a nineteen-year-old trumpeter, Don Cherry, who saw possibilities in Ornette's music. A small group of Los Angeles musicians began to gather around Coleman: bassists Charlie Haden and Don Payne, pianist Walter Norris, and drummers Ed Blackwell and Billy Higgins. Although they could not get work and had to practice in a garage, they came to the attention of Red Mitchell, the well-known jazz bassist. In February 1959 Mitchell arranged for the group to record some of Coleman's compositions. Although the recordings were not big sellers, they attracted the interest of Percy Heath, bassist in the Modern Jazz Quartet. Heath engineered the enrollment of Coleman and Cherry in the Lenox School of Jazz in Lenox, Massachusetts. John Lewis had organized this school in 1957 and had hired successful performers such as Dizzy Gillespie, Oscar Peterson, Max Roach, and many others to teach in three-week summer sessions for promising musicians.

After graduation, in November 1959, Coleman and Cherry opened at the

Five Spot, a nightclub in New York. Jazz followers responded with either enthusiasm or derision. No one was indifferent. That Coleman was playing a plastic sax and Cherry was blowing on a pocket trumpet did not help. Nevertheless, they became the momentary rage of the New York art world and were even endorsed by conductor and composer Leonard Bernstein. They signed a contract with the Atlantic Recording Company.

In spite of his recognition, Coleman never made more than twelve hundred dollars a week, from which he had to pay his sidemen. In 1962, when he saw other musicians making three times that much, he raised his fees. Jobs ended abruptly. For the next three years, he tried operating his own jazz club and running a music publishing company, but neither of these ventures worked out. When he relented and lowered his fees in 1965, he was engaged by New York's Village Vanguard, a well-known jazz club. He was received as though he had never been away.

In 1965 Coleman also began playing two new instruments, the trumpet and the violin, primarily for contrasting sound effects and rhythms. The distinctive sounds of each instrument stimulated new ideas. Together with the saxophone, these instruments enabled Coleman to express larger musical concepts.

Coleman's reputation continued to grow. At one point, he was commissioned to write a film score, and although it was rejected, he was paid substantially and used the money to organize a European tour in the fall of 1965, with drummer Charlie Moffett and bassist David Izenzon. The tour was not a financial success, but it spread Coleman's influence.

In the years since, free jazz, which Coleman calls "Harmolodic," has come to be taken seriously. Coleman traveled extensively and has received a Guggenheim grant to write a symphonic work; he also plans to write an opera. He has recorded an orchestral work called *Skies of America* and composed a piece for 125 voices to be sung in several languages at once. In the meantime, he has also taught himself the electric guitar. He appears regularly at the annual Kool (Newport–New York) Jazz Festival.

Although Coleman is associated with free jazz, most of his recordings are highly structured. Even his freest compositions have arranged moments, thus refuting some common notions about free jazz. He is significant in jazz history because he gave exposure to an already developing style and helped popularize a style of improvisation that relies on no prearranged harmonies.

Coleman has continued to branch out into new areas while preserving the accomplishments of his past. In 1986 he collaborated with Pat Metheny on the album *Song X*, wrote a string quartet, *Prime Design,* and worked regularly with his electric ensemble, Prime Time, which includes his son, Denardo, on drums. In 1987 he reassembled his original 1959 quartet of Don Cherry, Charlie Haden, Billy Higgins, and himself, and after recording the album *In All Languages,* he took the quartet on the road.

Ornette has had a reputation of asking more for his performances than was reasonable, which has idled him unnecessarily. He has stood firm on the matter of adequate monetary recognition, however, and has frequently been rewarded. In Paris, for example, a singer wanted Coleman to accompany him on a record. Ornette asked, and received, ten thousand dollars.

He has assigned the task of managing his professional life to his son, Denardo, and his public appearances and recording activities have increased. He is most heavily involved with the Fort Worth performance center, Caravan of Dreams, which not only stages performances but also produces records. Coleman is much sought after, and although he started out as an iconoclast, he has emerged as an elder statesman.

SUGGESTED LISTENING

Free Jazz. Double Quartet. 1960. Atlantic A2-1364-2.
The Shape of Jazz to Come. 1959. Atlantic A2-19238-2.
Song X. 1986. With Pat Metheny. Geffen 24096-2.

John Coltrane and Eric Dolphy 26

John Coltrane

JOHN COLTRANE (1926–1967)

The genius of John Coltrane lay in his philosophical approach to music, his intensity, and his dazzling technique, a technique that inspired Ira Gitler's famous description, "sheets of sound." He played notes so fast that he seemed to hang sheets of sound before the listener, playing through scales and patterns at a velocity previously unknown to the jazz world. He extended the upper range of the tenor saxophone to new heights and created his own unique sound.

Coltrane's deeply felt religion was the foundation of his intensity. It motivated his approach to the creative process. His belief in God took many directions. From the Christian philosophy espoused by the album *A Love Supreme* to the freer Eastern concepts of the album *Om*, Coltrane constantly declared his need to find what he hoped would be ultimate truth. The resulting sound was one of searching, searching with such intensity that he often seemed to be frustrated by the limitations of his instrument.

Coltrane's Life and Career

John Coltrane was born in Hamlet, North Carolina, in 1926. His father, a tailor, made a comfortable living, and his grandfather was a highly respected member of the community. Coltrane was always a shy, quiet boy but became even shyer when his father and grandfather died a few months apart when he was twelve. Through high school, he studied alto saxophone and later went to both the Granoff Studios and the Ornstein School of Music in Philadelphia. Drafted into the Navy in 1945, he spent his hitch playing the clarinet in the Navy band. After his discharge, he returned to Philadelphia and began his professional career doing rhythm and blues combo work, eventually playing with Eddie "Cleanhead" Vinson, who persuaded him to switch from alto sax and clarinet to tenor sax. By 1949 he was performing with Dizzy Gillespie, from whom he received a valuable bebop education. In 1952 he joined Earl Bostic and later that year began working with one of his first major influences, Johnny Hodges, with whom he remained until 1954.

Coltrane's first real exposure came with his recordings and performances with Miles Davis from 1955 to 1957. The modal jazz initiated by Davis gave Coltrane an opportunity for more harmonic freedom and with it a chance to become recognized. From the beginning with Davis, Coltrane was known for his intense sound and well-developed technique. Listen to the recording of "So What" (discussed in Chapter 22).

During his two years with Davis, Coltrane fluctuated between periods of abstinence and indulgence in alcohol and drugs. When he left the group at Davis's request, he went back to Philadelphia to his mother's house. While there, he awoke one morning with what he described as a revelation from God. He secluded himself in a room, consumed nothing but water, and in less than a week rid himself of alcohol and drug habits for good.

He joined Thelonious Monk in 1957 for a short but musically enriching period, then returned to stay with Davis until 1960. At that point, he formed his own quartet, composed of McCoy Tyner on piano, Elvin Jones on drums, and Steve Davis on bass (Davis was followed by Reggie Workman and finally by Jimmy Garrison). Of all the groups in which Coltrane worked, this one received the most acclaim.

LISTENING GUIDE

On his most famous recording, "My Favorite Things," Coltrane detaches himself from the rhythm section by creating a modal melody above a simplified modal chord progression. Coltrane's thoughts clearly establish this premise: "That's the way the song is constructed. . . . We improvise in the minor, and we improvise in the major modes."[1]

By performing quasi-modal solos over standard changes, Coltrane could create harmonic extensions that characterized his sound. "I could stack up chords—say, on a C^7,—I sometimes superimposed an $E\flat^7$, up to an $F\sharp^7$, down to an F. That way I could play three chords on one."[2]

The chords Coltrane mentions here are called **substitute harmonies;** one chord is replaced by another, creating a different but related sound. Such substitute harmonies, including *melodic extensions,* create sharp dissonances with the fundamental harmony played by the rhythm section.

Notice how the musicians reduce a melody with many chords to a repetitive rhythmic pattern. Coltrane and Tyner base most of their solo ideas on the first part of the song, with the first three notes receiving the greatest emphasis.

"My Favorite Things"—1960 (Intro. to Jazz Disc 2, Cut 1)

Soprano sax—John Coltrane
Piano—McCoy Tyner
Bass—Steve Davis
Drums—Elvin Jones

.00   Piano introduction.
.19   Sax plays melody.
.35   Piano vamp.

[1]Donald Demicheal, "John Coltrane and Eric Dolphy Answer the Jazz Critics," *Down Beat,* July 12, 1979, p. 16.
[2]Donald Demicheal and John Coltrane, "Coltrane on Coltrane," *Down Beat,* July 12, 1979, p. 53.

.44	Sax plays melody.
1.00	Solo improvisation by sax, piano continues to vamp.
1.18	3-note motive.
1.27	Return to melody.
1.54	Flash of technique.
2.05	Trills used in solo, piano vamp.
2.18	Piano solo begins.
2.25	Melody is outlined in top notes of chords (chord melody).
2.40	Vamplike solo.
3.10	Melody appears in right hand of piano part.
3.15	Chord melody.
3.26	Vamp again.
3.40	1-note solo with rhythmic interplay.
4.17	Syncopated rhythm in piano chords against the 3/4 **meter.**
4.49	1-note idea returns, followed by syncopated chord idea.
5.12	Tyner's right hand plays broken chords (chord trills).
6.30	Vamp.
6.48	Piano returns to the melody.
7.06	Sax takes up the melody.
7.32	Sax plays patterns and scales—extensions.
7.35	Sax continues with scale patterns into the upper register (modal scales used).
7.55	A flurry of activity on sax, unlike fast bebop.
8.16	Sax pushes against upper register.
9.25	Energy lessens, piano maintains similar chord vamp.
9.44	Melody returns.
10.03	Sax solo (improvised); notice the complicated interlocking patterns produced by the drums and bass.
10.13	Melodic patterns.
10.19	Large intervals used in pattern.
10.30	Upper register, syncopated chords by pianist continue.
11.25	Extensions in melody.
12.20	Melody returns.
12.36	2nd half of original melody used as an idea for the ending.
13.00	Activity slows down to the final accented ending.
13.39	End.

The Move to Free Jazz

In 1965 Elvin Jones and McCoy Tyner left the quartet, and Coltrane intensified his search for freer musical structures. A new group was formed with Pharoah Sanders on tenor sax, Rashied Ali on drums, and Coltrane's second wife, Alice McLeod, on piano. With this group Coltrane pursued ever-freer forms of jazz. Listeners found the music clashing and disorganized. Critics denounced it, and his records sold poorly. In later years, however, both critics and jazz fans have softened or even reversed their first reactions to the styles Coltrane developed in the 1960s.

Until his death from a liver ailment in 1967, Coltrane spent most of his time in New York City. He did enjoy a very successful tour of Japan in 1966, and that together with an apparent growing appreciation at home must have encouraged him. However, it has not been until after his death that his genius has been fully and generally recognized.

SUGGESTED LISTENING

A Love Supreme. 1964. MCA/Impulse MCAD 5660.
My Favorite Things. 1960. Atlantic SD 1361-2.
See Miles Davis.

ERIC DOLPHY (1928–1964)

The fact that Eric Dolphy, the woodwind player, lived only thirty-six years and the fact that he was a black, avant-garde jazz artist whose associates populated the 1950s and 1960s drug culture might lead one to suppose that here was another life wasted too soon by self-indulgence. Such was not the case. Eric Dolphy was a most admirable human being: gentle, devout, tolerant, creative, honest, generous, and dedicated. All the people whose lives he touched loved him.

He made disappointingly few recordings, considering the magnitude of his talent. Vladimir Simosko, in his discussion of Dolphy's brief place in jazz history, believed that ". . . in Dolphy intensity and passion reach a zenith as jagged, leaping, twisting patterns of notes pour forth in a torrent that constantly surprises the listener with unexpected directions and fantastic uses of intervals and phrasing."[3]

Dolphy died while critics were still waiting to see if he would establish a place among the greats. In his lifetime he was accepted and appreciated by musicians whose lifestyles were very different from his, and it is only in retrospect that wider recognition of his talent has emerged. His gentle personality and giving nature were rare qualities, especially in the aggressive, highly competitive world of jazz performance. In spite of his musical intellect, he never sounded

[3]Reprinted by permission of the Smithsonian Institution Press from *Eric Dolphy: A Musical Biography and Career Analysis*, by Vladimir Simoska and Barry Tepperman. Washington D.C., © Smithsonian Institution Press, 1974, p. 8.

sterile or analytical. He was unselfish when he played, always complementing the other musicians musically. It was this spirit that made his work successful when he performed with such strong personalities as Charles Mingus and John Coltrane. History probably will never elevate Eric Dolphy to the stature of Mingus or Coltrane, but that is not because he lacked comparable talent.

Although Dolphy was only eight years younger than Charlie Parker, his musical style was that of the next generation. Dolphy's artistry approached that of Parker's. His tone on the saxophone was less brittle, he had superb intonational command across the entire customary range of the instrument and beyond, and he was capable of intervallic leaps that left other saxophonists dumbfounded.

Dolphy's Life and Career

Eric Allen Dolphy was born in Los Angeles on June 20, 1928. His parents came from the West Indies, and when they took up residence in Los Angeles, they joined the People's Independent Church of Christ, which followed the European style of worship. The choir sang traditional hymns and the organist played Haydn and Bach. Both Dolphy's parents actively helped in the work of the church. It was natural, therefore, that young Eric would develop a love of music as well as a warm and compassionate nature.

His formal music training, on the clarinet, began in elementary school. When he graduated to junior high school, he expanded his studies to include the oboe and the bass clarinet. By 1942 Eric had won achievement awards in district band and orchestra festivals. While still in junior high school, he won a two-year scholarship to the University of Southern California Preparatory School of Music. His studies up to that time had been centered on classical woodwind music, but then jazz intruded. He heard recordings by Fats Waller, Duke Ellington, and Coleman Hawkins. This music swung, and its excitement infected Eric. While still in junior high, he began to earn money playing jazz at local dances. After high school, he studied at Los Angeles City College, where he matured quickly as a musician and was in demand by many local groups.

From 1948 to 1950, Dolphy was a member of Roy Porter's big band, and he made his first appearance on records with it. Although quite popular at the time, the band had not recorded extensively, and there is little evidence of Dolphy's soloistic role in the ensemble. In 1950 Eric joined the Army and was stationed at Fort Lewis, Washington, for two years. While there, he performed with the Tacoma Symphony and later studied at the Naval School of Music in Washington, D.C., receiving a certificate of excellence in 1952. Discharged in 1953, he returned to Los Angeles.

Throughout the 1950s, Dolphy worked with many bands around Los Angeles and eventually led his own band in 1956. His first national exposure came with the Chico Hamilton Quintet in 1958. He joined Hamilton in Los Angeles and toured with him until late 1959. When Hamilton disbanded the quintet in December 1959, Dolphy settled in New York City, joining Charles Mingus at the Showplace in Greenwich Village.

The partnership with Mingus nurtured the freedom Dolphy's style required. Dolphy's exposure in the Hamilton and Mingus groups led to his first recording sessions as a leader in April 1960. The album's title, *Outward Bound*, gave notice that Dolphy intended to head toward even more complex harmonic structures.

Beginning in 1960, Dolphy began to be heard on more records. He collaborated in a session with Ornette Coleman in May 1960. Among the most notable of his recordings during this period was the session with Ornette Coleman on the album *Free Jazz*, in which eight musicians participated. The double quartet format gave Eric the opportunity to introduce sound effects on the bass clarinet. Dolphy also played and toured with Charlie Mingus and recorded several Mingus compositions with the composer. These sessions were among his best. They led to engagements with Ron Carter on cello and later with the Latin Jazz Quintet, which showcased his flute.

Dolphy left Mingus late in 1960 to pursue a free-lance career. He played for a short time with George Russell in 1961[4] and then went to Sweden for a number of concerts. European audiences, particularly those in Scandinavia, had accepted his music much sooner than the American public. The selection "Oleo," recorded at a concert in Copenhagen, shows strong influences of bebop. In addition to the fast-flowing lines, the extreme upper register of the bass clarinet adds an element not common to bebop; flurries of notes also seem to blur together.

LISTENING GUIDE

"Oleo"—1961 (Intro. to Jazz Disc 2, Cut 2)

Bass clarinet—Eric Dolphy
Piano—Bent Axen
Bass—Eric Moseholm
Drums—Jorn Elniff

.00   No introduction, Dolphy begins with the 1st part of the melody (A), with the drummer playing melodic accents.
.06   2nd part (A).
.12   (B) section contains no written melody; improvisation, rhythm section plays time.

[4]This association produced a brilliant alto solo based on the Thelonious Monk tune "Round Midnight." The selection can be found on the record *George Russell: Outer Thoughts* (Milestone, M-47027).

.18   Last part (A): Only the bass clarinet and drums play.

.25   The bass clarinet begins an improvised solo with a long low note followed by a fast bebop melody.

.35   Dolphy plays over the entire range of the instrument.

.49   The piano sets up a static harmonic vamp.

1.02 Vamp ends, beginning of the bridge (B) section.

1.13 Bass clarinet plays in its extreme high range; a new chorus begins.

1.21 A flurry of notes that blur together.

1.31 Piano vamps again.

1.39 A rhythmic motive by the bass clarinet in the upper register starts a new chorus; extensions.

2.05 Another flurry, followed by exaggerated inflections blurring the notes.

2.27 Trills on the bass clarinet.

2.32 The bass clarinet plays a simple humorous melody that is picked up by the drummer.

2.44 Explosive attacks on the reed.

3.15 Piano solo employs a similar melodic structure and a similar use of extensions; fast bebop lines.

4.16 Drummer kicks more aggressively.

4.32 Sparse piano fades into an active walking-bass solo accompanied by splashes from the drummer.

4.55 A brief statement from Dolphy begins the drum solo.

5.18 Splashing hi-hat cymbals.

5.40 Bass clarinet enters with fast bebop lines, rhythm section returns to more familiar jazz patterns.

6.24 A repeated melodic-rhythmic motive.

6.32 Return to the melody, this time only the bass clarinet and bass, the (A) section is stated twice.

6.46 Drums and piano enter on the bridge (B).

6.51 Section (A), last 8 measures of the melody: Only the bass clarinet and drums play.

7.00 Everyone improvises an ending.

7.08 End.

The form is typically bebop, AABA. The (B) section has no written melody, only chords for improvisation. The melody, written by Sonny Rollins, is a standard in the bebop repertoire. This work is memorable for Dolphy's brilliant bass clarinet technique. Not only does Dolphy's tone command authority, it also projects a powerfully expressive quality, even in the extreme top range. Notice the large intervallic skips and the extended phrasing. Both are typical of avant-garde classical and jazz melodies; however, few performers can match Dolphy's control and logic in blending these techniques.

In September 1961 Dolphy and guitarist Wes Montgomery joined the John Coltrane quartet at the Monterey Jazz Festival. Dolphy and Coltrane had met in Los Angeles in 1954 and in the intervening time had followed one another's careers. They had a special rapport, particularly in their quest for new expression. The reviews in *Down Beat* by John Tynan were very critical of the new melodic freedoms and the long solos Coltrane and Dolphy played. The controversy was taken up by fans and critics across the country. Dolphy remained with Coltrane for several months, accompanying the group when it toured Europe late in 1961. In March 1962 Dolphy left Coltrane's group as a regular member and formed his own group. On the West Coast that same year, he performed Edgar Varése's *Density 21.5* on the flute. Other unique musical projects followed: experimental concerts involving simultaneous music, dancing, and painting, and musical dialogues accompanying poetry readings. Again, all these activities tied in with the third stream–avant-garde concepts popular in the 1960s.

In 1963 Dolphy rejoined Mingus, who was leading a new ten-piece band. In 1963 the group was booked on a European tour. While in Paris, Dolphy left Mingus to do free-lance recordings and concerts before returning to the United States to be married. The wedding was to have been in the summer of 1964, but on June 27, while playing for the opening of a nightclub in Berlin, Eric became ill and was hospitalized. He died two days later.

SUGGESTED LISTENING

The Essential Eric Dolphy. Prestige FCD-60-022.

Anthony Braxton and Cecil Taylor

27

Photo by Bill Smith

Cecil Taylor

ANTHONY BRAXTON (b. 1945)

Discussions about the direction an art form is taking usually include the term *avant-garde,* meaning ahead of its time. That designation remains with any new concept until it either becomes established and has received a name of its own or has faded away. A recent jazz form that appears to have outlasted its avant-garde classification was developed by a Chicago group called AACM (Association for the Advancement of Creative Musicians). One of its most prominent and articulate alumni, Anthony Braxton, refers to it as "creative music."

This jazz species is not as recognizable as Dixieland or bebop. It takes various forms from time to time and from performer to performer. Braxton's work in this form ranges widely. He is an experimenter in **timbres,** particularly in the sounds of woodwind (sopranino sax, contrabass clarinet, and flute). When an instrument is played in an unorthodox manner, its timbre can become so distorted as to sound unfamiliar or unrecognizable. Braxton not only plays normal woodwind sounds but also interjects squawks, squeaks, hisses, or pops that he has learned to control and manipulate in the process of improvising musical passages. His compositions run the gamut from conventionally notated marches to geometrically diagramed free improvisations. He has written a piece for one hundred tubas. He has composed a mammoth work for four forty-piece orchestras playing simultaneously in the corners of the same auditorium. His album *For Alto* (Delmark DS 420/421) contains over an hour's worth of unaccompanied solo sax.

Braxton was born in Chicago on June 4, 1945, and grew up on the South Side. He began studying the clarinet during his first year in high school. He confesses to having been withdrawn as a teenager, spending much of his time indoors listening to jazz and classical records. He liked Billie Holiday and rock-and-rollers Bill Haley and Chuck Berry. His formal music education was rather extensive and included study of clarinet and saxophone under Jack Gell, composition and harmony at the Chicago School of Music, and courses at the Chicago Music College. In 1962, at the age of seventeen, he became influenced by saxophonists Paul Desmond, Eric Dolphy, and Charlie Parker. Initially he was a bebopper, but when he was about twenty-one, following a two-and-a-half-year hitch in the Army, he began to alter his approach to playing. As it happened, this was about the time he became involved with AACM.

Braxton has since pushed out in directions beyond those of AACM. He studied philosophy at Roosevelt University and, in pursuit of further intellectual growth, became sufficiently adroit at chess to make a modest living as a chess hustler. The geometric-mathematic titles he has given many of his compositions reveal his analytical turn of mind. As of 1994 he is chairman of the Department of Music at Wesleyan University in Middletown, Connecticut.

In his solo performances, Braxton displays a facility for developing short motivic ideas. Although the motives may change in shape and length, they always retain the essence of their original character. Such motivic development in Braxton's improvisations is apparent from the first note to the last. The nontraditional sounds, melodic patterns, contrasts of tone, articulation, and pitch range are all bases for thematic development. Braxton's ability to manipulate unorthodox techniques gives him a vast platform from which to improvise. During concerts, he performs as many as a dozen numbers. Each succeeding composition is distinctly different, but the sequence is devised to create a progressive flow of ideas. Even listeners not familiar with this style of jazz can easily understand the logic inherent in such free solo performances.

It would be difficult to assess what Braxton's eventual importance in jazz history will be. He has great musical depth and is a superb technician. Perhaps what prevents him from being widely accepted is that his paths toward musical expression are too diverse ever to inspire a cult following.

SUGGESTED LISTENING

Anthony Braxton/New York, Fall 1974. Arista AL 4032. Out of print.
For Alto. Delmark DS 420/421.
DUO (LONDON) 1993. Leo 193.

CECIL TAYLOR (b. 1929)

To appreciate Cecil Taylor's music requires perseverance. Anyone who has not studied Stockhausen, Stravinsky, Schoenberg, or Shepp may be inclined to give up too soon. Taylor's music is difficult for those accustomed to traditional Western harmonic-melodic music to understand, but a persistent listener will find it full of unexpected beauty.

Taylor's piano technique is not timid. He startles the listener with loud, dissonant tone clusters, pounded out in forceful rhythmic patterns. Taylor exploits the piano's percussive capabilities as well as its melodic and harmonic ones. He has shocked listeners during concerts by using his fists or elbows to produce his intended sound effects.

Gary Giddins has described Taylor as being "the outermost concentric circle of the avant-garde."[1] Artists in such a position are not often well rewarded; nevertheless, Taylor has had a number of record albums released. He regularly appears at prestigious jazz festivals, and he has been highly regarded by members of the musical community. In the late 1970s and early 1980s, his concert engagements in the United States, Europe, and Japan increased substantially, and

---

[1]Reprinted from *The Encyclopedia of Jazz in the Seventies* by Leonard Feather and Ira Gitler, copyright 1976, by permission of the publisher, Horizon Press, New York, and Leonard Feather, p. 322.

his workshop seminars at the Creative Music Studio in West Hurley, New York, were fully subscribed.

Cecil Taylor was born in Long Island City, New York, on March 25, 1929. Although both of his grandmothers were American Indians and his father had Scottish great-grandparents, Taylor is most proud of his black heritage. His mother started him on the piano at the age of five. He was fortunate to live in a musical family and neighborhood. His mother played the piano, and Taylor took lessons from a Mrs. Jessey, who lived across the street. He also studied percussion, which was to affect his piano playing.

Taylor moved to Boston in 1950 and enrolled in the New England Conservatory. He remained there for four years, studying piano, arranging, and harmony. Despite his formal training, Taylor firmly contends that he learned more from listening to Duke Ellington and from other nonacademic sources than he did in class. He lists a number of artists who influenced him: Dave Brubeck, Lennie Tristano, Bud Powell, Horace Silver, and Erroll Garner. His view of instrumental technique also contradicts his conservatory training; if the performer logically brings forth musical sounds, the technique is right even though it may offend purists. Thus, the keyboard techniques of Vladimir Horowitz, who played with precise articulation, and Thelonious Monk, who used unorthodox fingerings, are equally valid. Each expresses a certain cultural heritage in a natural way.

The 1960s and early 1970s were discouraging years for Taylor. He washed dishes rather than abandon his kind of music to take the commercial music jobs he could have had. His following was small, although enthusiastic, and he lacked patronage, but as time passed and he persisted, his reputation grew. He was invited to play at the famous 1978 White House concert, and his concert schedule, particularly in Europe and Japan, has filled up. He was able to buy a two-story brownstone in Brooklyn in 1983, and although his performances probably will never draw as well as a rock concert, his stature as a musician will overshadow those of most of the wealthy rock stars.

LISTENING GUIDE

As in the music of Ornette Coleman, Taylor's free jazz style fashions long energy curves, which novice listeners have to learn to recognize and follow. Some striking sounds occur in the recording of "Enter Evening." The most difficult to identify is the high violin sound produced by one of the string bass players. It is produced by bowing harmonics, which are created when a string is lightly touched instead of being firmly pushed down to the fingerboard;

the resulting note is much higher than the lower fundamental expected. This technique allows the bassist to play in the same range as the trumpet and oboe. Other striking sounds are produced on the piano, with Taylor creating clouds of sharply contrasting sounds by using tone clusters.

"Enter Evening"—1966 (SCCJ Disc 5, Cut 5)

Piano, bells—Cecil Taylor
Trumpet—Eddie Gale Stevens
Alto sax—Jimmy Lyons
Alto sax, oboe, bass clarinet—Ken McIntyre
Bass—Henry Grimes
Bass—Alan Silva
Drums—Andrew Cyrille

.00	1st phrase: Independent motives uttered by the oboe, sax, and muted trumpet with staccato piano notes sounded in the low register.
.10	2nd phrase is played by the oboe, which predominates, muted trumpet, and alto sax.
.19	3rd phrase: Notice the bass-note activity on the piano.
.28	4th phrase.
.40	Bowed bass leads into next idea, no piano.
.56	Oboe still dominates the texture, piano uses the entire range of the keyboard, phrasing continues.
1.48	A more detached, separated new texture is introduced, played on the triangle, and bowed string bass.
2.20	Activity increases.
2.32	A new section is played by muted trumpet, string bass (harmonics), and piano (short chords).
3.22	A climax builds.
3.32	Thick texture, high activity level.
3.36	Activity decreases, walking bass creates a temporary feeling of swing.
4.04	No piano, light percussion, bass very high, muted trumpet also high, "white noise" effect (no sense of pitch).
4.30	Oboe enters.
5.00	Piano plays repeating pattern.
5.25	Piano adds chords to pattern, long bowed note on bass.
5.50	Climax.
6.06	Alto sax becomes soloist starting very melodically, piano continues activity, brushes on snare drum.

6.50	Alto sax and high bass increase the speed.
7.12	Percussive effects on piano.
7.34	New section, piano solo.
7.53	Tone clusters on piano.
8.09	Fast succession of tone clusters.
8.23	Long, difficult runs on piano.
8.45	Slower, thinner texture leads to **cadence.**
9.01	Return to 1st texture, oboe is again prominent.
9.43	Everyone holds long note, piano returns to low bass-note activity.
9.58	Silence.
10.02	New idea in long notes appears.
10.13	Long-note idea continues and phrasing returns.
10.45	An ending is created as everyone plays in the extreme high range, with a roll on the triangle.
11.00	End.

Taylor confronts many contemporary social problems head on. He is a forthright, serious individual. His music is a direct outgrowth of his philosophy. It is brilliant, sobering, and overpowering. It leaves the listener drained. Joy and humor are hard to find in it. Whatever its message, Taylor says it with supreme force.

SUGGESTED LISTENING

Unit Structures. 1966. Blue Note B21Y-84237.

FREE JAZZ INTO THE '80s AND '90s

Many of the original free jazz musicians went on to form their own groups and strike out in different musical directions. For example, Don Cherry, from the Ornette Coleman band, developed a unique sound that incorporated elements of Indian, Indonesian, and Arabic music. Besides the new melodic and rhythmic ideas, Cherry uses instruments from Eastern cultures to add exotic timbres and sounds to the musical texture.

Three influential tenor saxophone players, Pharoah Sanders, Albert Ayler, and Archie Shepp, carried on where Coltrane left off. All three continued to develop the explosive sound Coltrane used in the album *Om.* The most intense performer was Albert Ayler. Under his skillful control, moving, folk-song-like melodies could suddenly turn into harsh squeaks and squawks. Archie Shepp combined free jazz with more traditional Afro-American jazz. His style combined the lyricism of Coleman Hawkins with the aggression of Albert Ayler. Pharoah Sanders took a course somewhere between Ayler and Shepp.

New free jazz styles were also developed by musicians outside the mainstream. The Sun Ra Orchestra provides a striking example. A self-proclaimed prophet of free jazz, Sun Ra directed a unique big band structured like a communal family. Many of its members were with him several years. The band performed wearing costumes designed to express Sun Ra's belief in galactic inspiration. Sometimes called the Solar Arkestra, sometimes the Intergalactic Myth-Science Arkestra, its performances presented startling visual effects. At times, movies of the band appeared in the background while the wildly costumed musicians performed onstage. Aside from the visual spectacle, the music was rich in ideas using free jazz concepts within a big-band structure that varied in size containing as many as twenty musicians or more, including vocalists.

Sun Ra was not a newly arrived musical rebel. He was born Herman Poole Blount in 1917 but legally changed his name to Le Son'y Ra in 1952. He lived

The World Saxophone Quartet. *Clockwise from top left: Hamiet Bluiett, Julius Hemphill, David Murray, Oliver Lake.*

through most of the major events in jazz history. Ra's later devotion to free jazz was a renunciation of the more conservative jazz he favored in the 1950s. Ra died in May 1993 following three strokes and a questionable operation. Although saxophonist John Gilmore and trumpeter Michael Ray hope to perpetuate the band, the disorganized conditions of Ra's estate together with uncooperative survivors may make that difficult.

THE WORLD SAXOPHONE QUARTET

Early in 1976 Professor Ed Jordan of Southern University in New Orleans invited saxophonists Julius Hemphill (hem-fill), Hamiet Bluiett, Oliver Lake, and David Murray to come from New York to his campus to participate in some clinics and concerts. Hemphill, Bluiett, and Lake shared a common background in progressive music during the 1960s with the Association for the Advancement of Creative Musicians and the Black Artists Group in Chicago. Murray came from a church tradition, and all four had played together previously, although not on a formally organized basis.

At Southern University, in addition to their clinics, the quartet played twice at a local nightclub. Some of their sets were played with a rhythm section, but some were unaccompanied and these were so well received that the four decided to establish the quartet permanently and to perform with a rhythm section.

In the beginning, all their music was originally composed, mostly by Hemphill. They attracted a devoted, if limited, following but were unable to get an American recording contract. They did record three albums for a progressive Italian label, "Black Saint," which received very little distribution in the United States. Then, in 1986, the quartet did an album, *Plays Duke Ellington,* for Nonesuch, a subsidiary label of Warner Brothers, and the American marketing together with the widely recognized Ellington songs generated a much enlarged audience. Their next album, *Dances and Ballads,* contained only originals and, unfortunately, did not do well, but their third for Nonesuch, *Rhythm and Blues,* containing cleverly adapted rhythm and blues standards, was very successful.

The quartet has achieved more permanence than many groups, although in early 1991 Hemphill departed and was replaced by Arthur Blythe, a highly regarded avant-garde saxophonist. One reason for its stability is that the group is democratically organized. Decisions in all matters have always been by consensus. Quartet members have musical careers outside the group, because they believe that this will ensure continued sources of new ideas, but the World Saxophone Quartet remains at the center of their musical universe. Realistically, the group probably can never expect to become a national craze, but they admire and strive for creativity and are certain to have an effect on the progress of the music.

Instrumentation of the quartet most frequently is one baritone, one tenor, and two alto saxophones, but all the musicians are multi-instrumentalists. Listen to *Steppin'* for an unusual mix of timbres.

LISTENING GUIDE

"Steppin'"—1981 (World Saxophone Quartet; Intro. to Jazz Disc 2, Cut 3)

Alto flute—Hamiet Bluiett
Soprano sax—Julius Hemphill, Oliver Lake
Bass clarinet—David Murray

.00   The piece opens with the bass clarinet and one of the soprano saxes playing a rhythmic motive.

.09   The alto flute and the other soprano sax play a line above the other two. Soon all four combine into a soli line.

.41   The above section is repeated.

1.23   Improvised section begins using the same texture as the opening. All players move to more independent ideas. The bass clarinet maintains a similar bass pattern built on short notes.

2.00   Blues inflections and motives.

2.20   The improvised melodic lines begin to swing harder.

2.39   The texture expands, becoming freer.

3.10   The melodic interchanges become more rapid.

3.12   The bass clarinet plays longer, smoother notes.

3.37   Bass clarinet is now freed from patterns, playing lines similar to those of the other players.

4.00   Extreme high range is used by the bass clarinet.

4.20   The range of all the instruments moves upward.

5.00   Moment of cadence. The momentum slows and the texture thins.

5.18   Motive appears briefly and is shared.

5.30   Large range sweeps, distorted notes.

6.06   Another moment of cadence followed by a return to the original melody over the initial rhythmic motive.

6.32   Soli section returns.

6.48   Rhythmic texture returns and the volume decreases.

7.07   Final long note.

In this performance, the improvised section stands out from the main theme, which is clearly arranged. The group improvisation (collective) is one of the group's strongest attributes. Notice how the texture of the arranged sections that open and close this performance is maintained to some degree throughout the improvised section.

FREE JAZZ IN EUROPE

The impact of jazz on other countries has grown steadily since the first Dixieland bands toured Europe in the 1920s. Dixieland is still very popular in Europe, especially in Poland. Later jazz styles are also popular in Europe, but generally speaking, these styles have followed the innovations of Afro-American musicians. Free jazz improvisation merged with the traditional European orchestra in the late 1960s, primarily in England, France, and Germany. The mixture of a formal structure with the free elements of jazz is truly a Western European cultural statement.

The list of active jazz musicians in Europe has grown very long. Free jazz has brought forth a new generation of performers; composer and pianist Alexander von Schlippenbach, trombonist Albert Mangelsdorff, and trumpeter Manfred Schoof are but a few of the leaders in this style. They all bring traditional styles to bear on totally free structures. The closest counterpart in the United States is perhaps the Art Ensemble of Chicago under the leadership of Roscoe Mitchell.

Free jazz was introduced in Europe by American records and by visiting performers, especially those who went to France in the 1960s. In addition, classical music was turning toward freer musical concepts. It is no wonder, then, that Europe has taken free jazz and developed it so extensively.

SUGGESTED LISTENING

Sun Ra: *Strange Celestial Road.* Rounder CD-3035.
Alexander von Schlippenbach: *Globe Unity.* BASF MPS20630. Out of print.
World Saxophone Quartet: *Rhythm and Blues.* Nonesuch 9 60864.
    Dances and Ballads. Nonesuch 9 79164-1.
    Plays Duke Ellington. Nonesuch 9 79137-1.

Fusion: Chick Corea

28

A new musical style appears either because the listening public, or musicians, have grown tired of the old or because a succeeding generation wants a style of its own. The intermingling of jazz and rock, known as *fusion,* was unusual because it created something new out of two existing styles. This was not the first time jazz had been combined with a recently popular form; it had happened in the swing era, and as was the case then, the product was highly successful. Jazz and rock fused to form an exciting new style of music. This music was freed from purely rock or jazz restrictions.

The incorporation of traditional jazz styles, especially bebop, with contemporary rock and roll gave birth to fusion. Although the separate traditional elements undergo a change when combined into fusion, they do not lose their identities entirely. Fast-swinging bebop melodies now appear above a persistent, even eighth-note beat. Traditional jazz imparts a feeling of swing to rigid rock rhythms, and in return rock provides a driving rhythmic pulse. The influence of each style is not always necessarily equal. Within a given performance, the music may fluctuate between swing, two-beat, jazz/rock, or basic funk. In each case, the dominant style is continually modified by the others. (Refer to Appendix C for a brief overview of rock history.)

Bitches Brew, recorded in 1970 by Miles Davis, successfully set the stage for the growth of jazz/rock.[1] This album was the first to show that this style was more than a wedding of rock and jazz. Prior to this recording, groups such as Blood, Sweat, and Tears and Chicago featured arrangements that leaned heavily on a jazz heritage. The term most often used to describe them was rock-jazz. The musical product was essentially rock "with" jazz. *Bitches Brew* not only redirected efforts to amalgamate jazz and rock, it also demonstrated that musicians drawn from the whole jazz spectrum could contribute equally. John McLaughlin, guitarist on *Bitches Brew* and director of the now-defunct Mahavishnu Orchestra, startled the rock world in 1972 with his "sophistifunk" approach to rock. The influence of Miles Davis permeated McLaughlin's performances, although the group was not considered a jazz ensemble. Saxophonist Wayne Shorter, another *Bitches Brew* soloist, and pianist-composer Joe Zawinul went on from the Davis group to form the nucleus of the successful fusion group Weather Report. Although a number of other personnel changes occurred, Zawinul and Shorter remained together for fourteen years, finally going separate ways in 1985. When that happened, Zawinul renamed the group Weather Update. Another keyboard player from *Bitches Brew,* Chick Corea, organized another outstanding group, Return to Forever.

The 1970s witnessed an explosion of activity in the jazz/rock idiom. The popularity of this new style rivaled any in jazz history. Its influence is reflected in commercial music as well. For the first time since the big-band era, the debate regarding what is true jazz and what is commercial resurfaced.

---

[1] See the discussion of this album in Chapter 22.

ELEMENTS OF FUSION

The style that first came to be called fusion had three easily identifiable qualities: (1) Instruments were electronically modified to alter their sounds. (Many
groups did retain some acoustic instruments to supply backups to vocals and
even to solo: Chicago, Earth, Wind and Fire, and Spyro Gyra, for example.) (2)
The keyboard player used synthesizers to create a multitude of new effects. (3)
The basic rhythmic presence drew from the heritage of swing but inclined toward the more pervasive rock beat, and Latin-influenced percussionists playing
wood blocks, cowbells, congas, bongos, chimes, gourds, and whistles began to
be featured.

Growing knowledge of electronics influenced the musical product partly
by sophisticated recording techniques and partly by using public-address systems designed to amplify as well as modify sound. The step from employing
electronics to enhance normal musical sound to creating new sounds was a
small one. The turning point came with the discovery that a simple amplifier
could do more than just make an instrument louder. Guitarist Jimi Hendrix
found that if he turned toward an amplifier while playing he could use the **feedback** for added effect. The ear-splitting volume produced distortions that added
new dimensions to his solos. The building of electronic devices to reproduce
the same effects but with greater control was just around the corner.

The most sophisticated musical electronics were first developed in studios
by classical avant-gardists. Modern classical music had already devised synthesizers capable of the most remarkable sounds. (The exploratory electronic compositions of Karlheinz Stockhausen were typical of classical composers in the
1950s.[2]) The research into electronics was destined to influence all developing
styles of music, especially the increasingly electronic world of rock and jazz.

Fusion keyboard players require four or five synthesizers in addition to the
traditional piano. Electronic organs capable of imitating traditional instruments such as clarinets, violins, and trumpets are commonplace. Along with organs, which are themselves synthesizers, other sound synthesizers create entirely
new sound effects. Using a pianolike keyboard to trigger the new sounds, players manipulate or program synthesizers to exploit endless possibilities.

Examples of the electronic revolution are plentiful, but there are few more
representative than a recording by Return to Forever. "Musicmagic," recorded
in 1976, mixes the traditional sounds of piano, saxophone, trumpets, and trombones with many synthesized sounds. The Mellotron, a keyboard instrument
that allows a musician to selectively replay previously taped sounds, demonstrates the versatility of electronics. In this case, the vocal ensemble (choir) is
composed only of Chick Corea and his wife, Gayle Moran. They recorded a sep-

---

[2]For example, "Gesang der Juenglinge" (1956) is a song for human voice and electronically
generated tones.

arate vocal pitch on a short tape for each key of the Mellotron. When several keys were depressed at once, as on a piano, a vocal ensemble was synthesized. The Mellotron can also reproduce drums, strings, woodwinds, or any other sound. This instrument is only one of the many resources available to the keyboard player. Notice the number of keyboard instruments listed with Chick Corea's and Gayle Moran's names.

LISTENING GUIDE

"Musicmagic"—1976 (Intro. to Jazz Disc 2, Cut 4)

Acoustic piano, Fender Rhodes, Mini Moog, Clavinet, Moog 15, ARP
*   Odessey, vocals—Chick Corea*
Hammond B3 Organ, Polymoog, acoustic piano, vocals—Gayle Moran
Electric bass, piccolo bass, acoustic bass, vocals—Stanley Clarke
Tenor sax, soprano sax, flutes, piccolo—Joe Farrell
Trumpets—John Thomas, James Tinsley
Trombones—Jim Pugh, Harold Garrett
Drums—Gerry Brown

.00	Introduction, acoustic piano.
.09	Melody by flute.
.22	Acoustic piano interlude.
.33	Flute enters.
.41	Short brass shout.
.50	Flute and piano.
1.01	End of 1st idea.
1.11	Low bass note, synthesized melody.
1.20	Brass statement.
1.24	Keyboard melody, noise effects in background.
1.41	Brass statement.
1.48	Synthesized guitar sound (piccolo bass?).
2.09	3rd section: Stringlike sounds.
2.37	New sound (melody).
2.55	Return of guitarlike sound, piccolo bass.
3.27	New section: Fender Rhodes solo, blues figures.
3.36	Mellotron creates a vocal background.
3.49	Vocal duet by Corea and Moran, brass background, funk rhythm with an active bass.
4.10	Vocal continues, Fender Rhodes accompanies.
4.27	Fundamental rhythmic background.

4.40	Hammond B3 solo (Moran).
5.10	The solo quotes the beginning to "Mary Had a Little Lamb."
5.19	Musical quote from J. S. Bach.
5.32	Stop time.
5.41	Fender Rhodes solo, organ accompanies, melody swings, bebop references.
6.32	Brass interlude.
6.38	New sound (solo melody), piccolo bass.
6.49	Brass statement.
6.56	Return of new solo sound, piccolo bass.
7.11	Stop time, solo continues, Fender Rhodes accompanies.
8.02	Brass interlude, keyboard plays in unison.
8.21	Bass fill.
8.26	Drum solo (brass stop time).
8.41	Vocal returns, guitar sound accompanies.
8.57	A mixture of funk and Dixieland textures (collective improvisation), soprano sax in the upper register.
9.10	Soprano sax solo (melody).
9.26	Acoustic piano returns, similar to the introduction.
9.38	Brass statement.
9.44	Flute enters.
10.03	Piano plays alone.
10.14	Tutti ensemble.
10.24	Final section.
10.37	Coda.
10.58	End.

Volume

Increased volume levels were a natural side effect of the adoption of electronic instruments. In the 1950s, rock and roll was the first style to turn almost exclusively to amplified instruments, primarily guitars. It was played loudly to project intensity. Fusion also needed elevated volume to preserve its identity; however, the dynamic contrasts between loud and soft were more pronounced than were generally found in rock. Rock and roll's early performers used volume to cover their lack of technique. Fusion, on the other hand, demanded greater facility from the performers than any preceding rock style. Consequently, volume levels had to be carefully controlled for the musician's technique to be heard. To control the total sound during performances, engineers mixed the many sources into a final, well-balanced product.

There has been much discussion concerning extreme volume, most of it having to do with the physiological damage that can occur to listeners' ears. But the sociological implications have also been examined. The influence of 1960s social upheaval can still be felt. The Woodstock generation used loudness as an identifying statement. The "generation gap" was clearly articulated by musical tastes, the chief element being volume. Nonetheless, the mountain of amplifiers that emitted earshattering sounds also opened a door to new subleties.

From Acoustic to Electric Bass

The emancipation of the jazz string bass from rhythm-keeper to soloist occurred slowly. At first, a bass solo required that the other musicians stop playing or play softly enough for the unamplified bass to be heard. The next step was amplification of the acoustic instrument, and the final step was the development of the electric bass guitar. The last stage was greatly influenced by the rock and funk techniques practiced by soul artists associated with James Brown and Stevie Wonder. There is a marked difference between the acoustic and electric bass. The acoustic bass is, in fact, the same contrabass viol found in classical orchestras. For rhythmic effect, it is usually played **pizzicato** (plucked) in jazz, although it has also been bowed to good effect, notably by Slam Stewart. The bass guitar is not merely a variant of the acoustic bass; it produces a different sound and requires a different technique. Two musicians at the forefront of fusion bass innovation were Stanley Clarke and the brilliant, troubled Jaco Pastorius, who died in 1987 from a beating.

FROM JAZZ TO ROCK TO JAZZ

Over the years, there has always been a clear demarcation between jazz and rock performers. However, with the rise of fusion, jazz critics' attention has been drawn to historically important rock performers. Rock guitarist Eric Clapton, clearly influenced by blues singer B. B. King, personifies the circle of musical evolution from jazz to rock and back to jazz. His blues-oriented playing marked

---

Stanley Clarke (b. 1951)

Stanley Clarke is one of a handful of bassists who play brilliantly on both the acoustic bass and the bass guitar. He was first known for his bass guitar work with rock groups in and around Philadelphia in the 1960s. Most of his fans were unaware of his abilities on the acoustic bass until he became involved in jazz with Horace Silver in 1970. He later worked with Joe Henderson, Pharoah Sanders, and Stan Getz. Since rock enthusiasts are rarely jazz fans, Clarke's following dropped off when he moved from rock to jazz. Not until he joined Chick Corea in Return to Forever in 1976 did he regain his popularity, especially for his acoustic bass playing. His technical displays on both electric and acoustic bass in traditional jazz, funk, and jazz/rock have influenced bassists in both rock and jazz.

Jaco Pastorius (1951–1987)

Standards for aspiring bass players were extended even further by Jaco Pastorius, the virtuoso with Weather Report. His blistering speed and pinpoint control created "Jaco licks," which every young bassist worked to imitate. (Listen to "Teen Town" on Heavy Weather, *by Weather Report [Columbia PC 34418].) Pastorius also introduced the use of other electronic devices, such as tape loops and phase shifting, during live performances to create additional soloistic textures.*

    The correlation between the popularity of certain fusion groups and the popularity of their bass players is not just a coincidence. The bassist in fusion groups is often called on to carry the melodic weight of the ensemble. Before fusion the bassist was forced to solo on an unadorned harmonic progression. With the advent of fusion, the bassist has been freed because keyboard synthesizers are capable of carrying the bass line.

---

rock's heyday. The circle of evolution is also represented by Mike Bloomfield, Paul Butterfield, and Jimi Hendrix. The transition of styles has not been confined to the United States, however; European interest is also widespread. "Electric jazz" groups such as Pork Pie, led by the Danish keyboard player Jasper van't Hof, represent a shift from pure rock to jazz-flavored rock. The shift may not be sufficient to classify these groups as fusion, but it does show the mutual influence of the two styles.

In the United States another musician, Chick Corea, has risen to prominence and influence in the realm of fusion. This keyboard player's career has been similar to Miles Davis's in that he has favored widely varying styles.

CHICK COREA (b. 1941)

Born in Chelsea, Massachusetts, in 1941, Chick began studying classical piano at age four. His father, Armando, is an Italian-American jazz trumpeter and bassist who led his own band during the 1930s and 1940s. Corea's earliest exposure came from his father's collection of 78-rpm records. He first modeled his playing after Horace Silver's; he transcribed onto paper every recorded solo he could find. After Silver, the pianists who had the most influence on Corea were Bud Powell and Bill Evans. While listening to and copying these pianists, he began playing dinner-dance music jobs with his father at country clubs around Boston and Cape Cod.

Before graduating from high school in 1959, Chick was introduced to Latin music by a friend. This single element has played an increasingly important role in Chick's music. He moved to Manhattan the same year to attend Columbia University. Immediately upon his arrival, he went to hear Miles Davis at Birdland. The group featured John Coltrane on tenor sax and Winton Kelly on piano. Inspired, Chick returned to Boston after two months and prepared for an audition at the Juilliard School of Music. At Juilliard, Chick realized he needed training somewhere other than in a classically oriented conservatory, so after two months he dropped out of school to play in several New York Latin/jazz groups. In 1960 he joined the Billy May band and, later, the Warren Covington orchestra. His first major jazz association came in 1962 when he performed in the Latin-flavored Mongo Santamaria band. The experience led to short stints with Willie Bobo, Herbie Mann, Blue Mitchell, and finally in 1966, Stan Getz.

In 1966 he also recorded his first solo album, *Tones for Joan's Bones,* later retitled *Inner Space.* The fact that these were his own compositions added luster to his already growing reputation as a pianist. After backing Sarah Vaughan for a short time in Las Vegas, he was recommended to Miles Davis by drummer Tony Williams. In 1967 he joined one of Miles's legendary quintets and recorded several albums, one being the pivotal *Bitches Brew.* In 1970 Miles moved him from acoustic to electric piano. Chick left Davis after three years to form a group of his own.

Circle

Chick's first group was called Circle and featured bassist Dave Holland (also from Miles's group), drummer Barry Altschul, and reed player Anthony Braxton. There are only two albums available from the group's one-year existence. The music, freely structured and highly dissonant, was influenced by John Coltrane, Ornette Coleman, and Albert Ayler. The time spent working with this group marked the most experimental period of Chick's career. He openly admits that even then he had a strong desire to return to more flowing melodies and harmonies.

Chick became a disciple of L. Ron Hubbard, the controversial writer who advocated a system of personal improvement called Scientology. According to Corea, Scientology was responsible for his change to a musical style that communicated to audiences more effectively. He felt that the music he wrote for Circle did not represent his true feelings, and he wanted to replace it with music that would have something pleasant to say, even to the musically unschooled. This commitment pointed him in a new direction and put him in touch with other musicians. He had taken the first step toward jazz/rock.

Return to Forever

The first composition he wrote in the new style was titled "Return to Forever," which also became the name of his new group. The group featured bassist Stanley Clarke, saxophonist Joe Farrell, and vocalist Flora Purim and percussionist Airto Moreira, a Brazilian husband-and-wife team. Moreira stimulated Chick's growing interest in Latin rhythms and melodies. The music, as represented by the album *Light as a Feather* (Polydor PD 5525), was played on acoustic instruments. In 1973 the group moved to an electric format; major personnel

Photo courtesy of GRP Records

The Chick Corea Elektric Band. *Left to right: Frank Gamble, Eric Marienthal, Chick Corea, John Patitucci, Dave Weckl.*

changes also occurred, with only Stanley Clarke remaining. Drummer Lenny White and guitarist Bill Connors, later replaced by Al DiMeola, helped lead the group toward jazz/rock. The new sound established Return to Forever as a leading instrumental group in both jazz and rock. The addition of keyboard-vocalist Gayle Moran and the return of Joe Farrell on reeds helped to expand the musical textures. The group became very popular and in 1977 was nominated for a Grammy award for the album *Musicmagic.*

Elektric Band

After 1980, when he disbanded Return to Forever, Corea followed several diverse paths, including the study and recording of compositions by Wolfgang Amadeus Mozart. He was not so much searching for his niche as he was indulging his numerous enthusiasms. In 1985 he became convinced that electric instruments drew the largest audiences, so to reach the greatest number of listeners, he organized the Elektric Band. This band consisted of Corea, virtuoso drummer Dave Weckl, and bassist John Patitucci. Corea used a variety of fixed and strap-on, MIDI-interfaced, synthesized keyboards capable of creating virtually any conceivable sound. In 1991, when his cycle of preference swung away from synthesized sound, Corea reconstituted the band's instrumentation and, with the same personnel, called it the Akoustic Band. In 1993 he formed the Elektric Band II with guitarist Mike Miller, bassist Jimmy Earl, and drummer Gary Novak. Then in 1994, he toured with yet another Akoustic Band called Quartet featuring Patitucci, Novak, and saxophonist Bob Berg.

Corea's place in musical history seems assured if his thirty-year record of continued popularity is an indication. He is a complete musician, able to compose, arrange, perform, lead, and, perhaps most important, organize.

WEATHER REPORT: JOE ZAWINUL

Although jazz/rock grew from two directions, to say that jazz became more like rock or rock became more like jazz would be an oversimplification. In reality, the two styles fused into a new concept. Musicians who play jazz/rock are forced to reevaluate their approach to composition and performance. Josef Zawinul and Wayne Shorter, leaders of Weather Report, the group that set the standard for fourteen years, were not young proponents of rock; they both originally performed with mainstream jazz musicians. However, to play jazz/rock, they had to abandon their traditional jazz groups. Zawinul, for example, says he felt a need to try something new. Oddly enough, jazz/rock was developed by musicians with relatively little background in rock; the only member of Weather Report who was well grounded in rock was Jaco Pastorius, the group's bassist from 1976

Joe Zawinul

to 1982. Together, however, Zawinul, Shorter, and Pastorius created the nucleus for one of the most exciting fusion bands.

Weather Report's musical contributions have influenced both rock and jazz. The most stimulating aspect of the group's sound came from the variety of its compositions. Wayne Shorter's pieces written for Miles Davis, "Nefertiti" in particular, display his absorption in angular rhythms and modal sonorities. Zawinul became famous for his writing in the Cannonball Adderley group. When first introduced to electric piano, he wrote "Mercy Mercy Mercy," which won a Grammy award for best instrumental performance in 1967 and was one of Adderley's biggest hits. Zawinul's talent for conceiving synthesized sounds and Shorter's melodic and rhythmic sense set the direction for Weather Report. Later, Jaco Pastorius also began writing, thereby further diversifying their repertoire. His compositions often featured the electric bass as a melodic instrument. With three identifiably talented composers, Weather Report became the most innovative jazz/rock group in America. Of the three composers, Zawinul has been the most prolific. His compositions are conceptually free and are capable of tremendous energy. The rhythmic pulse is most often based upon a driving rock beat. Lyric melodies float above a heavy beat with compelling authority. The solo improvisations naturally follow the same design. The diversity of sound and texture gives depth to each composition as well as to entire albums.

The first album in which all three composer-performers participated was *Heavy Weather* in 1977. It incorporated a well-defined rock performance, "Teen Town," by Pastorius, as well as more jazz-flavored works by Zawinul and Shorter. The album offered a broad cross-section of musical textures and moods. Weather Report's jazz/rock identity had now become well established. Each succeeding album presented new material. Even old jazz standards appeared in totally new settings without upsetting the jazz/rock definition. In the album *Mr. Gone,* three drummers were used: Tony Williams, Steve Gadd, and Peter Erskine.

Two selections from the album *Night Passages* (ARC Columbia JC36793) best show the remarkable diversity this group achieved. The first selection, "Port of Entry," was written by Wayne Shorter and strongly emphasizes soloing by both the tenor sax and the bass. Shorter's solo focuses on a rhythmically punctuated melody. Jaco's lightning solo is built on the rhythm section's double-time patterns. Zawinul also has an interesting solo, but his main role in this performance is to maintain the rhythmic funk patterns with synthesized keyboard effects. The performance has an undeniable rock feeling constructed carefully by the drummer, bass player, and comping keyboards. Listen to the driving rhythm and notice how the energy level peaks at the very end.

LISTENING GUIDE

"Port of Entry"—1980 (Intro. to Jazz Disc 2, Cut 5)

Piano—Joe Zawinul
Saxes—Wayne Shorter
Bass—Jaco Pastorius
Drums—Peter Erskine
Hand drums—Robert Thomas, Jr.

.00	Introduction: Bass plays.
.06	Drums enter; conga drums play against a sitarlike sound (East Indian) in the background.
.24	Melody on the keyboard; the rhythmic pattern suggests Middle Eastern influences.
.38	Dissonant chords in the background.
.48	Sax starts with the melody but quickly moves into a solo; jazz/funk background.
1.30	New synthesized melody; sax plays detached notes, feeding the texture.
1.45	Jazz/funk pattern continues in bass; heavy rock texture.
2.07	The keyboard plays a strong rhythmic riff.
2.22	Stop time played by the entire ensemble.
2.27	Bass solo, accompanied by conga drums and a tambourine; double-time feeling.
2.56	Bass plays melodic patterns in his solo.
3.21	Keyboard enters, also double time; bass continues.
3.38	Vocal shouts and calls in background; the bass continues a very fast pattern.
3.46	Sax enters with the original melody; double time continues.
4.00	Keyboard solo.
4.27	Stop-time effect becomes an ending.
4.37	A musical tag starts with the same double-time texture; ensemble punches lead into another ending.
4.50	End.

Weather Report's Beginning

Weather Report was organized in 1971 after Joe Zawinul left Cannonball Adderley and Wayne Shorter left Miles Davis. The other original members were Miroslav Vitous on bass and Alphonse Mouzon and Airto Moreira playing percussion. Zawinul and Shorter had worked together only once before, in

Weather Report. *Left to right: Joe Zawinul, keyboards; Jaco Pastorius, bass; Wayne Shorter, tenor sax; Manolo Badrena, percussion; Alex Acuna, drums.*

Maynard Ferguson's band in 1959. Drummer Peter Erskine, who played with the group from 1978 to 1982, was also a Ferguson alumnus.

Weather Report's jazz/rock style grew slowly from 1971 until 1973, when rock rhythms, electric bass, and synthesizer carried the scope of the group into a true fusion concept. The use of more sophisticated studio techniques helped to further clarify the ensemble's sound. Although the group's music is widely admired, certain aspects have come under criticism. There have been several unfavorable comments about overdubbing on recordings. *Overdubbing* is the process of recording parts of a performance separately and having an engineer add them together. Zawinul maintains the process is used for clarity only and is not a necessity. Recordings of live concerts seem to bear him out. Because of the limitless possibilities for creating sounds and textures, the group took great care in developing its ensemble arrangements. It included fewer solos and put greater emphasis on creating new ensemble sounds.

By 1974 the group's swing toward jazz/rock was nearly complete. Vitous was replaced by Alphonso Johnson, and reed player Joseph Romano joined the group. The personnel was not stabilized until Jaco Pastorius joined as a partner in 1976. Peter Erskine had sufficient technique to replace two percussionists. Until 1982 additional percussion parts, when needed, were played by one of the other members. In 1982 the group was almost entirely reconstituted, with only Zawinul and Shorter remaining. The drums were taken over by Omar Hakim, the bass by Victor Bailey, and percussion by Jose Rossy. Weather Report, in name, became defunct in 1985 when Shorter decided to branch out elsewhere. Zawinul was the only charter member left. He continued with a group, temporarily called Heavy Weather, experimenting and inventing timbres, scales (fifteen notes per octave), harmonies, and melodies. In the mid-1990s Zawinul's recording and touring band, *Zawinul Syndicate*, consists of drummer Mike Baker, Robert Thomas, Jr., on hand drums and flute, bassist Gerald Veasley, guitarist Randy Bernsen, and, of course, Zawinul on electronic keyboards.

Wayne Shorter (b. 1933)

Wayne Shorter was born in Newark, New Jersey, in 1933. He studied music education for four years at New York University. During his enlistment in the Army, he played with Horace Silver, and when discharged he worked with Maynard Ferguson before joining Art Blakey in 1959. At that time, Shorter became well known as a powerful tenor sax player in the mold of Sonny Rollins and John Coltrane. He stayed with Art Blakey's Jazz Messengers until 1964. During the next six years, he worked for Miles Davis. His compositions, including "E.S.P.," "Footprints," and "Nefertiti," established him as a sophisticated jazz composer. He left Miles Davis in 1970, and one year later joined Zawinul to form Weather Report.

Joe Zawinul (b. 1932)

Zawinul was born in 1932 in Vienna, Austria. In his early youth, he studied at the Vienna Conservatory of Music, and after World War II, he performed with his own trio for the United States military occupation forces in Special Service clubs in France and Germany. He worked with leading bands in Vienna until 1959, when he came to the United States. He worked briefly for Maynard Ferguson, and then after accompanying Dinah Washington for a short time, he joined the Cannonball Adderley quintet. His writing and fluid piano technique helped sustain Adderley's popularity. After ten years with Adderley, he worked with Miles Davis on several albums, the most significant being In a Silent Way. *He wrote the title song for that album and was one of three electric piano players. That recording was followed by* Bitches Brew, *on which Shorter and Zawinul both performed.*

Married for over thirty years, Zawinul and his wife Maxine have three grown sons, one of whom, Ivan, is the sound engineer with the current band.

SUGGESTED LISTENING

Chick Corea: *Now He Sings, Now He Sobs.* Blue Note B21Y-90055.
    Elektric Band. GRP Records GRP-D-9535.
Weather Report: *Heavy Weather.* 1977. Columbia CK-34418.
    Mr. Gone. 1978. Columbia. Jazz Contemporary Masters CK-46869.
Zawinul Syndicate: *Lost Tribes.* Columbia.

Fusion to Crossover

29

Photo by Robert Farber

David Sanborn

As in all stylistic development, definitions change with the appearance of new concepts and, in the case of fusion, with the expansion of the equipment available to musicians. The arena of greatest development in the last few years has been the recording studio. Musicians find new stimulation working in this environment because it is possible to engineer "perfect" performances and to layer sound effects into the finished product with a precision previously unattainable. As a result, the sounds commonly associated with studio recording have become a very important part of the new jazz fusion (also termed *crossover*). It is new in the sense that it differs from the earlier fusion style introduced by Weather Report and Return to Forever.

The differences are described in many ways. The new sound has been called studio jazz or commercial instrumentals, and the similarity to commercial sound tracks and popular songs is obvious. It is not, however, the first time jazz and commercial music have appealed to audiences for the same reason. For example, dancing has frequently been associated with the various jazz styles; in fact, it is a common misconception that to be jazz it must be danceable. The move from swing to bebop, third stream, and free jazz was an attempt, among other motives, to refute such an association. Late fusion, on the other hand, is an unmistakable return to dance rhythms.

ELEMENTS OF CROSSOVER

1. *Studio effects.* The word *commercial* is widely used to describe sounds, styles, and effects that are immediately agreeable to large sections of the populace, where success is measured by monetary return. The term is not necessarily derogatory or demeaning. However, commercial influence on all musics has had significant and not always beneficial effects on the continuance of a style. The pressures of producers and record promoters to increase sales have resulted in the injection of more pop-song sounds into fusion. The mixture has proved to be very popular. The attraction derives from the music's basic timbre and rhythm. Basic instrumentation remains similar to that of the groups Weather Report and Return to Forever; the difference lies in the **effects (signal processing)** used in the recording process. That is not to say that the music is simplified. Dealing with the studio and its many possibilities requires new skills, which many traditional musicians have not practiced. Groups like David Sanborn, Dave Grusin, Kenny G, and Pat Metheny exemplify the new standards being set for the quality of fusion instrumental sounds.

Studio techniques are used to enhance and even alter the sound of instruments, electronic acoustic alike. The same sounds are reproduced in a concert situation by applying the same techniques to the sound amplification system. In the case of David Sanborn, the saxophone is heavily effected electronically to achieve its contemporary sound. Compare his sound with that of Charlie Parker or John Coltrane. Because of this development, saxophonists who wish to perform in this fusion style must acquaint themselves with all the possible electronic treatments and practice using them.

2. *Rhythm-section patterns.* Many of the more commercial-sounding fusion groups replace or supplement the live drummer with electronic rhythm machines. Live drummers themselves are amplified or recorded using effects to emulate drum machines. This sound can readily be found on sound tracks to films and television shows. Use of these machines creates rigidly precise, structured patterns.

3. *MIDI (Musical Instrument Digital Interface).* Not only are drum machines used to create patterns, they may also be tied into electronic keyboards and synthesizers through a computer to supply even more contemporary studiolike sounds. Once a musician plays a part on the drum machine or keyboard, the computer stores the decisions made and, upon command, will replay those decisions on any synthesizer at any speed. Needless to say, there have been many discussions as to whether this music is "real music" or merely "gimmicks."

4. *New melodic structures.* The acoustic instruments, such as the saxophone, still must work within a given pitch range. However, since modern musicians have pushed instrument ranges higher and higher, new realms of intensity and expression are being heard. Synthesized keyboards may be adjusted to almost any range, from very low bass notes to almost imperceptible high notes. During performances, improvisational moments are shared by acoustic instruments when present. The style of the melody lies somewhere between the screaming rock-and-roll sax sound of the 1970s and the highly developed bebop lines of the 1980s. This hybrid style can also be used by guitar and keyboard soloists; however, they borrow melodic structures more commonly associated with contemporary rock and pop-rock. Fusion composers such as Dave Grusin and Bob James disdain the rigid eight-bar AABA format of swing and bebop and write in freer form. "Maputo" by Bob James and David Sanborn (see the Listening Guide) presents an eight-bar A section, a ten-bar B section, in which the critical harmonic resolution occurs in the sixth bar, and a return to the A section. Another good example of these melodies is found in the album *TUTU* by Miles Davis. Notice the quality of the entire rhythm section and the melodies used by the soloists.

5. *Improvisational control.* As in the big bands of the swing era, organization of the musical arrangements takes precedence over freedom of improvisation. In the case of fusion, and especially crossover, the same stricture exists. The amount of improvisation permitted in any given arrangement varies as much as in the arrangements of the swing era. Extended, laboriously developed solos are rare. Instead, quickly developing, short solos are found in the highly arranged pieces of the more commercial fusion groups, paralleling the formulas found in the more commercial swing bands.

6. *Solo heritage.* Modern fusion soloists have drawn inspiration from several sources: bebop, acid rock, rhythm and blues, swing. Frequently the source is difficult to pin down. In the case of Chick Corea and Joe Zawinul, the move was

from traditional jazz to fusion. However, most contemporary groups rely on a blend of soloistic heritages. Controversy comparing swing solos with bebop solos has now been replaced by speculation of lineage. Was a solo born of rock or of traditional jazz (usually bebop)? Guitarists in the mid-1980s bands of Miles Davis and Chick Corea demonstrate a powerful rock lead-guitar heritage. The trend to incorporate multiple soloistic heritages is now desirable. This blend of heritages of rock and jazz solo styles produces some of the most interesting moments of late fusion jazz.

7. *Jazz inflections versus rock inflections.* Screaming rock vocalists creating intensity by distorting their voices and fusion saxophone soloists playing in the upper register are the heart of the fusion experience. It is difficult to determine if these expressive inflections owe their genealogy to jazz or to rock. This is not a dilemma; it merely indicates how completely rock and jazz have fused in this style. Notice the clear similarities between a rock vocalist such as Joe Cocker and the distorted intensity of a solo lead guitar in a rock or fusion group. The same comparison can be made between saxophone soloists in bebop and fusion groups.

There are many examples of crossover groups following independent routes. Pat Metheny, Herbie Hancock, Michael Brecker, David Sanborn, and Kenny G all demonstrate the diversity this style has to offer. The underlying commonality is a reliance on the fusion of jazz, rock, and commercial music.

LISTENING GUIDE

"Maputo"—1986 (Bob James, David Sanborn; Double Vision, WB 253934)

Keyboards and synthesizers—Bob James
Sax—David Sanborn
Bass—Marcus Miller
Drums—Steve Gadd
Guitar—Paul Milton Jackson, Jr.
Rhythm arrangements—Marcus Miller

.00 Fade-in, synthesizer chord.
.05 Bass and rhythm begin, a single harmony.
.22 Keyboard chord punctuations.
.25 Sax enters with a two-beat anticipation to 8-bar section (A); notice the effects.
.33 Synthesized whistle.
.47 10-bar bridge, section (B), changing harmonies especially from the 5th to the 6th bar, thicker accompaniment.

1.11   Return to section (A), notice the accompaniment changes. Descending alto line.

1.33   Repeat of bridge with full accompaniment. String and bass timbres.

1.59   New melodic idea, duet between sax and keyboard.

2.20   Sax solo over extended (A) section.

2.55   Sax figures derivative of bebop.

3.00   Section (B) with highly improvised sax line.

3.12   Slurred scream from sax.

3.26   Keyboard solo with active rhythm and percussion.

3.49   Section (B) with full synthesized string background.

4.08   Sound effects added.

4.12   Sax returns to original melody, notice background effects.

4.34   Section (B).

4.53   Bells, bass lead into the next chorus.

5.00   Repeat of duet passage.

5.20   Sax and keyboard exchange 4-measure statements, then enter a call-response dialogue.

6.24   Fade-out.

6.28   Final screaming glissando from the sax.

MICHAEL BRECKER (b. 1949)

Such dissimilar artists as Frank Sinatra, Frank Zappa, John Lennon, Eric Clapton, Billy Joel, Kazumi Watanabe, Charles Mingus, and dozens of other pop, blues, rock, and jazz musicians for years have been eager to include saxophonist Michael Brecker in their recording sessions. His ensemble playing is impeccable, but it is for his burning, inventive solos that enhance each of the different styles that he is in such demand. Although he plays flute, piano, drums (which he particularly likes), and all the reeds, his principal instrument is the tenor sax, which he plays with full-throated intensity, rarely resorting to the unnatural squawks and squeals favored by some avant-garde musicians. His mastery of the instrument permits him to cover its full range at blazing speed in unexpected intervallic leaps when such playing is called for, or to contribute to a ballad with sensitivity and simplicity.

Michael and his older brother, Randy, an equally sought-after trumpet player, were born and raised in Philadelphia, sons of a piano-playing father. Their early musical training predictably was on the piano, but as they continued through school, each gravitated to the instruments that best permitted him to express himself, and to the instrumentalists who best exemplified his need for

Michael Brecker

expression. Michael credits John Coltrane as his first and most influential inspiration, and Randy names Clifford Brown.

Both boys attended Indiana University, but Michael left after a year to find his fortune in New York City, where he arrived in 1969. He was soon recognized for his virtuosity, and he and Randy, together with drummer Billy Cobham, guitarist John Abercrombie, and bassist Will Lee, formed an adventurous band called Dreams that incorporated jazz inflections with rock rhythms. They were, in fact, at the forefront of fusion. This band made two albums, *Dreams* and *Imagine My Surprise,* both of which are still considered textbook examples of the new form. From 1975 to 1980 the Breckers fronted their own band and recorded six albums. During that time, a Japanese producer heard Michael jamming with vibraphonist Mike Mainieri, keyboardist Warren Bernhardt, drummer Peter Erskine, and bassist Eddie Gomez and asked them to play in Japan; they formalized the group, naming it Steps Ahead. It has been a very successful and durable band and one that probably comes closest to defining the true Michael Brecker in spite of the wide assortment of gigs he has played.

Brecker personifies the modern jazz artist. His musical roots are firmly attached to traditional bebop, but he is intrigued by the possibilities of developing styles. Lately, he has added an EWI (Electronic Wind Instrument) to his arsenal and features it frequently. He also has been playing the synthesizer and writing music. He has been a member of Paul Simon's touring Afro-Brazilian production *The Rhythm of the Saints* and has formed his own touring band as well, but he feels his life is stabilized around his wife, Susan, and daughter, Jessica, and sees no reason his career should not continue at the same pace.

LISTENING GUIDE

"Itsbynne Reel"—1989 (from *Don't Try This at Home;* Intro. to Jazz Disc 2, Cut 6)

Composers—Michael Brecker and Don Grolnick
Tenor sax and Akai EWI—Michael Brecker
Guitar—Mike Stern
Piano—Don Grolnick
Acoustic bass—Charlie Haden
Fretless electric bass—Jeff Andrews
Drums—Jack DeJohnette
Violin—Mark O'Connor

.00	Introduction, solo melody (EWI), hoedown-style melody.
.08	Violin joins the EWI.
.16	Piano pattern is added.
.54	The violin and the EWI become independent, they dialogue back and forth.
2.12	Full rhythm section, drums, bass, and keyboards, extended rock rhythmic patterns. Brecker now plays tenor sax.
2.40	Chordal sounds from the sax and synthesizers.
3.17	Notice the acoustic piano sounds.
3.40	Complex ensemble patterns, drummer accents all ensemble patterns.
4.18	Tenor sax solo (improvised).
4.47	Tenor sax plays rhythms with the ensemble background momentarily.
5.25	Rhythm section maintains a static harmonic texture with varying accents. Brecker builds the melodic line to a climax.
6.11	Climax of solo.
6.20	Return to hoedown theme, violin joins the melody.

6.56   Repeat of theme with slight variations.
7.01   Violin and sax become very soloistic and independent.
7.40   End.

This selection displays the use of a wind controller (Akai EWI) capable of playing any of the settings available to keyboard synthesizers. It is played like a saxophone and is capable of breath accents and articulations. The opening duet that sounds like traditional bluegrass features Brecker on EWI and Mark O'Connor on violin. Mike Stern on guitar is representative of the strong influence of rock soloing styles. All the musicians have virtuoso technique and perform together in a highly improvisational relationship. Their communication is extraordinary and very responsive to the soloist. Their ability to improvise large architectural solos is truly remarkable. The rhythmic patterns supporting the texture are a hybrid of rock and jazz elements. The fusion of the two styles is complete.

Photo by Carl Studna

Yellowjackets. *Left to right: Jimmy Haslip, William Kennedy, Russell Ferrante, Bob Mintzer.*

Yellowjackets

The nucleus of the group came into existence in the late 1970s as the rhythm section of guitarist Robben Ford's blues band: bassist Jimmy Haslip, keyboardist Russell Ferrante, and drummer Ricky Lawson. In 1980 the trio persuaded Ford to join them on an instrumental demo tape, and the results were so pleasing that Warner Brothers Records signed them to a contract. Their first album, Yellowjackets, *released in 1981, found wide acceptance, and the name became firmly established.*

Robben Ford played with the group for two years, but his primary interest was in being a soloist and he left. The group disbanded temporarily in 1982, but when they discovered that their second album, Mirage à Trois, *had been nominated for a Grammy, they decided to reform but with a somewhat different sound. Alto saxophonist Marc Russo came on board in 1982, and drummer Will Kennedy replaced Lawson in 1986. The quartet has achieved great success, having produced nine albums and received two Grammys, even though their style defies categorization. They do not totally reject the word* fusion, *although they feel it to be too much a 1970s term, but* rhythm and jazz *does not quite fit, either. They are serious about perpetuating jazz but are willing to pursue it along diverse branches. They admire the works of Billy Strayhorn as well as those of Keith Jarrett, the almost avant-garde pianist; however, most of their recorded tunes are the compositions of Ferrante and the others. It is a democratic organization that accepts input from all its members.*

Group names seem to have become the vogue in the fusion era: Acoustic Alchemy, Uncle Festive, Sea Wind, and so on. One advantage of this is the preservation of group identity irrespective of personnel turnover, but it is those groups whose membership has remained relatively stable that have had the greatest success. Testimony to this can be found in Spyro Gyra, four of whose seven members—altoist Jay Beckenstein, keyboardist Tom Schuman, vibraphonist Dave Samuels, and drummer Richie Morales—have been together for fifteen years or more. Stability of the cadre of Ferrante, Haslip, and Kennedy is central to the longevity of Yellowjackets; however, infusion of new talent as a stimulus to further development continues by the acquisition of saxophonist Bob Mintzer in 1991 following the departure of Marc Russo in 1990.

The expanding multimedia world of music reaches every active style of jazz today. Vocal jazz has incorporated many of the new electronic sounds and recording techniques that we have seen in the music of Sanborn and Brecker. The New York Voices is a high-energy vocal group much like Manhattan Transfer. There is, however, a strong instrumental influence in the group because of the writings of Darmon Meader, who plays sax and sings in the group. The background material is as vital as the singing. The arrangements are balanced and complete.

LISTENING GUIDE

"Round Midnight"—1989 (Intro. to Jazz Disc 2, Cut 7)

Arranger—Darmon Meader
Vocals—Peter Eldridge, Kim Nazarian, Sara Krieger, Darmon Meader,
  Caprice Fox
Piano—John Werking
Bass—Chuck Bergeron
Drums—Peter Grant

.00 Piano introduction, melodically angular, very free rhythmically.
.53 Vocal tutti, *a cappella*, dissonant thick chords; notice the contrasting unison lines.
1.49 Rhythm section enters, piano fills during the solo vocal line.
2.24 Tutti vocal again with lush chords.
2.49 Big-band-like texture, solo voice accompanied by ensemble punches from the other singers.
2.58 Return to rhythm section and vocal solo but with another vocalist.
3.31 Ensemble vocal shouts, rhythm section is more aggressive. A short drum solo leads into the next section.
3.43 Swing rhythm patterns, walking bass, ride cymbal, vocal improvisation by Darmon Meader.
4.24 Double-time bebop improvisation.
4.44 Bass solo, sparse piano chords, drum continues a swing pattern, with kicks.
5.44 Vocal soli using scat syllables.
5.58 Double-time scat, unison.
6.16 New texture, more independence between voices rhythmically.
6.42 Return to the text.
7.13 Slower ballad texture (suddenly), like the beginning.
7.41 *A cappella*, ensemble.
7.53 Ending section, in time. Vocal improvisation above the other voices.
8.28 End.

Notice how the voices work in ensemble textures such as tutti, soli, and shouts, which imitate the sounds heard in big bands. In this arrangement, the vocalists are asked to deal with very difficult harmonies and fast bebop melodies, creating interesting and colorful textures and sonorities. The vocal traditions of both rock and jazz are brought to a high level of refinement and virtuosity in this group and others like it.

Photo courtesy of GRP Records

The New York Voices. *Left to right: Sara Krieger, Peter Eldrige, Kim Nazarian, Darmon Meader, Caprice Fox.*

SUGGESTED LISTENING

Miles Davis: *TUTU*. Warner Bros. WB 25490-2.

Herbie Hancock: *Sound System*. Columbia CK-39478.

Pat Metheny: *Still Life (Talking)*. Geffen 24145-2.

David Sanborn: *Double Vision*. Bob James and David Sanborn. Warner Bros. WB 25393-2.

Yellowjackets: *Four Corners*. MCA Records MCAD 5994.

Epilogue
Jazz in Action

In the preceding chapters, we have seen jazz styles develop in many directions. There should be a single thread in all of these styles relating them to an overall definition of jazz. However, jazz resists definition because the elements of its founding music have been scattered and absorbed by so many other musical styles. There are some who believe that only the kind of music played in New Orleans between 1900 and 1918 is jazz; everything else is a hybrid needing another name. Others find jazz in anything with a beat, a lick, an improvised solo, or some blued notes. We have seen in both fusion and free jazz the incorporation of other musical styles; in the case of fusion, a new jazz/rock style developed, and in the case of free jazz, there are times when little or no distinction can be made between it and avant-garde classical music.

The crux is probably that *jazz* is a noun intended to describe a style, one that can be thought of as constantly changing or, conversely, as something frozen in time. If it is supposed to define a product, then that product is at once so big and so varied that everyone and no one is an expert. Even to some jazz musicians, such as Miles Davis and Anthony Braxton, the word has either lost its meaning or, through distasteful association, become anathema. On the other hand, maybe Duke Ellington was correct in predicting that eventually there will be no musical styles, only music.

The authors feel that the single, elusive thread is most probably that shared experience of jazz musicians and listeners: In the absence of a better word, call it "swing." Jazz musicians always have swung and always will swing, not in the literal sense, but in the sense that they create sounds that communicate and stimulate feelings. It follows that jazz is any music that has this essence of "swing."

Jazz is everywhere. Jazz styles can be seen and heard in television and radio commercials, in film and theater music, and even in new gospel music. It is taught in schools and used as therapy. It has risen from an object of contempt and ridicule to one of esteem.

What is the future of jazz? Will it be a new fusion with new restrictions or a new sound with new instruments? Historians cannot predict its future and should not try; it is the musicians who will continue to lead jazz into areas they feel are expressive and real and, above all, still jazz.

Regardless of anyone's position on the future of jazz, the history of jazz continues to be written by many excellent jazz musicians active today. The following are a few we encourage you to listen to.

Photo by Richard Laird

John Abercrombie

John Abercrombie   A native of Connecticut, guitarist John Abercrombie graduated from the Berklee School of Music in Boston in the mid-sixties. He usually plays as leader or sideman in a trio or small group consisting of drums and bass or, preferably, the Hammond B-3 organ. Sometimes a saxophone is added. Abercrombie became enamored of the guitar synthesizer in the mid-eighties but returned to the pure electric instrument about 1990. Listen to: *Speak of the Devil* (ECM 21511).

Photo by Tom Lau

Jane Ira Bloom

    Jane Ira Bloom   One of the most highly regarded jazz soprano saxophonists in the world, Jane Ira Bloom began her musical development on piano. Nearing completion of her studies at the Yale School of Music in the mid-seventies, she found that the soprano sax best expresses her inner voice. She has developed a "live electronics" method, the extemporaneous selection of various electronic effects by use of a foot pedal or by moving the bell of her instrument past microphones. Her object is only to augment her personal sound, not falsify it with gadgetry. She has applied this concept to her orchestrations for symphony orchestras, wind ensembles, and small jazz groups. Listen to: *Art and Aviation* (Arabesque AJ-0105).

Brian Lynch

Brian Lynch   Trumpeter Brian Lynch, a 1980 graduate of the Wisconsin Conservatory of Music, has earned soloistic, compositional, and organizational credentials with the elite of mainstream and Latin jazz. He has played in the bands of Charles McPherson, Horace Silver, Toshiko Akiyoshi, Art Blakey, Benny Golson, Phil Woods, David "Fathead" Newman, Jim Snidero, Mark Murphy, Mel Lewis, George Russell, Paul Simon, and the Latin giants Angel Canales and Eddie Palmieri. He has led and recorded with his own band. Critics such as Leonard Feather and Scott Yanow have placed him among the top rank of all jazz trumpeters of the nineties. Listen to: *Back Room Blues* (Criss Cross 1041) and *Palmas* (Electra/Nonesuch).

Photo by Nana Watanabe. Courtesy of Sony Music.

Marcus Roberts

Marcus Roberts Marthaniel (Marcus) Roberts, born in Jacksonville, Florida, in 1963, has been blind since the age of four. He began piano studies when he was eight and graduated from the University of Tallahassee with a music degree. While winning the competition at the annual convention of the Association of Jazz Educators in 1982, he met Ellis Marsalis. Later, he met Wynton Marsalis, who hired him as band pianist in 1985. He remained for more than six years. When Wynton was appointed the New York Lincoln Center Jazz series director, he made Marcus music director as well as pianist in the jazz orchestra. Roberts is comfortable with, and has recorded, both classical and jazz standard compositions. Listen to: *Alone with Three Giants* (Novus 63130-2).

Photo by Hans Neleman. Courtesy of Sony Music.

Terence Blanchard

Terence Blanchard   Trumpeter Terence Blanchard is another New Orleans native in the line of descent from Ellis Marsalis through Art Blakey to a position of esteem in his own right. He began studying classical piano at his father's urging but switched to trumpet in grade school. He began his apprenticeship with the Lionel Hampton band while he was still a scholarship student at Rutgers. He joined the Blakey band in the mid-eighties and remained for four years. In the late eighties, Blanchard began writing scores for film director Spike Lee, doing the music for *Malcolm X, Do the Right Thing, Mo' Better Blues, Assault at West Point,* and *Crooklyn.* Listen to: *Terence Blanchard* (Columbia 47354).

Sherrie Maricle

    Sherrie Maricle Women jazz instrumentalists in the past have been primarily pianists, but recently names like trumpeters Stacy Rowles and Rebecca Coupe Franks, saxophonists Jane Ira Bloom and Jane Bunnett, and percussionists Terri Lyne Carrington and Cindy Blackman have become recognized as first-class musicians. Drummer Sherrie Maricle is certainly one of the best, not only as an instrumentalist, but also as a composer. She has played with the Virginia Symphony, the New Jersey Symphony, and the Palm Beach Symphony, but also with Bucky Pizzarelli, Dizzy Gillespie, Lionel Hampton, and Clark Terry. She is the driving force behind a superior fifteen-piece all-woman jazz band called Diva, No Man's Band, which not only swings as an ensemble but also has a number of spectacular soloists. Listen to: *Something's Coming* (PSCD 1216) and *Cookin' on All Burners* (Stash ST-CD 24).

Photo by Michael Tighe

Michael Wolff

Michael Wolff   By age twenty, Michael Wolff had already toured the world with vibist Cal Tjader, played piano in the Jazz/Brazilian group Fingers with Airto Moreira and Flora Purim, and become the feature pianist for the Cannonball Adderley Quintet. He went on to tour with other leading jazz musicians, such as Sonny Rollins, Jean-Luc Ponty, and the Thad Jones/Mel Lewis Orchestra. For five years, Michael was the pianist-arranger for Nancy Wilson. During that period, he met the comedian Arsenio Hall, who was Nancy's opening act for a short time; that meeting led to Michael's becoming the musical director of the Arsenio Hall Show for five and one-half years. Michael is a talented pianist and composer with a developing personal style. Listen to *Jumpstart* on the Evidence Music label. He is joined by Christian McBride on bass and Tony Williams on drums.

An Essay on Jazz
and the Creative Spirit

Without appearing pretentious and for the purpose of discussion, we have undertaken the responsibility of exposing various concerns every creative individual encounters. These concerns are especially intense during the process of learning to improvise jazz. It is the purpose of this discussion to investigate without the need to espouse concrete conclusions. The ideas expressed here have been collected from talking to music historians and critics, reading biographical depictions of the creative act, talking to the musicians themselves, and, finally, listening, playing, and listening.

We hope that this discussion will be a springboard to new avenues of expression while you struggle with the creative process. Whether you are a virtuoso or a dilettante, the joy of creativity is an important personal goal in playing music.

THE INTUITIVE LEAP

There has been considerable discussion of right-brain and left-brain activity and how a person's dominant side will not only influence but also shape the manner in which a person perceives himself or herself and the world. To begin a creative act, there must be a nominal act of faith so that the first note can be played, listened to, and evaluated. This intuitive leap provides the forward thrust necessary to begin any project laden with personal expression.

Intellect usually provides the formal structure of what could, should, or may happen. However, one's factual intellect (left brain?) can prove to be the biggest obstacle to creativity and especially to improvisation. Once critical skills are developed in a musician, a fear develops that one's own product may not live up to self-imposed standards. This position of inactivity was cleverly labeled "musical constipation." The intuitive leap is that act of faith in which the process of improvisation alone is worth the effort and one's own or anyone else's critical perceptions will not inhibit that creativity.

CREATING AND RECREATING

In a world where doing anything correctly is usually the goal, it is often difficult to pursue what is different. In fact, it is considerably more difficult to believe in something that is a little different from the standard than it is to insist on an expression that is radically different. The real issue is comparison with the past, especially historical expressions that the literary community has canonized. In the difficult world of improvisation, the images of jazz greats loom above and around us. Their expressions have been reviewed, analyzed, categorized, and transcribed. The result is that no mere mortal, especially a contemporary one, could ever experience like genius. The musical phobia is stroked once more.

It is true that recreating a style in the manner of a jazz great can enliven a feeling of sharing common creative goals. The danger arises when the comparison forces the performer to be "as good as" or "just like" or "as inspired as" rather than showing a unique personality that should defy comparison.

The role of creating while playing another performer's music is naturally diminished and to many musicians becomes frustrating. However, all music, jazz included, borrows from tradition and is not ever totally new. Jazz improvisation is not different from other forms of improvisation found in the vast musical heritage. The need to be expressively unique has been the goal of all performing musicians. Why, then, should anyone want to perform a Beethoven concerto again and again? Even the moments of improvisation in the cadenzas have been reduced to frozen notation. The soloist can, however, add interpretive gestures to the music, personalizing the performance.

In the case of classical music, the argument is not really one of creativity versus recreativity. The argument usually centers on the amount of personal freedom for the soloist. If this were not true, any great recording should meet all our needs.

SHOULD ONE STOP IMITATING AND, IF SO, WHEN?

We often sing along with our favorite recorded performances. It is uplifting. They inspire and enlighten those of us who can understand what the musicians are doing, but we are usually limited by technical comparisons. Although images of possibility help drive us to greater heights, the problem still exists: We feel that we must continue to imitate until our technique is sufficient to allow us equal means of expression, until we or someone else deems us "talented" or of comparable worth. Once we have attained this level, we believe, we will be accepted by whomever to perform for the masses of talented listeners. This also assumes that we must perform for others to be successful. It is hoped, however, that any great performance imparts to the listener a feeling that the musician would have been as productive artistically with or without an audience.

With a certain feeling of guilt, individuals pass up opportunities to go to concerts by great performers in order to have a jam session with "ungreat performers." Should there be any hesitation in telling musical colleagues that it is more enjoyable to "make mistakes with musical friends than to attend a promising concert of established greats"? Comparing musical perceptions or abilities is futile and usually destructive to creative tendencies; indeed, there is a unique enjoyment musicians feel when actively exercising their expressive skills with others. These experiences are usually rich, regardless of style, especially when musicians play with other listening and expressive musicians. Such experiences would naturally be coined "collective creativity."

CREATIVITY AT RISK

Musicians must create within the bounds of tradition to communicate to other musicians. They are still free to reorder, restructure, and invent musical material that speaks directly from their personal skills and expression. Pressures from historians, critics, friends, and tradition often become the greatest influences on the creative act. Nevertheless, jazz history has been sprinkled by personalities willing to experiment and challenge the "obvious direction" of jazz, leaving a legacy of creativity and expression for all students of jazz and the arts to witness. In looking at and listening to these individuals, we must constantly be aware that the creative act is free to all, not to be imitated, but to be shared. Creativity is at risk only when external pressures dominate the individual rather than stimulating skillfully executed expressions.

Appendix A
The Elements of Music
for the Nonmusician

The major elements of music are rhythm, melody, and harmony. To study jazz—or any other kind of music—one needs to recognize these elements and their relationships to one another.

RHYTHM

Rhythm is the heartbeat of music. It is the organization of time, the regularly recurring pulses or beats that are in turn arranged into regularly recurring groups usually consisting of multiples of two or three pulses. Organization within the groups determines meter, and the rate at which the pulses proceed determines the tempo.

The groupings are created by adding **accents**—that is, by placing emphasis on certain beats. For example, most dance music consists of groups of four beats with an accent on the first beat. Each group is called a **measure.** Measures can be made up of two, three, four, or any number of fundamental beats, but rarely are there more than twelve beats in a measure. A simple dance pattern can be created by clapping:

CLAP-clap-clap-clap, -CLAP-clap-clap-clap

The first clap should be louder (accented) than the following three, and the interval between claps should be uniform.

The accents define the groupings and give character to what would otherwise be a colorless ongoing beat. The term for such groupings is **meter.** The meter is indicated on written music by a **time signature,** such as 4/4, 3/4, and 2/4. This fraction tells the musician two things: In 4/4, for example, the upper 4 indicates the number of beats per measure, and the lower 4 indicates the kind of note each beat represents, in this case a quarter note (note values will be explained later in this appendix). In other words, there are four quarter notes per measure. Meter is the organization of rhythm, and rhythm is the foundation on which the other two major elements of music, melody and harmony, are constructed.

TEMPO

Tempo is the speed of the basic beat. Classical composers specify tempo with Italian words that mean fast, slow, quick, very slow, and so forth, but jazz composers usually specify tempo in beats per minute. Thus, a composition with a tempo of 120 would have two beats per second.

MELODY

A melody is a series of notes that progress in a logical manner. A melody may be a simple, easily remembered tune, such as "Row, Row, Row Your Boat," or a long, complex aria, such as those in Bach's B Minor Mass. Melodies can convey emotions such as joy, sadness, excitement, and pride; or they can be abstract and appeal to the intellect; some may be incomprehensible to all but a few. All melodies, however, share the quality of completeness. Sing "Row, Row, Row Your Boat." The melody is in two large **phrases.**

> Row, row, row your boat, gently down the stream,
> Merrily, merrily, merrily, merrily, life is but a dream.

Notice how the melody ascends and descends in pitch, creating a feeling of completion.

PHRASES

Musical phrases are similar to grammatical sentences in that they make complete statements. Written sentences end with a period, signifying a pause, just as spoken sentences are followed by a pause. Composers try to write melodies in phrases that flow in a series of curves much like the rising or falling vocal inflections heard at the ends of questions and answers. Each phrase ends with a sequence of notes that signals an approaching pause. This sequence of notes is called a **cadence.** Composers often follow a phrase that has a rising cadence by one that has a falling cadence; this creates a kind of question-and-answer effect. The two phrases in "Row, Row, Row Your Boat" clearly show the question-and-answer effect.

"Row, Row, Row Your Boat" is a *tuneful* melody because it contains a sequence of notes in a familiar scale: Do, Re, Mi, Fa, Sol, La, Ti, Do. Melodies do not have to be tuneful in the ordinary sense to be musically valid. A melody that proceeds from note to note in unexpected leaps and twists will be *angular,* not tuneful. All melodies move horizontally (from left to right on a page of music)—that is, one note follows another in time until the musical thought has been stated.

HARMONY

Three or more different notes that are played at the same time create **chords** (also called **harmonies**). The flowing of one chord (or harmony) into another creates a forward motion in the music. People from Western cultures regard certain note combinations as pleasing and restful, or **consonant,** and other combinations as discordant, or **dissonant.** Composers use chords in support of their melodies to add richness, increase texture, and reinforce mood. They employ discordant harmonies when they want to build tension, and pleasing harmonies to create tranquility or to resolve tension.

TEXTURE

Musically, the word **texture** signifies thickness or thinness. Thickness could be characterized by a fast-moving melody, agitated rhythm, and quickly changing chords of many notes and ranges. A thin texture might be produced by a single instrument playing with no accompaniment. A thin texture can also be created by reducing or slowing down the musical activity.

Musical composition can be thought of in structural terms. As the melody winds along horizontally, the vertically constructed chords move with it, changing when necessary to support the notes of the melody or to control the degree of tension. The changing chords that occur during a composition are called chord or harmonic **progressions.**

THE SYMBOLS OF MUSIC

The written symbols for musical notes, scales, rhythms, meter, and harmony form a balanced system of musical notation. The Western European notational system that developed over the centuries is now generally accepted throughout most of the world. To perform all styles of music, a musician must be able to recognize specific notes and rhythms. All notes or pitches are named and have a specific place on the familiar five-line **staff** (see Figure A1). Each line and each space between lines represents one unchanging note, and each has a letter name from A to G.

A composer can add any number of **ledger lines** (short horizontal lines like the one in Figure A2) above and below the staff to designate the higher and lower pitches. Ledger lines are extensions of the same lettering sequence. In addition to ledger lines, it is customary for composers to use staffs in two **clefs.** The staff in Figure A1 is in the treble clef—identified by the sign 𝄞 —and is

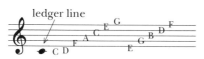

Figure A1. The staff and notes (treble clef)

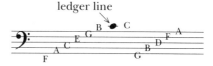

Figure A2. The bass clef

used for high instruments. The staff in Figure A2 is the bass clef (𝄢) and is used for low instruments. The bass and treble clefs are separated by only one ledger line—hence the term *middle C.*

Key Signature

The notes of the major scale—Do, Re, Mi, Fa, Sol, La, Ti, Do—are not equally spaced in pitch (specific tone). The change in pitch is only half as much between Mi and Fa and between Ti and Do as it is between all the others. This arrangement makes the first and last notes of a scale (which are the same note an octave apart) sound more stable and gives the key its name. When composers write in any key but C, they have to indicate by a symbol on the staff the notes that must be played a half step higher or lower to fit into the key. To lower a note a half step, composers write the symbol for a **flat** (♭) immediately in front of the note. To raise it a half step, they write a **sharp** (♯). The sharps or the flats needed for a particular key are written on the staff at the beginning of the composition. This is called the **key signature.** Figure A3 shows the signature for the key of D in the treble clef with a 4/4 time signature.

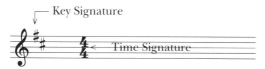

Figure A3. Key signature and time signature

If composers want to flat or sharp a pitch later in the composition, they place the appropriate symbol in front of that note. To cancel a sharp or a flat, they place a **natural** (♮) in front of the note.

Scale

The sequence Do, Re, Mi, Fa, Sol, La, Ti, Do is the familiar major scale. By changing the distance between notes, composers can construct different scales; for example, by lowering Mi, La, and Ti one half step each, they can create a minor scale.

An **octave,** the distance from one Do to the next Do, represents the closest relationship two notes can have. Compare it to colors in the spectrum. Suppose the bottom Do (a very low bass note) is a large yellow circle. Re, Mi, and so on are circles of red, purple, blue, and green. The next higher Do would then be another yellow circle, but only half the size of the first. If the progression is continued, the circles will get smaller and smaller until they become too small to see, just as pitches will become too high to hear. Each succeeding yellow circle represents the separation of an octave. Purple to purple, green to green, and so on, are, naturally, also octaves.

Notation

Note symbols tell the musician two things: *what* pitch (note) to sing or play, and *how long* each pitch should last. Duration is designated by the shape of the symbol. Whole notes (o) last four beats—in other words, the whole measure. Half notes (♩) last two beats; quarter notes (♩) one beat; eighth notes (♪) half a beat, and so on, through sixteenth, thirty-second, and sixty-fourth notes.
A **triplet** (♪♪♪) requires the playing of three notes in the time span of one beat.

The pauses between notes are not left to chance, either. Silent moments are called **rests** and are written into the music just as pitches are. A whole-note rest (▬) lasts four beats, a half-note rest (▬) lasts two beats, and so on.

Musical notation is logical and mathematically precise. Figure A4 presents the most common note and rest values.

Chords

A chord is sounded when three or more notes in a scale are played at once. The most basic harmony is created by a chord consisting of the first note of a scale, Do; the third note, Mi; and the fifth note, Sol. The kinds of chords, major

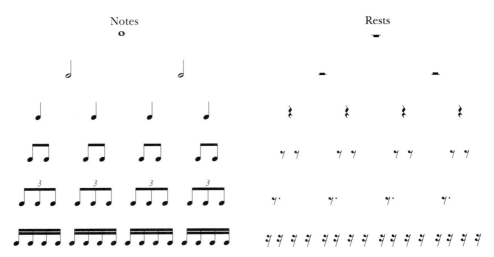

Figure A4. Note and rest values

or minor, depend on the specific distance between each two notes of the chord. These distances are referred to as **intervals.** In addition to major and minor chords, there are augmented and diminished chords. All these chords are built upon three fundamental notes.

Jazz musicians use a shorthand notation for common chords (Figure A5). In addition to writing these notes on a staff, they also use letter symbols.

When more than three notes are used in a chord, a number is added after the letter name of the chord—for example, C^7, $F\#^9$, $E\flat^7$. This number represents the distance (interval) from the bottom note of the chord up to the additional note.

Finally, if you use the basic information just discussed, Figure A6 should have some meaning.

The song is "Row, Row, Row Your Boat." 4/4 meter is used so often it is called *common time.* It is often shown on the staff as in Figure A7. As an exercise, sing the melody first, using the familiar words of the song, and then try it using the syllables Do, Re, Mi for each pitch. Identify the note values and notice where the chords change.

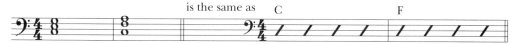

Figure A5. Shorthand notation for chords

Figure A6.

Figure A7. Common time (4/4)

Appendix B
The Elements of Jazz

Many aspects of jazz are neither clearly defined nor adequately represented by standard musical notation. In the early days of jazz, aspiring young performers learned by listening intently to older professionals and imitating what they heard. It was quite common for a young player to develop into a leading performer without being able to read a note of music. However, as jazz became more and more complex, composers and musicians adopted the Western European system of musical notation. Since traditional notation could not completely capture all the individual qualities of this kind of folk expression, jazz musicians invented a jargon to compensate for notation's shortcomings.

SWING AND LAY BACK

Compare a traditional rendition of a simple melody with one based on a jazz concept. When a performer plays exactly what is written, it sounds "square"— that is, stilted and uninteresting. Look at the melody written in Figure B1.

Notice how the eighth notes divide each beat exactly in half and the quarter notes come directly on the beat. A very literal performance would sound mechanical and lifeless. Jazz musicians would flavor this tune in two ways: They would *swing* it (Figure B2) and *lay back* (Figure B3).

In Figure B2, the treatment of the eighth notes imparts a lilting, swinging feel to that time-honored schoolyard taunt, "Suzy Has a Boyfriend." The notation closely approximates the way jazz musicians would interpret the basic melody. The triplets stretch out the first note of each group and reduce the following note. Most of the big bands of the 1930s and 1940s swung this way or with the variation shown in Figure B3.

Musicians lay back when they purposely delay notes so that they are slightly

Figure B1. A straight melody

Figure B2. A swing melody

Figure B3. The lay-back effect in a melody

behind the beat. Laying back creates the impression of relaxation. An entire band, with the exception of the basic rhythm instruments (string bass, left hand of the piano, and hi-hat cymbal of the drums) may lay back, and the amount varies from band to band. Lay back is not always used, however. Fast (often called *up-tempo*) numbers do not lend themselves to it as readily as slow, easy swing tunes. It is an effective device in the hands of a mature band in which all the musicians lay back equally while the rhythm section maintains the beat.

The feelings of lay back and swing personalize the jazz sound. Using these techniques, jazz musicians create a sense of spontaneity, which is the essence of the jazz feeling. The final step toward true spontaneity comes when musicians invent melodies and accompaniments while playing. Such spontaneous playing requires that every musician listen carefully to the other performers.

Every aspect of musical performance depends heavily on a musician's ability to listen. Classical musicians must be constantly listening to their own sound and comparing it with that of others in the orchestra to be certain their **intonation** (accuracy of pitch), **dynamics** (volume), and rhythm conform to the group and to the requirements of the conductor. In even greater measure, jazz musicians must listen to others to be compatible, to hear ideas being germinated, to feed those ideas to the other musicians, and to contribute new ideas.

IMPROVISATION

Musicians improvise when they create new music during a performance. An established composition with a prearranged chord (or harmonic) *progression* serves as the foundation for each improvisation. The harmonic progression dic-

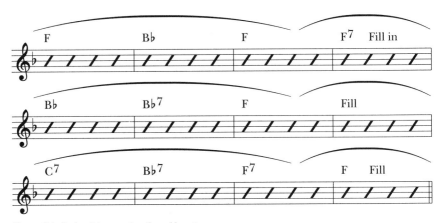

Figure B4. A chord progression for a blues tune

tates which notes the musician may use at any one time. The freedom to impro-vise also carries the responsibility of avoiding wrong notes. Many competent musicians find this responsibility too intimidating; and even successful impro-visers, once they have developed a pleasing new melody, will, rather than hazard another new one, leave it unchanged in subsequent performances. Ideally, im-provisation should go beyond mere technical compliance with the harmonic structure. The solo should convey a mood or a message that expresses the mu-sician's interpretation of the song. Although a jazz player may repeat a success-ful solo, he is free to make a fresh, new statement out of it by modifying the phrasing and accentuation at each playing. Every improvised solo thus becomes a new composition.

One can best illustrate how the various elements of jazz go together by building up a simple blues tune. The example in Figure B4 contains twelve mea-sures of 4/4 meter; each measure has one chord, which is sometimes carried over to the next measure.

At the end of the twelfth measure, the musicians would start over again at the beginning (each twelve measures is called a *chorus*). As the musicians im-provise over the same progression of chords, they are then able to anticipate the harmonic pattern. With the upcoming harmonies already fixed, they are then free to improvise melodies on the spot while playing. Figure B5 adds a melody to the chord progression of Figure B4.

There are actually thirteen measures in Figure B5. At the end of the twelfth measure, there is a double bar with two dots before it. This "repeat" sign tells the musician to go back to the beginning and continue playing. The twelfth measure also has ⌐1.   ⌐ above it, meaning "first ending." When the mu-sicians play the chorus for the second time, they go from the end of the eleventh measure right to the thirteenth, which has ⌐2.   ⌐ above it, meaning sec-ond ending. This is the final **cadence,** a sequence of notes that indicates the end of a phrase.

Figure B5. A head arrangement

The notation in Figure B5 contains all the essential elements that would enable a group of musicians to play the tune: meter, melody, and harmony. This is called a **head** arrangement, and it is often all the music (if it is written down at all) that a performer has to work from. The head itself may last only fifteen to thirty seconds, whereas the whole composition lasts as long as the performers want to continue improvising on the given progression of chords. Figure B6 shows the notation for a performance of the same blues tune with one improvised chorus by the saxophone. The performers play the head first, then the saxophonist plays a solo, and finally the performers return to the head. The number of choruses each performer takes may vary greatly. If there are several players and each is moved to take a solo, the performance could be quite long.

THE RHYTHM SECTION

Three or four musicians in the background support the soloist. These instrumentalists, referred to as the **rhythm section,** commonly use the same group of instruments: drums, bass, piano, and/or guitar. Each performer has a distinct function in establishing harmonic and rhythmic support for the soloist. The drummer maintains a constant pulse while adding color through numerous sounds made by instruments such as cymbals, tom-toms, and bells. The drummer also supports changes of intensity and excitement through various levels of activity, and helps punctuate the melody. The bass player helps generate the metric pulse while furnishing the fundamental harmonic progression. The bassist can also change the texture by means of various melodic and rhythmic devices such as scale patterns, rock-and-roll patterns, and Latin beats. The keyboard or guitar player supports these stylistic shifts while playing chords in

Figure B6. An expanded head arrangement

rhythmic patterns, a technique called **comping.** These chords increase the activity (thickening the texture) behind the soloist. When the pianist plays a solo, he plays a melody with his right hand while he comps with his left; in this way, the pianist supplies the background for his own solo. All the members of the rhythm section *comp*lement or ac*comp*any the soloist at one time or another. Musicians use comping to create moods in everything they play—from soft, pretty ballads to intensely active swing tunes. The rhythm section, therefore,

Figure B6 (cont.)

generates the stylistic atmosphere that feeds the soloist ideas, and provides the basic rhythmic and harmonic foundation. No one member is entirely responsible for the harmonic or rhythmic development; the more sophisticated the rhythm section, the more evenly distributed and integrated are their contributions.

Most stylistic settings, such as those for swing, rock, and Latin music, are not notated any more fully than most head arrangements. The musician must

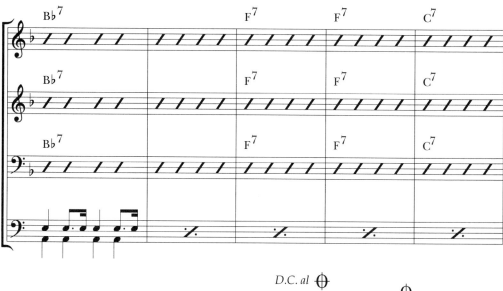

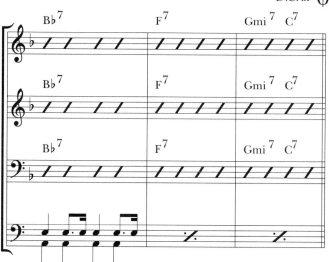

Figure B6 (cont.)

convert such brief outlines into living performances. The bass player and the pianist may be given only a page with the harmonic progression written down. The drummer may be told only which style to play. The melody that the soloist sees looks much the same for all three styles, but the performance would differ in each case. The soloist need be told only that it is a rock, medium swing, or basic Latin tune. The rhythmic patterns that make up the melodic line sometimes help determine the style. The veteran performer recognizes these groupings

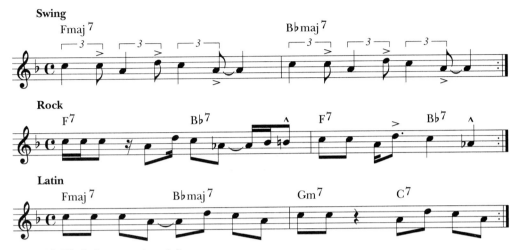

Figure B7. Rhythmic patterns in melodies

and plays accordingly. The rhythms shown in Figure B7 reflect these distinctions; however, even these examples would sound stiff if they were performed exactly as written.

Each style, though similar in notation, differs in jazz feeling. Notice the *accents* in the swing notation (above the second, fourth, and sixth notes) in Figure B7. These notes are on the *offbeat,* meaning that they fall between the normally accented beats. *Syncopation* is the deliberate placement of accents on the weak spots of the beat (when a foot tapper's toe is in the air) or on unaccented beats; it also can be the omission of a strong note in an important place or sometimes the tying of a weak note to a strong one. The result is rhythmic surprise.

The melody in each case is stylized to conform with the rhythm section. The rock passage takes on a more rigid character because of the strict use of **straight rhythms.** The two-note groupings do not swing, and most of the melodic figures end on the offbeat. This kind of rhythmic grouping is an essential characteristic of rock. The swing passage uses a smoother type of syncopation. The primary distinction between rock and swing syncopation is the placement of the syncopated notes between the beats. The rock offbeat is exactly halfway between beats, whereas the swing offbeat occurs slightly after the midpoint.

Because of the vital nature of jazz, the performer can convert a basic unit of musical material into a creation that responds instantaneously to the contributions of the other members of the ensemble. As the excitement of the individuals present, listeners included, increases, so does the energy level of the creation. Only in the realm of jazz are the acts of creation, performance, and listening so actively integrated.

Appendix C
Rock to Fusion: An Overview

ROCK—1950 TO PRESENT

In the early 1950s a musical style evolved that shared many of the same roots as jazz. Although it has been suggested that rock and roll is a descendant of jazz, it actually developed independently, albeit along similar paths. In recent years the two styles have converged and, in places, merged. Rock's current importance to jazz has shed new light on many developing styles.

Jazz and rock share a heritage of country blues, rhythm and blues, work songs, rags, gospel, and even country and western. As the two styles matured, they grew apart stylistically; not until the seventies did they combine. The principal arena in which these two styles mingle today is the recording studio, where electronic effects have become essential. In this atmosphere, the wedding of jazz and rock into a popular musical fusion was natural. The terms *commercial, jazz/rock, rock/jazz,* and *contemporary fusion* are negative terms to some traditionalists, but they still accurately describe rock's place in society today. Elements of rock can be found in most aspects of commercial writing, such as film scores, commercials, radio jingles, albums, and videos. Although it has infiltrated much of the music in our society, it has maintained a singular stream of development.

There are several terms being used today to describe different parts of the popular music industry. More often, they are used interchangeably. *Commercial music* usually refers to movie sound tracks and jingles; however, it has grown to include activities in the music industry such as playing in studios for sound tracks, and popular songs. The term *commercial* is used when the music business is a primary concern. *Popular music* is an even bigger term, encompassing packaged music that enjoys a large listening audience for a relatively short period of time. Many musical styles make up the larger category of pop music. One could even say the waltzes of Strauss fell into the definition of popular music.

Photograph by Roger Marshutz

Elvis Presley

Although rock is a large part of the popular and commercial music world, it must share that position with country and western, jazz, (especially swing), folk, and even contemporary gospel.

The Fifties

As in the popular ballads of the 1940s, lyrics of songs were indispensable to the shaping of rock's musical style. Pop music from Tin Pan Alley (an area of music publishing in New York City) provided a basis for lyric development in the most popular songs of the day. Lyrics were not provocative and usually centered on romance and falling in love. Bill Haley and the Comets used a combination of rhythm and blues and country to forge the beginning of a new vocal sound. Elvis Presley further intensified and personalized it with vocal tones in the black tradition borrowed from the blues. The techniques used by those performers contributed to the library of inflections that identify rock performers today. Rhythm-and-blues singers such as Chuck Berry and Bo Diddley gave further definition to the 1950s sound of rock and roll. By adding amplified sound, early rock became aggressive and vibrant.

Elvis Presley (1935–1977)

Elvis Presley was born in 1935 in Tupelo, Mississippi. His early musical education consisted of exposure to church music, gospel concerts, and country music. He first appeared in public at a State Fair talent contest in 1945. During the 1950s Elvis formed a band through connections at Sun Studios in Memphis; they toured the South and became locally popular. In 1954 Colonel Tom Parker became Elvis's manager and began to build a solid career for him based on personal appearances, recordings, and films. RCA Victor purchased Elvis's contract from Sun Studios. In 1956 the recording "Heartbreak Hotel" catapulted Elvis into stardom; he made Love Me Tender, *the first of his thirty-three motion pictures, that year. From 1956 to 1961, nearly all his recordings made the top ten in the United States, including such hits as "All Shook Up," "Don't Be Cruel," "Hound Dog," "Jailhouse Rock," and "Love Me Tender"; Elvis successfully combined elements of country-and-western music with rhythm and blues, and was a tremendous influence on rock performers in the United States and England. Elvis was drafted into the U.S. Army and served two years in Germany (1958–1960). In 1967 Elvis married Priscilla Beaulieu, daughter of an Army officer; they had a daughter, Lisa Marie. Elvis's popularity declined during the 1970s, although he still had a large following of faithful fans who packed his Las Vegas stage shows and bought his recordings. Elvis died in Memphis, Tennessee, in 1977; although his death was officially declared a result of natural causes, his long dependency on drugs undoubtedly led to his early death at the age of forty-two.*

Like jazz, rock adopted the tenor sax as the principal melodic instrument. Unlike jazz, rock seldom used brass instruments. The tenor saxophone still plays a primary role in both styles. The rhythm section mirrored the structure of rhythm-and-blues bands. The following table compares a typical 1950s small jazz group with a rock-and-roll band of the time.

Comparison of Rhythm Sections

Traditional Jazz Instrumentation	*Rock Instrumentation and Function*
Piano	Rhythm guitar (comps by playing simple strummed patterns)
String bass	Electric bass (less active melodically, usually 4/4 patterns built around the chord)
Drums	Drums expanded sets (rigid patterns with simple but forceful fills)
Solo horns (trumpet and sax)	Lead guitar, saxophone (call-response to the vocal part, relatively short solos, repeated riffs as accompaniment to voice)

The importance of the 12-bar blues and the style of rhythm and blues cannot be overemphasized. These two structures provided an environment for new vocal sounds, new lyrics, and new recording techniques to establish a foothold. The 12-bar-blues structure was basic and easily memorized. Rock, using such a simple structure, could easily be passed from individual to individual by imitating records. Everything was imitated—the music, vocal inflections, guitar styles, even accompaniment figures. There was little need for notated music.

Teenage audiences of the 1950s did not discriminate exclusively between

Photo courtesy of Capitol Records, Inc.

The Beatles. *Clockwise from top: George Harrison, John Lennon, Paul McCartney, Ringo Starr.*

the rock offerings of Buddy Holly and Little Richard and even the more conservative popular music produced by singers like Pat Boone and Paul Anka. Then, as now, the line between soft-rock and rock music was difficult to draw. The lines between jazz and rock, or rhythm and blues for that matter, have been equally indistinct. For instance, historians justifiably consider Ray Charles and Muddy Waters vital contributors to both rock and jazz.

The Sixties

The sixties brought a new generation of listeners and several different cultural identities that would influence the direction of rock. The Beatles probably exemplified this era most prominently. Their worldwide, lasting impact was unprecedented. (Re-releases of their albums on compact disc twenty years later sparked unbelievable sales.)

The Beatles took rock and roll into uncharted territory. They explored the use of classical concepts (rock's third stream), new recording techniques, jazz ideas, and experimental sounds. As John Lennon, Paul McCartney, and George

Paul McCartney (b. 1942)

Paul McCartney was born in Liverpool, England, in 1942. Influenced as a teenager by Elvis Presley, he traded in the trumpet his father gave him for a bass guitar. In 1957 he joined his friend John Lennon in the group the Quarrymen; they began writing music together and played locally in pubs. Lennon picked the name "Beatles" after Buddy Holly of the Crickets died in a plane crash in 1961; that same year, the group was discovered by Brian Epstein, who became their manager and promoter. Capitol Records released "I Want to Hold Your Hand" in 1963; already popular in the British Isles and Europe, the group gained American recognition. The Beatles' debut in the United States in 1964 brought them instant fame; between 1962 and 1970, they recorded several hit albums, including Hard Day's Night, Revolver, Rubber Soul, Abbey Road, *and* Sgt. Pepper's Lonely Hearts Club Band. *McCartney married Linda Eastman in 1969; because Paul had been considered the most charming and handsome Beatle, this union was a blow to single female fans everywhere. He took the other Beatles to court in 1970 to have their partnership legally dissolved; he released his first solo album,* McCartney. *The following year, McCartney formed the group Wings, with his wife, Linda, on keyboards and vocals. Their most successful album was* Band on the Run. *He recorded a hit duet, "The Girl Is Mine," with Michael Jackson in 1982. In 1985, his movie production* Give My Regards to Broad Street *was a commercial failure. A multimillionaire, McCartney continues to write music and perform. He runs his own company out of an office in London.*

Harrison matured musically, their importance became more and more far reaching. Their musical styles fall into three periods, the first involving simple lyrics and musical arrangements, the second dealing with lyrical symbols and growing electronic experimentation, and finally well-rehearsed and studio-perfect performances that dealt with mystical and abstract ideas.

The success of the Beatles by 1965 allowed them to take their audience with them as they experimented with new instrumental combinations and song structures. Such activities normally would blur a group's identity, spelling failure in the marketplace. The pinnacle album of the Beatles and of all rock at that time was *Sgt. Pepper's Lonely Hearts Club Band.* It was a concept album based on scenes from a concert with heavy psychedelic overtones. The album has sitars (a stringed instrument from India), strings, brass, crowd noises, and sound effects. This album also marked a new level of recording techniques that would stimulate the recording industry tremendously.

Rock and roll, like jazz, has had many tangent styles, which have met with varying degrees of acceptance. Sudden improvements in recording techniques encouraged variations of singing and playing that were not possible before; sound effects like echo and distortion were the first to appear. Groups also began to reflect geographical locations and cultural backgrounds. For example, surfing music became associated with good times and security, whereas acid rock spoke of rebellion and a demand for change. The untroubled and dissident worlds, respectively, of the Beach Boys and Jefferson Airplane seem even further apart now than when they were both active on the West Coast. West Coast, or cool, jazz was centered in Los Angeles at the same time as surfing music, while in San Francisco, acid or psychedelic rock flourished. The sixties was indeed a time for rock styles to splinter from the earlier 12-bar rhythm-and-blues structures.

Cultural diversity was expressed in another segment of sixties rock, **soul.** Soul was a mixture of the emotions of gospel, rhythm and blues, and the urban black community. The music was produced in Detroit by the record company Motown. The name of the company became a stylistic term. **Motown** stars such as Stevie Wonder, Diana Ross, Aretha Franklin, and Michael Jackson carry a strong lineage of the emotion-packed style of soul.

The guitar has remained the most important instrument in rock and was given a new dimension by Jimi Hendrix in the late 1960s. His ability to coordinate the new electronic effects such as the **wah-wah pedal,** the toggle switch, and the tremolo bar set higher standards for guitarists today. His use of feedback as a musical sound shocked some and excited others. He delivered a historic performance of "The Star-Spangled Banner" at Woodstock using only feedback.

The Vietnam War greatly affected the youth of the sixties and was reflected in rock music of the period. The social structure of each era necessarily adopts avenues of escape and encounter through music. It is no coincidence that music from the times when our country was at war has always inspired nostalgia for those who lived through the turmoil and insecurity. Many of the folk-rock singers of the sixties and seventies sang of individual freedom and respect; they decried governmental structures that denied them a sense of identity.

The Seventies

The seventies produced technological advances in music that offered new musical formats; better recording techniques led to more realistic products. The goal to imitate "live" music was not the single purpose of the studio. The music business led in experimental use of storage, synthesis, and processing sound. The art of studio recording had matured far beyond the revolutionary recordings of the Beatles. The jazz and classical communities of acoustically oriented musicians, however, were initially uncomfortable with electric applications for their instruments. Amplification's association with rock and roll was considered demeaning. Today, however, jazz and classical artists do not hesitate to acquire sound systems and sound engineers to help enhance otherwise totally acoustic performances.

American and English musicians and their promoters controlled rock and roll's direction. English groups and artists like the Rolling Stones, Elton John, and The Who became models for young players in America to emulate. Meanwhile, in America, groups like Peter, Paul and Mary, Joni Mitchell, and Bob Dylan pursued a more folk-oriented rock style. Jazz, having had a strong hold in Europe and Scandinavia since the 1920s, continued to exert an ever-

Elton John

increasing influence on modern rock. Instrumental soloists, especially on sax, were increasingly showing backgrounds in jazz.

The late 1970s saw further development of progressive rock, which expanded musical structures and developed more-complicated musical textures. This was also the beginning of rock's journey toward fusion. Groups started to use brass instruments. Blood, Sweat, and Tears and Chicago are prime examples of the move to using several horn players. Blues and jazz ideas began appearing within the standard rock-and-roll structures. Then, to further modify the style, Santana, among others, brought Latin rhythms into rock. The elements of jazz/rock were at hand.

The Eighties

Rock styles of the eighties returned to a danceable format. Like jazz, rock's most popular styles were those associated with dance rhythms. **Disco,** perhaps the most obvious dance rhythm, was the popular music industry's answer to progressive rock. New Wave groups like the Stray Cats brought back the simplicity of Elvis Presley combined with highly developed recording techniques. Punk, an aggressive and extremely loud style of basic rock, and several parallel styles in

---

Elton John (b. 1947)

In 1947 Elton John was born Reginald Kenneth Dwight in Middlesex, England. He began studying the piano at an early age. After graduating from high school in 1964, John worked as a messenger for a music publisher and played piano at night in the local pubs. One year later he joined the band Bluesology, which provided backup for American soul stars touring England. John began collaborating with lyricist Bernie Taupin in 1967. After working for several other groups, they began writing for John's voice, and in 1969 his first song, "Lady Samantha," was released; this led to his first album, Empty Sky. *The album* Elton John *became a hit in England and the United States in 1970; the Elton John Band was a huge success at the Troubadour Club in Los Angeles. The album* Madman Across the Water *made the top ten in the United States and Europe the next year. From 1971 to 1976, John became one of the world's most famous and highest-paid solo rock performers; he performed to packed audiences, who were drawn by the elaborate stage sets and costumes as well as the music. During this time, John established his own record company, Rocket Records. In 1974 he performed on stage in New York with John Lennon singing "Lucy in the Sky with Diamonds"; it was Lennon's last public performance. John performed in the film musical* Tommy *as a pinball wizard in 1975. From 1976 through the 1980s, he continued to tour and perform throughout the United States and Europe; his visit to Russia inspired the 1985 hit "Nikita." In 1987 he had successful throat surgery performed in Australia. Elton John continues to thrill audiences and fans all over the world.*

England carried on the rock tradition of cultural separation from the perceived establishment.

But most important, musicians with true virtuoso abilities, like John McLaughlin, emerged from rock and were capable of bridging the gap to jazz convincingly. The floodgates then seemed to open, with musicians like keyboardist Herbie Hancock and violinist Jean-Luc Ponty able to generate great musical excitement in the worlds of both rock and jazz. In the later part of the decade, musicians were passing from rock to jazz as freely as from jazz to rock. Such previous jazz hardliners as Miles Davis and Chick Corea have blended musicians of both worlds into groups that became headline attractions.

Record production and **multitrack** recording possibilities have restructured the definition of bands. It is common for one individual to perform more than one musical part and store it on tape to be **mixed** together later. As a result, there are many recordings with only two or maybe three musicians who are made to sound like five or six. The job of producing albums is critically important and is often done by someone not in the band. The producers' objectivity and knowledge of the industry and the market make them critical to the success of a project. Producers such as George Martin for the Beatles, Berry Gordy for Motown, and Quincy Jones for Michael Jackson are prime examples of the importance of producers in the recording industry.

Michael Jackson

Michael Jackson (b. 1958)

In 1958 Michael Jackson was born in Gary, Indiana, into a large family of performers; still a young child, Michael stepped in as the youngest brother of the original Jackson Five singing group. His sisters, LaToya and Janet, later become solo stars in their own right. At the age of thirteen, Michael had his first solo hit, "Got to Be There." During the years 1971–1976, he recorded six best-selling albums with the Motown label and starred with Diana Ross in the movie The Wiz, *from which came the hit duet "Ease on Down the Road." In 1979 Jackson teamed up with producer Quincy Jones for his solo album* Off the Wall; *this was the beginning of a long-standing personal friendship and professional relationship. In 1982 Jackson recorded the hit duet "The Girl Is Mine" with Paul McCartney. The same year, Quincy Jones produced Jackson's hit album* Thriller, *which sold over thirty million copies, and produced several single hits as well; the video "Thriller," directed by John Landis, showcased Jackson's unique dancing style. The album* Bad *followed in 1987, also produced by Jones; it rivaled* Thriller *in sales and popularity. Jackson's popularity was at an all-time high when he went on tour in 1988. Although Jackson is reputed to be somewhat of a recluse with bizarre personal habits, his music continues to be successful all over the world.*

Heavy Metal and Rap

Rock, like any musical style, has branched into separate entities, which contrast with each other and other parts of its heritage. Heavy metal has come into focus in the last few years. Beginning in the sixties as acid rock, an extremely loud and loose style, metal has retained its definition with excessive volume levels projecting a very thick texture of electronic power. The vocals are mixed into the texture without the up-front placement of more commercial rock. The topics of the songs further separate metal from mainstream rock. They discuss more rebellious topics associated with street culture. Until recently, the music had been simple and direct; however, with groups like Quennsrÿche, the style has developed musically and technically with larger, more sophisticated forms. Their album *Operation: mindcrime* is an excellent example of a concept album in which the composers and the musicians alike display very mature musical and studio techniques. As has happened with other groups from this genre, the songs, volume, topics, and performances have been dismissed as outside sophisticated musical taste; however, heavy metal has found quite a large audience.

Alongside these metal groups is an international music underground of highly experimental rock, punk, and metal. The recordings are homegrown and sold mostly in a tape format. The east and west coasts of America and London are the primary areas of activity. The music is caustic and angry, pulling away from mainstream cultural identity. The subject matter is threatening and can be interpreted as revolutionary. This musical style is very possibly an example of musical development farthest removed from academic environments. In fact, the academic arena is often not even aware of its existence.

Rap is at the other end of the acceptance spectrum from metal. It enjoys a surprising popularity, especially as an expression of black identity. Rap first appeared in the 1940s and was associated with the beginning of bebop. It may be easier to describe rap performances as a rhythmic literary form rather than a developed musical structure. Rap minimizes harmonic motion and intensifies rhythmic and metric patterns. Speech patterns with minimal melodic shape ride above the rhythm with highly developed soloistic freedom. Like metal, rap is strongly associated with cultural pockets in America, often quasi-revolutionary and angry. To a lesser degree, the style has recently invaded more mainstream commercial rock groups like Vanilla Ice.

There are many splinter styles associated with a vast number of cultural developments. Elements of folk music are woven into many styles such as reggae, Latin, rhythm and blues, gospel, and experimental. Rock is immediately responsive to trends in society and culture. Popularity and success continue to shape rock's path. In time, the various styles will be placed into greater perspective.

Music Video

The most dramatic addition to rock in the eighties was the development of **music videos.** This format is indeed a theatrical musical entity. At first, videos merely showed performances. Later, they became elaborate interpretive extensions of the song. Some are entertaining, provocative, or bizarre. The video alone can change a listener's impression about a song and the group who wrote and performed it. Videos are a vital part of some performers' outputs. There are many groups who do not perform live; they just produce recordings and videos. The music industry has changed dramatically from the days of the early rock-and-roll bands of the fifties. Music is now presented visually, adding new and extended interpretation. As in the study of opera and tone poems, the debate once again surfaces: Should music be able to stand alone without other elements such as staging, text and video?

Both rock and jazz have spawned many tangential styles that became popular and then were absorbed into the more global commercial music industry. Such trends give music historians and critics much food for thought, argument, and, occasionally, despair, but they are healthy indications of the viability of the art. New styles and new names will continue to reflect societal changes, cultural shifts, and world conditions.

SUGGESTED LISTENING

Bill Haley: *Golden Hits.* MCA Records C2-4010.

Elvis Presley: *Golden Records.* Vols. 1–5. PCD1-5196, PCD1-5197, 2765-2-R, 1297-2-R, PCD1-4941.

Bo Diddley: *Two Great Guitars.* Chess CHC 9170.

Chuck Berry: *Golden Hits.* Mercury 826256-2.

Beatles: *Abbey Road.* Capitol C212-46446.

Jefferson Airplane: *Bless Its Pointed Little Head.* RCA 4545-2-R.

Glossary

AABA   Symbols representing sections of a song; each letter usually signifies eight measures; in this form, all the A sections have the same melody and chords, while the B section has a different melody and chords.

Accent   A stressed note that is played louder to make it stand out from the other notes before and after it.

Acoustic   Instrumental and vocal sounds that have not been electrically or electronically altered or amplified.

Bar   *See* Measure.

Beat   A rhythmic pulse; a strong, regular beat is fundamental to all dance music.

Blue notes   Notes that are sung or played below the intended pitch; the most commonly blued notes are the third and seventh notes of the major scale.

Bombs, Dropping bombs   A bebop drumming technique; bombs are accented notes that do not correspond with other rhythmic ideas in the ensemble.

Boom chuck   A left-hand piano figure in which a bass note is followed repeatedly by a chord; used extensively in ragtime, stride, and Chicago Dixieland.

Bridge   B section of a standard, 32-bar AABA composition.

Cadence   The flow of melody and harmony that anticipates the end of a musical phrase or composition; the cadence of a short musical phrase is usually much shorter than the final cadence of a complete composition

Cadenzas   Solos played with no accompaniment; often there is no sense of rhythm, and the soloist is free to progress at any rate desired.

Call-response   A musical dialogue consisting of two unequal musical statements; one musician states a phrase and the other fills in the gaps between the phrases. In an earlier form of call-response called "lining out," a leader would sing a line of text and the congregation would respond with the same line. Both derive from African rituals, in which a gathering would respond to a leader with recurring chants or short phrases.

Canon, Canonic   A musical form in which a melody is followed by and overlaps the same melody; also called a "round." The most well-known canon is "Row, Row, Row Your Boat."

Changes   The move from one chord to the next; a soloist is said to "play the changes" when the improvised notes fit properly into each succeeding chord.

Chart   The musical composition or arrangement for a jazz ensemble. This term is used most often to describe the notated music used by a jazz musician in a large jazz band where every player has his or her own part.

Chops   The term for one's ability to play or sing. It is used to describe a performer's technique and stamina or the ability to play in an ensemble or read music.

Chord   The simultaneous sounding of three or more notes that have specific harmonic relationships to one another; chords are used to accompany melodies.

Chord-melody (homophony)   A solo technique of pianists and guitarists who play a flowing sequence of chords; the melody is traced in the top notes of the chords.

Chorus   A single rendition of a song or a jazz composition in its basic structure; a "jazz chorus" is an improvised melody superimposed on the chords of the original song; when used in jazz, the term should not be confused with the refrain of a popular song.

Chromatic scale, interval   Sequence of ascending or descending notes that proceed by half steps.

Clef   *See* Staff.

Coda   The epilogue of a song, often presented like an afterthought; its musical function is to clarify the ending. Short codas are sometimes called tags.

Comping   A rhythmic activity supplied by the chording instruments and the drummer to help fill in the texture. The left hand of the pianist supplies chords that complement the melodic activity. A guitarist comps with chords sounding much like the pianist's left hand. The drummer uses the snare drum, playing rhythms similar to those used by the pianist and the guitarist.

Consonance   The pleasing sound of two or more notes; a consonant sound is stable and does not create tension.

Counterpoint, Contrapuntal   The addition of related, independent melodies to the basic melody.

Creole   The name given to descendants of French and Spanish settlers of the Louisiana and Gulf Coast regions. The culture retains localized dialects incorporating French and Spanish. The term is also applied to those with Negro and Indian ancestry as well as Creole. This subculture played an important role in the creation of early New Orleans bands.

Disco   A dance style typified by a heavy bass drum on each beat of the measure. A contemporary style of the late seventies.

Disjunct   An unusual or unexpected progression of notes over a wide interval or from a scalar to a nonscalar note.

Dissonance   A combination of notes that seem unrelated or harsh; too many dissonant sounds make most listeners uncomfortable.

Dixieland   The term white musicians gave to New Orleans jazz after it had been brought north to Chicago and other cities.

Double   A musician who performs on more than one instrument doubles—or triples, depending on the number of instruments; the most common doubles occur in the woodwind section. A saxophonist may double on clarinet and triple on flute.

Dynamics   Various volume (loudness) levels, as well as gradual changes in volume; the Italian terms used by musicians are variations of the words *piano* (soft) and *forte* (loud).

Echo-plex, reverb, phase shifting   Effects produced by feeding the normal sounds of instruments into electronic devices that distort them, make them echo and reverberate, or produce entirely new sounds; such sounds can be made only with the aid of electronic synthesizers and amplifiers.

Effects   Electrically or electronically generated sounds or augmentation not possible on acoustic instruments.

Extensions (harmonic and melodic)   Dissonant notes that are added to harmonies or introduced in melodies to create different sound colors; these notes are theoretical extensions of the chords.

Feedback   The harsh, piercing squeal sometimes heard on public-address systems. It occurs when a sound is emitted by a loudspeaker, is picked up by a microphone, and is sent back to the speaker, and so on, in an endless cycle; it can be interrupted if the microphone or the speaker is moved.

Field holler   A musical form used by plantation slaves; one individual would usually sing a lead solo part, which was answered by the others. Field hollers were sometimes used to communicate escape plans and the whereabouts of separated family members.

Fills   Short transitions from one musical phrase to the next; they are an essential part of the call-response technique.

Flat   To lower a note by half a step; the symbol ♭. The term is also used to describe an intonation below the intended note.

Flat-four beat   New Orleans–style Dixieland is characterized by four even beats in each measure; the 4/4 beat is created by the strong strumming sound of the banjo.

Free jazz   A modern style of jazz that observes none of the traditional melodic or harmonic rules; performers are free to play anything at any time.

Gig   A job or appearance obligation of a working musician. Musicians are hired to play gigs for dances, concerts, and even background music.

Glissando   A slide of rapidly played or slurred notes.

Harmonic extensions   *See* Melodic extensions.

Harmonics   Very high notes that are produced on stringed instruments instead of the fundamental pitch when a string is lightly touched; harmonics can also be played on wind instruments to extend their normal range.

Harmony   The result of sounding two or more different notes at the same time; the grouping of notes into chords; or the progression of chords and their relationship to one another.

Head   The term for one chorus of a jazz composition in its simplest form—that is, the basic melody supported by only the essential chords; applies to either the written musical notation or its performance. Improvised solos are built on the framework of a head.

Horn   In jazz, any wind instrument; in classical music, a specific brass instrument, the French horn.

Improvisation   The instantaneous creation of music. Horn players improvise melodies, pianists and guitarists improvise melodies and harmonies, bass players improvise bass lines, drummers improvise rhythms. Texture is improvised by all the musicians working together.

Interval   The specific distance between two notes of a chord or melody, such as a 3rd, 4th, 5th, 6th.

Intonation   Accuracy of pitch; good intonation is the exact sounding of a specific pitch without being slightly above or below.

Jam, Jam session   An informal gathering of musicians who play without pay for the fun of it; jam sessions usually occur after the normal hours of nightclubs.

Key signature   The symbol representing the tonal area of a song—for example, the key of A, or the key of B-flat; the key signature is specified by sharps or flats written on the staff at the beginning of a composition.

Kicks   Rhythmic accents played primarily by the drummer and aided by the pianist and the bassist; the accents coincide with rhythms being played by the horns. Kicks add a feeling of precision to the ensemble.

Lay back   Melodies played slightly behind the beat; the effect imparts a feeling of improvisation to the solo.

Ledger lines   Short lines that are added to extend the staff when notes must be written above and below it.

Lick   A short melodic idea.

Measure   Small equal units of a composition that contain a certain number of beats, designated in written music by vertical bar lines.

Melodic extensions   Notes that are dissonant to a chord's fundamental three notes but are still theoretically related to the chord; such unfamiliar dissonances produce a feeling of instability.

Melody   A logical series of notes that expresses a musical thought; angular melodies, which are not very singable, are not considered any less melodic than the tuneful melodies common to simple folk songs.

Meter   The number and kind of beats grouped in each measure—for example, 3/4 meter means 3 quarter notes per measure; 6/8 means 6 eighth notes; and so on. Various meters form the bases of dance forms—for example, a waltz is always written in groups of 3 (3/4 time), cha-cha is always in groups of 4 (4/4 time).

Mix (mixed)   The process of blending instruments together in a proper musical whole. In the modern studio, the mixing is performed electronically by engineers. In orchestras and ensembles, the mixing is performed by the instrumentalists.

Mode, Modal   A specific sequence of pitch changes between the eight ascending notes of the scale. There are seven common modes, including the major and minor scales; the Dorian mode is frequently used in jazz.

Motive   A complete musical phrase, usually of short duration.

Motown   A name for the musical style that emanated from Detroit. It is a black rock style with a strong emphasis on rock rhythms.

Multitrack (recording)   The process of recording individual parts separately and mixing them together at a later time. Modern studios have as many as 64 tracks available to record and mix later.

Music video   The video production that accompanies a song or interprets the song.

Natural   A symbol (♮) that is used to bring a flatted or sharped note back to its natural pitch.

Notation   The system of written symbols that indicates what notes are to be sung or played.

Note   The sound of a pitch; also the symbol for a pitch that is written on the staff.

Octave   The distance (in terms of pitch) between the lowest and highest notes of a scale. The two notes are entirely consonant because the higher note vibrates at exactly twice the frequency per second of the lower. The two notes share the same name.

Ostinato   A repeated short, rhythmic, musical figure.

Pedal point   A long, sustained note, usually in the bass range, above which melodies and chords proceed; the term came from its use on the bass pedals of the pipe organ.

Phrase   The musical equivalent of a spoken phrase, clause, or sentence; a melodic statement with a recognizable beginning, middle, and end. A composer may use several phrases in a composition, repeating them from time to time, possibly with subtle variations, to create familiarity and interest.

Pitch   The highness or lowness of a note, dictated by the speed of its sound vibrations.

Pizzicato   Plucking a stringed instrument; drawing a bow across a string is called *arco*.

Polyrhythm   The simultaneous use of two or more contrasting rhythms; such rhythms often conflict with and blur the beat.

Progression (chord or **harmonic)**   The flow of harmonies toward a cadence or resting point; harmonic progression determines the length and stability of phrases.

Quarter tones   The division of the octave into 24 steps instead of the familiar 12 half steps. Eastern music is based on this arrangement; however, Western European music does not divide the octave into such small parts. The notes sound so close together that each pitch seems to melt into the next.

Reed(s)   The term applied to any reed-articulated wind instrument: clarinet, saxophone, oboe, bassoon, and so on.

Rest   A silence of a specific duration; rests carry the same values as sounded notes—whole, half, quarter, eighth, and so on.

Rhythm   The regularly recurring pulses or beats that are in turn arranged into regularly recurring groups consisting of multiples of two or three pulses that establish meter; refers to the flow of harmonies and the activity of the melody, hence harmonic rhythm and melodic rhythm.

Rhythm and blues   A highly rhythmic dance form of the blues. It led to the development of rock and roll.

Rhythm section   A group of instruments—usually consisting of a string bass (acoustic or electric), a piano or guitar, and drums—that supplies the basic rhythmic and harmonic drive to a band or an ensemble.

Ride   Usually refers to a long–short swing pattern played on the "ride" cymbal to accompany the other musicians; also refers to accents played by horns to increase a swinging rhythm.

Riff   A short melodic idea (motive) or a simple short melody using very few notes; a rifflike melody is built by repeating a riff several times to create phrases.

Scale   Any of several sequences of pitches dividing an octave into whole-tone (T) and semitone (S) steps. In Western music, the octave contains 12 semitones: the chromatic scale. It also may be divided into 5 whole tones and 2 semitones thus: TTSTTTS—a major scale; or thus: TSTTSTT—a minor scale; or any of several other combinations.

Scat singing   Vocal improvisation using stylized nonwords.

Segue ("to connect")   To move without pause from one musical section or idea to another.

Serial (12-tone, atonal) music   A modern classical procedure for writing music. Devised by Arnold Schoenberg, it arranges the twelve tones of the octave into an arbitrary tone row without assigning them a key area. Serial melodies leap and zigzag from one octave to another and sound illogical to an untrained ear.

Sharp   To raise a note by half a step; the symbol is ♯. The term is also used to describe intonation above the intended note.

Shout, Shout chorus   A loud, climactic section of a big-band arrangement in which the trumpets, trombones, and saxes exchange a melody and supporting themes. The brass most often play short rhythmic chords above a melody played by saxes or trombones; these punches, or shouts, give definition to the shout chorus.

Sideman   Any musician in a band other than the leader or featured vocalist or soloist.

Sight-read   The ability to play or sing accurately from a written musical score at first sight.

Signal processing   The technique of enhancing or modifying an electrically transmitted sound.

Soli   A musical direction for an instrumental section to play a melodic line in harmony. A soli features one section; all the other sections play an accompaniment.

Soul   A blues style defined by the black musical tradition of slow rock (1970s) that emanated from Detroit (Motown).

Staff   The five lines on which pitches (notes) are written; also called a *clef*.

Stanza   The words that make up one section of a song.

Stop time   Interludes within a chorus when the rhythm instrument(s) plays only the first beat of every, or every other (or more), measure, leaving the soloist to play over the implied pulse.

Straight rhythms   Equally divided beats that do not swing; "straight eights" are used specifically in Latin and rock compositions.

Strain   A thematic section of a song.

Stride   Piano style in which left-hand single-note runs are interspersed between boom-chuck patterns.

Substitute harmonies   Related chords that are substituted for the original chords; they serve the same musical function but yield different sound colors.

Swing   A style of playing two notes of equal value within a beat. A classical musician makes the duration of each note exactly equal; a jazz musician makes the first note last longer than the second. The result is a swinging, dancelike feeling.

Syncopation   Placing an accent upon a normally unaccented part of the beat or measure; for example, a Viennese waltz is counted "ONE, two, three," but a jazz waltz goes "go-PARK-the-car."

Tag   *See* Coda.

Taxi dance hall   An establishment where unaccompanied men bought tickets that could be exchanged for dances with girls available for that purpose.

Tempo   The speed of a musical composition; the basic pulse can be designated to proceed slowly or quickly as well as to change gradually between fast and slow. An "up-tempo" tune is a lively song that sounds fast.

Texture   The activity level of the musicians. When the activity is high, the texture is thick; when the activity is low, the texture is thin.

Third stream   Jazz that incorporates elements of classical music such as modern classical sounds, orchestral instruments, and classical composing techniques.

Timbre   The individual, unique sound or tone color of an instrument or a voice; for example, the sound quality that lets the listener distinguish between the sounds of a flute and those of a violin.

Time signature   The numerical fraction at the beginning of written music indicating the number of beats per measure and what value of note will be counted as one beat—for example, 3/4, 6/8, 4/4. *See also* Meter.

Tone   The sound quality of an instrument or a voice; for example, the tone of a voice may be nasal, shallow, full, or deep.

Tone clusters   Notes unrelated by chords or key area played very close together at the same time, producing a discordant sound.

Tones   *See* Pitch; Note.

Transpose   To rewrite or play musical notation in another key.

Triplet   Three equal notes played within one beat.

Tune   A term that refers to almost any jazz composition or arrangement, and not to a specific melody; can also refer to a head arrangement, song, or jazz standard.

Tutti   A musical direction for all sections of a band to play together. The horns play in the same rhythm, but usually different notes. The term is sometimes used when all sections play at once but not specifically in the same rhythm.

Two-beat   A rhythmic pattern played by the bass instruments, tuba, bass sax, or string bass; the term comes from playing *only* the first and third beats of each measure.

Up tempo   Fast tempo.

Vamp   A repeated melodic and/or harmonic idea that anticipates the beginning of a new section.

Vibrato   The rapid fluctuation in pitch that gives intensity and warmth to a sustained note.

Wah-wah pedal   The pedal used by guitarists to vary the level of distortion and volume from the guitar amplifier. When used well, it can sound like vocal inflections.

Walk, Walking bass   A rhythmic-melodic pattern employed by a swing-style bass player; when a note is played on every beat of the measure and notes are organized into a scale, the impression is one of "walking" up and down the scale.

Bibliography

ALBERTSON, CHRIS, *Bessie*. Briarcliff Manor, N.Y.: Stein & Day, 1982.

ARMSTRONG, LOUIS, *Satchmo: My Life in New Orleans*. Jersey City, N.J.: Da Capo Press, 1986.

BALLIETT, WHITNEY, *American Musicians*. New York: Oxford University Press, 1986.

BERENDT, JOACHIM, *The Jazz Book: From Ragtime to Fusion and Beyond,* trans. Dan Morgenstern and Helmut and Barbara Bredigkeit. Chicago: Chicago Review Press, 1982.

BLESH, RUDI, AND JANIS HARRIET, *They All Played Ragtime*. New York: Grove Press, 1959. Rev. ed., New York: Music Sales, 1971.

CHILTON, JOHN, *Who's Who of Jazz*. Jersey City, N.J.: Da Capo Press, 1985.

COKER, JERRY, *Listening to Jazz*. Englewood Cliffs, N.J.: Prentice Hall, 1982.

COLLIER, JAMES LINCOLN, *Louis Armstrong: An American Success Story*. New York: Macmillan, 1985.

——, *The Making of Jazz*. New York: Dell Pub. Co., Inc., 1986.

DANCE, STANLEY, *The World of Duke Ellington*. Jersey City, N.J.: Da Capo Press, 1980.

ELLINGTON, EDWARD "DUKE," *Music Is My Mistress*. Jersey City, N.J.: Da Capo Press, 1976.

FEATHER, LEONARD, *From Satchmo to Miles*. Jersey City, N.J.: Da Capo Press, 1987.

——, *The Encyclopedia of Jazz in the Sixties*. Jersey City, N.J.: Da Capo Press, 1986.

——, AND IRA GITLER, *The Encyclopedia of Jazz in the Seventies*. Jersey City, N.J.: Da Capo Press, 1987.

GRIDLEY, MARK C., *Jazz Styles*. Englewood Cliffs, N.J.: Prentice Hall, 1991.

HARRIS, SHELDON, *Blues Who's Who*. Jersey City, N.J.: Da Capo Press, 1981.

HASKINS, J., *Scott Joplin*. Chelsea, Mich.: Scarborough House, 1980.

HENTOFF, NAT, *The Jazz Life*. Jersey City, N.J.: Da Capo Press, 1975.

——, AND A. J. MCCARTHY, *Jazz*. Jersey City, N.J.: Da Capo Press, 1974.

HODEIR, ANDRE, *Jazz: Its Evolution and Essence,* trans. David Noakes. Jersey City, N.J.: Da Capo Press, 1975.

HOLIDAY, BILLIE, WITH WILLIAM DUFFY, *Lady Sings the Blues*. New York: Penguin, 1984.

JEWELL, DEREK, *Duke*. New York: W. W. Norton & Co., Inc., 1980.

MCCALLA, JAMES, *Jazz: A Listener's Guide*. Englewood Cliffs, N.J.: Prentice Hall, 1982.

MEGILL, DAVID W., AND PAUL O. W. TANNER, *Jazz Issues*. Dubuque, Iowa: WCB Brown and Benchmark, 1995.

MORGENSTERN, DAN, *Jazz People*. Englewood Cliffs, N.J.: Prentice Hall, 1978.

MORITZ, CHARLES, ed., *Current Biographies*. New York: H. W. Wilson, 1984.

NANRY, CHARLES, *The Jazz Text*. New Brunswick, N.J.: Transaction Pubs., 1988.

RAMSEY, DOUG, *Jazz Matters*. Fayetteville, Ark.: University of Arkansas Press, 1989.

RAMSEY, FREDERIC, AND C. E. SMITH, *Jazzmen*. New York: Limelight Editions, 1985.

RUSSELL, ROSS, *Bird Lives*. New York: Charterhouse, 1973. Out of print.

SCHULLER, GUNTHER, *The Swing Era*. New York: Oxford University Press, 1989.

SHAPIRO, NAT, AND NAT HENTOFF, eds., *The Jazz Makers*. Jersey City, N.J.: Da Capo Press, 1979.

SIMON, GEORGE T., *The Big Bands*. New York: Schirmer Books, 1981.

SIMOSKO, VLADIMIR, AND BARRY TEPPERMAN, *Eric Dolphy*. Jersey City, N.J.: Da Capo Press, 1979.

SPELLMAN, A. B., *Black Music: Four Lives*. New York: Limelight Editions, 1985.

TANNER, PAUL, DAVID MEGILL, AND MAURICE GEROW, *Jazz*. Dubuque, Iowa: Wm. C. Brown, 1992.

TERKEL, STUDS, *Giants of Jazz*. New York: Harper & Row Junior Books, 1975.

TIRRO, FRANK, *Jazz, A History*. New York: W. W. Norton & Co., Inc., 1977.

WALLER, MAURICE, AND ANTHONY CALABRESSE, *Fats Waller*. New York: Schirmer Books (Macmillan), 1977. Out of print.

WILLIAMS, MARTIN, *Jazz Masters of New Orleans*. Jersey City, N.J.: Da Capo Press, 1979.

Many out-of-print books may still be located in public libraries and specialty book stores.

Discography

This discography is only as current as the date of its compilation. The reader will realize that by the time it is printed, many new recordings will have been issued, and, inevitably, some of those listed will have gone out of print. The present-day record collector is faced with complications unknown to those who started when there were only a few labels producing the fragile 78-rpm discs. Now there are tapes and LPs and CDs and even videos. The collector searching for an obscure but valued pressing may have to seek out a store dealing in old 78s or 45s, or defunct labels. On the other hand, companies detecting the resurgence of admiration for past artists are resurrecting discarded master plates and reissuing them in collections, so by keeping a weather eye peeled, collectors can find treasures. There are, also, a few caches of previously unissued recordings that are being brought to light. We have endeavored to reference all suggested listenings and the discography to current CDs; however, a number of examples of important artists are still available only on LPs and/or cassettes, so we have included them when we felt it appropriate.

The best advice to the record seeker is to go to the current catalog at your record store; however, the following list should prove helpful.

Collections

The Best of Blue Note. 2 vols. Blue Note BST 2 84429, BST 2 84433.
Capitol Jazz Classics. Out of print, except vol. 1: *Birth of the Cool.* Capitol Jazz CDP7-92862.
The Encyclopedia of Jazz on Records. 3 vols. MCA Records MCA2-4061, 4062, 4063. Out of print.
Jazz. 11 vols. Folkways Records 2801-2811.
Jazz: The Bebop Era. Columbia Jazz Masterpieces CK-4097392.

Piano Giants. 2-Prestige. 24052.

The "Real" Sound of Jazz. Pumpkin 116 (TV sound track).

The Sound of Jazz. Columbia Jazz Masterpieces CK-45234 (studio recordings).

The Smithsonian Collection of Classic Jazz. 5 CDs. Columbia Special Products PS 11891.

Blues

Ray Charles: *A Life in Music.* Atlantic Deluxe CS-37005. 5 cassettes.

Eric Clapton: *Time Pieces.* 2 vols. Polydor 800014-2 and 811835-2.

> *Journeyman.* Reprise 26074-2.

Robert Johnson: *The Complete Recordings.* Columbia C2K-46222.

B. B. King: *Best of B. B. King.* MCA Records MCAD-31040.

Bessie Smith: *Nobody's Blues but Mine.* Columbia CGT-31093.

> *Bessie Smith: The Collection.* Columbia Jazz Masterpieces CK-44441.
>
> *Empress of the Blues.* Columbia Jazz Masterpieces C2K-47091.

Muddy Waters: *The Best of Muddy Waters.* Chess CHD-31268.

> *Muddy Waters at Newport.* Chess CHD-31269.

Piano

Albert Ammons/Meade "Lux" Lewis: *The Complete Blue Note Recordings.* Mosaic Records MR3-103. Out of print.

> *Barrel House Boogie.* RCA Bluebird 8334-2-RB.

Bill Evans: *Bill Evans: Sunday at the Village Vanguard.* Fantasy/Orig. Jazz Classics OJCCD-210-2.

> *Bill Evans: Complete Riverside Recordings* (1956–1963). RCD-018-2. 12 CDs.

Erroll Garner: *Concert by the Sea.* Columbia Jazz Masterpieces CK-40589.

> *Long Ago and Far Away.* Columbia Jazz Masterpieces CK-40863.

Earl Hines: *With Roy Eldridge at the Village Vanguard.* XANADU 106.

> *Live at the Village Vanguard.* Columbia Jazz Masterpieces CK-44197.

Pete Johnson: *Boogie Woogie Mood.* MCA Records MCAC-1333. Cassette.

Scott Joplin: *King of Ragtime Writers.* Biograph BCD-110.

> *Scott Joplin—1916.* Biograph BRC-1006Q. Cassette only.

Art Tatum: *Piano Starts Here.* Columbia PCT-9655E. Cassette only.

> *Solos.* MCA Records MCAD-42327.

Fats Waller: *Piano Solos (1929–41).* 2-Bluebird AXK2-5518. Cassette.

> *The Joint Is Jumpin'.* RCA Bluebird 6288-2-RB.

New Orleans and Chicago Dixieland

Louis Armstrong: *Laughin' Louis.* RCA Bluebird 9759-2-RB.

> *Pops: The 1940s Small Band Sides.* RCA Bluebird 6378-2-RB.

The Hot Fives. Vol. 1. Columbia Jazz Masterpieces CK-44049.

Sidney Bechet: *The Complete Blue Note Recordings.* Mosaic MD4-110. 4 CDs.

    The Victor Sessions/Master Takes. RCA Bluebird 2402-2-RB. 3 CDs.

Bix Beiderbecke: *Bix Lives!* RCA Bluebird 6845-2-R.

    Singing the Blues. Columbia Jazz Masterpieces CK-45450.

    At the Jazz Band Ball. Columbia Jazz Masterpieces CK-46175.

Jelly Roll Morton: *Jelly Roll Morton and His Red Hot Peppers.* RCA Bluebird 6588-2-RB.

    The Jelly Roll Morton Centennial: His Complete Victor Recordings. RCA Bluebird 2361-2-RB. 5 CDs.

King Oliver: *King Oliver's Jazz Band, 1923.* Smithsonian Collection. 2 LPs.

Swing

Louis Armstrong: *Swing That Music.* MCA Records MCAC 1312. Cassette only.

Count Basie: *The Essential Count Basie.* Columbia Jazz Masterpieces CK-40608, CK-40835, CK-44150.

Bunny Berigan: *The Complete Bunny Berigan.* Bluebird. Vol. 1, AXM2-5584. Vol. 2, 5657-4-RB. Vol. 3, 9953-1-RB.

Nat "King" Cole: *Jumpin' at Capitol! The Best of the Nat King Cole Trio.* Rhino R21S-71009.

Bob Crosby: *The Best of Bob Crosby.* MCA Records 2-MCA 4083. Out of print.

Duke Ellington: *The Blanton–Webster Band.* RCA Bluebird 5659-2-RB.

    The Great Times (with Billy Strayhorn). Riverside OJCCD 108-2.

Ella Fitzgerald: *The Duke Ellington Songbook.* VERVE 837035-2. 3 CDs.

    With Louis Armstrong: Porgy and Bess. VERVE 827475-2.

Benny Goodman: *This Is Benny Goodman.* RCA Bluebird PK-6040, PK-5120. 2 cassettes.

    The RCA Victor Years. RCA Bluebird 5704-4-RB. 16 cassettes.

    The Carnegie Hall Jazz Concert. Columbia Jazz Masterpieces G2K-40244. 2 CDs.

The Great Dance Band Era. Available only through Reader's Digest.

Coleman Hawkins: *Body and Soul.* RCA Bluebird 5717-2-RB.

    The Hawk Flies. Fantasy/Orig. Jazz Classics OJCCD-027-2.

Fletcher Henderson: *Hocus Pocus: Fletcher Henderson and His Orchestra, 1927–36.* RCA Bluebird 9904-2-RB.

Billie Holiday: *The Quintessential Billie Holiday.* 8 vols. Columbia CK-40646, CK-40790, CK-44048, CK-44252, CK-44423, CK-45449, CK-46180, CK-47030.

Jimmy Lunceford: *For Dancers Only.* 1936–37. MCA Records MCAC-1307.

    The Last Sparks. 1941–44. MCA Records MCAC-1321.

The 1930's Big Bands. Columbia Jazz Masterpieces CK-40651.

Mel Tormé: *The Duke Ellington and Count Basie Song Books.* VERVE 823248-1. Cassette.

Sarah Vaughn: *The George Gershwin Song Book.* Emarcy Jazz Series 822526-4. Cassette.

    With Billy Eckstine; The Irving Berlin Song Book. VERVE 822526-4. Cassette.

Mary Lou Williams: *The Best of Mary Lou Williams.* Pablo 52405-412. Cassette.

Lester Young: *Jazz at the Philharmonic Bird and Pres, The '46 Concerts.* VERVE VE-2-2518. 2 LPs.

Lester Swings. VERVE VE-2-2516. 2 LPs.

Bebop

Art Blakey: *Art Blakey with The Jazz Messengers, Moanin'.* Blue Note CDP7-46516.

Art Blakey and Horace Silver: *A Night at Birdland.* 2 vols. Blue Note CDP7-46519, CDP7-46520.

John Coltrane: *My Favorite Things.* 1960. Atlantic A2-1361-2.

Blue Trane. Blue Note CDP7-46095.

Giant Steps. Atlantic A2-1311-2.

Miles Davis: *Kind of Blue.* Columbia Jazz Masterpieces CK-40579.

Bitches Brew. Columbia Jazz Masterpieces G2K-40577. 2 CDs.

Decoy. Columbia CK-38991.

The Chronicle. Prestige PCD-012-2. 8 CDs.

Dizzy Gillespie: *Jazz at Massey Hall* (with Charlie Parker, Bud Powell, Charles Mingus, and Max Roach). Fantasy/Orig. Jazz Classics OJCCD-044-2.

Branford Marsalis: *Royal Garden Blues.* Columbia CK-40363.

Renaissance. Columbia CK-40711.

Wynton Marsalis: *Wynton Marsalis.* Columbia CK-37574.

Resolution of Romance. Columbia CK-46143.

Bobbie McFerrin: *Spontaneous Inventions.* Blue Note CDP7-46298.

The Voice. Electra Musician 60366-2.

Thelonious Monk: *Genius of Modern Music.* 2 vols. Blue Note CDP7-81510, CDP7-81511.

The Best of Thelonious Monk: The Blue Note Years. Blue Note CDP7-95363.

Charlie Parker: *The Bird You Never Heard.* Stash ST-CD-10.

Bird's Night. Savoy Jazz SJL-2257.

Bud Powell: *The Complete Blue Note Recordings.* Mosaic MR 5-116.

Sonny Rollins: *Saxophone Colossus.* Fantasy/Orig. Jazz. Classics OJCCD-337-2.

Way Out West. Fantasy/Orig. Jazz Classics OJCCD-340-2.

Third Stream

Barney Kessell: *Plays Carmen.* Fantasy/Orig. Jazz Classics OJCCD-269-2.

Shelly Manne: *The West Coast Sound.* Fantasy/Orig. Jazz Classics OJCCD-152-2.

Charles Mingus: *Mingus Ah-Um.* Columbia Jazz Masterpieces CK-40648.

Pithecanthropus Erectus. Atlantic A2-8809-2.

The Modern Jazz Quartet: *The Art of the Modern Jazz Quartet.* 1957–66. Atlantic CS2301. Cassette.

Three Windows. Atlantic A281761-2.

Thelonious Monk with Gerry Mulligan: *'Round Midnight.* Fantasy/Orig. Jazz Classics
  OJCCD-301-2.
Gerry Mulligan: *The Complete Pacific Jazz and Capitol Recordings of the Quartet and Tentet.*
  Mosaic MD3-102. 3CDs.
Shorty Rogers: *Short Stops.* RCA Bluebird 5917-4-RB.
George Russell: *New York, New York.* Decca Jazz MCAD-31371.

Modern Big Band

Count Basie:*Best of Basie.* Pablo 2405-408-2.
  April Paris. VERVE 825575-2.
Duke Ellington: *At Newport.* Columbia Jazz Masterpieces CK40587.
  Second Sacred Concert. Prestige PCD-24045-2.
  The OK'eh Ellington. Columbia Jazz Masterpieces CK-46177. 2CDs.
Maynard Ferguson. *The Birdland Dreamband.* RCA Bluebird 6455-2-RB.
  Primal Scream. Columbia PCT-33953. Cassette.
Woody Herman: *50th Anniversary Tour.* Concord CCD-4302.
  Giant Steps. Fantasy OJC 344.
Stan Kenton: *The Comprehensive Kenton.* Capitol 4XVV- 12016. Cassette.
  New Concepts of Artistry in Rhythm. Capitol Jazz CDP7-92865.
Rob McConnel and the Boss Brass: *Present Perfect.* VERVE/MPS 823543-2.

Free Jazz

Anthony Braxton: *Anthony Braxton/New York, Fall 1974.* Arista AL 4032. Out of print.
  For Alto. Delmark DS 420/421.
Ornette Coleman: *Free Jazz.* Atlantic A2-1364-2.
  Tomorrow Is the Question. Fantasy OJCCD-342-2.
  Virgin Beauty Portrait. RK-44301.
Eric Dolphy: *The Essential Eric Dolphy.* Prestige FCD-60-022.
Herbie Hancock: *Maiden Voyage.* Blue Note CDP7-46339.
Sun Ra: *Strange Celestial Road.* Rounder CD-3035.
Cecil Taylor: *Cecil Taylor.* 1979. New World Records NW201.
  3Phasis. New World Records NW303.

Fusion

Michael Brecker: *New York See It (Now You Don't).* GRP GRD-9622.
  Don't Try This at Home. Impulse MCAD 42229.
Chick Corea: *Return to Forever—Light as a Feather.* Polydor 827148-2.
  Elektric Band. GRP Records GRP-D-9535.
Al Jarreau: *All Fly Home.* 1978. Warner Bros. 3229-2.

Weather Report: *Heavy Weather.* Columbia CK-34418.
    Night Passage. Columbia CK-36793.
Manhattan Transfer: *For Vocalese.* Atlantic 81266-2.
New York Voices: *New York Voices.* GRP Records GRD-9589.
Yellowjackets: *Four Corners.* MCA Records MCAD 5994.

Addresses

Reader's Digest: Attention Music Division; Pleasantville, New York 10570.
Mosaic Records: 35 Melrose Place, Stamford, Connecticut 06902-7533.

Index

Abba Labba, 43, 44
Abercrombie, John, 282, 290
Acuna, Alex, 275
Adderley, Julian "Cannonball," 273, 274, 276, 296
Ahern, Bob, 223
Akiyoshi, Toshiko, 292
Akiyoshi, Toshiko–Lew Tabackin, 230
Akoustic Band, 271
Ali, Rashied, 247
Almeida, Laurindo, 223
Altschul, Barry, 270
Alvarez, Chico, 224
Ammons, Albert, 52, 53
Ammons, Gene, 221
Anderson, Cat, 106, 226
Anderson, Ivy, 105
Anderson, John, 223
André, Maurice, 181
Anka, Paul, 317
"Another Night in Tunisia," 187
Anthony, Al, 223
Armstrong, Louis, 21, 24, 46, 57–58, 60–61, 63–67, 68, 70, 80, 82–83, 86, 94, 107, 117, 119, 127–28, 131, 142, 157, 161, 211, 226, 230
Arnheim, Gus, 222
Art Ensemble of Chicago, 261
"Artistry in Rhythm," 225

Association for the Advancement of Creative Musicians (AACM), 254, 260
Auld, George, 97, 115
Austin High Gang, 63
Ayler, Albert, 258, 259, 270

Babs, Alice, 108
Bach, Johann Sebastian, 194, 248
Badrena, Manolo, 275
Bailey, Buster, 94, 96
Bailey, Mildred, 126
Bailey, Victor, 276
Baker, Ginger, 29
Baker, Mike, 276
Baquet, George, 80
Barksdale, Everett, 147
Barnet, Charlie, 160, 227
Barris, Harry, 70
Bartók, Béla, 99
Basie, William "Count," 92, 96, 98, 99, 107, 113–16, 118, 120, 123, 128, 137, 138, 158, 219, 220, 227, 230
Bauduc, Ray, 70, 123
Beach Boys, 318
Beatles, 317, 318, 319, 321
Bechet, Sidney, 80–82
Beckenstein, Jay, 285
Beethoven, Ludwig van, 194